35 – N/N

# MATH INTO TeX

## A SIMPLE INTRODUCTION TO

# AMS-LaTeX

# GEORGE GRÄTZER

# MATH INTO TeX

## A SIMPLE INTRODUCTION TO
## AMS-LaTeX

**Birkhäuser**
Boston • Basel • Berlin

George Grätzer
Department of Mathematics and Astronomy
University of Manitoba
Winnipeg, Manitoba
Canada  R3T 2 N2

**Library of Congress Cataloging In-Publication Data**

Gratzer, George A.
   Math into TeX  : a simple introduction to AMS-LaTeX /
George Gratzer.
      p.     cm.
   Includes  bibliographical references.
   ISBN 0-8176-3637-4 (alk. paper).  --  ISBN 3-7643-3637-4
(alk. paper)
   1. AMS-LaTeX.  2.  Mathematics printing--Computer programs.
3. Computerized typesetting--Computer programs.  I.  Title.
Z253.4.A65G7    1992                             92-6320
686.2'2544536--dc20                              CIP

Printed on acid-free paper
© Birkhäuser Boston 1993  *Birkhäuser*

ISBN 0-8176-3637-4
ISBN 3-7643-3637-4

Typeset  by the Author in $\mathcal{A}_{\mathcal{M}}\mathcal{S}$-LaTeX
Printed and bound by Edwards Brothers, Ann Arbor, MI
Printed in the U.S.A.

9 8 7 6 5 4 3 2 1

# CONTENTS

### PART I
### A SHORT COURSE

**PART II**
**A LEISURELY COURSE**

**PART III**
**CUSTOMIZING**

## 1. What is TEX and $\mathcal{A}_{\mathcal{M}}\mathcal{S}$-LATEX?

TEX is a typesetting language created by Donald E. Knuth. $\mathcal{A}_{\mathcal{M}}\mathcal{S}$-LATEX is a "dialect" of TEX designed by the American Mathematical Society ($\mathcal{A}_{\mathcal{M}}\mathcal{S}$) to facilitate the writing of mathematical articles.

Look at the typeset sample article in $\mathcal{A}_{\mathcal{M}}\mathcal{S}$-LATEX following the Introduction (pages xviii–xx). You do not have to invest much time *learning how* to produce such high-quality typeset articles. In fact, you will be able to begin typing articles after completing PART I.

### What is the Source File?

Think of $\mathcal{A}_{\mathcal{M}}\mathcal{S}$-LATEX as a *mark up* (or coded) *language*. The text and the set of codes for an article make up what is called the *source file*. These codes convey instructions to a typesetting device—instructions as to **how to print** what has been typed. The coding is actually quite easy to learn. Observe in the abstract of the sample article (page xxii) the instruction (\em) for italicizing (**em**phasizing) the phrase "complete-simple distributive lattice":

```
{\em  complete-simple distributive lattice}
```

On pages xxii–xxix we show the source file and the typeset version of the sample article together; the source file is framed. The coding in the source file may appear somewhat bewildering and perhaps even forbidding if you previously worked on a WYSIWIG (what you see is what you get) word processing program. But the typeset article is a rather pleasing-to-the-eye polished version of that same coded material.

### Several Powerful Features of $\mathcal{A}_{\mathcal{M}}\mathcal{S}$-LATEX

- $\mathcal{A}_{\mathcal{M}}\mathcal{S}$-LATEX deals with *mathematical formulas* as well as text. Formulas are produced by typing sequentially, as ordinary text. For example, to get $\sqrt{a^2 + b^2}$, simply type \sqrt{a^{2} + b^{2}}. No need to worry about constructing the square root. In addition, $\mathcal{AMS}$-LaTeX has excellent tools to deal with *multiline math formulas requiring special alignments*. For instance, in the following formula, the $=$ signs are aligned as well as the explanatory text:

$$
\begin{aligned}
x &= (x + y)(x + z) \text{ (by distributivity)} \\
&= x + (yz) \qquad \text{(by Condition (M))} \\
&= yz
\end{aligned}
$$

This is easy to accomplish in $\mathcal{AMS}$-LaTeX:

```
\begin{alignat}{2}
  x &= (x + y) (x + z)  &&\text{ (by distributivity)}\\
    &= x + (y z)        &&\text{ (by Condition (M))}\\
    &= y z
\end{alignat}
```

In each line, & marks the first and && marks the second alignment point. See the sample article (pages xxvii and xxviii) for two more examples.

• $\mathcal{AMS}$-LaTeX relieves you of tedious *bookkeeping chores*. Consider a completed article, with the theorems and equations numbered and properly cross-referenced. On the final reading, some changes must be made—for example, Section 4 has to be placed after Section 7, and a new theorem has to be inserted somewhere in the middle. Such a minor change can cause a major headache! But with $\mathcal{AMS}$-LaTeX, it becomes "almost" a pleasure to make the changes. $\mathcal{AMS}$-LaTeX does *all the renumbering*.

• Typing the same *bibliographical references* in article after article is a tedious task. With $\mathcal{AMS}$-LaTeX, you can create and continually add to a "bibliographic database" so that retyping is no longer necessary for each article. $\mathcal{AMS}$-LaTeX is able to select the references needed for each article from the database.

• An article is divided into such *logical units* as the abstract, sections, theorems, bibliographic items, and so on. $\mathcal{AMS}$-LaTeX takes full charge of the *visual design*. The logical units are typed separately. Then, after all the units are typed, $\mathcal{AMS}$-LaTeX organizes the placement and formatting of all of the elements.

Notice line 5 of the source file of the sample article (page xxii). Here is where the visual design is specified—by the "stylesheet". In this case, amsart is designated; amsart is the $\mathcal{AMS}$ article stylesheet. When submitting the article to a journal that is equipped to handle $\mathcal{AMS}$-LaTeX articles (and the number of such journals increases very rapidly), only the *name of the stylesheet* will be replaced by the editor. *No errors shall be introduced into your article* since the source file will not be touched in any other way. This topic is further discussed in Section 2-10.

• $\mathcal{AMS}$-LaTeX is *platform independent*. This means that whether you work on a mainframe IBM, a DEC minicomputer, an IBM compatible personal computer (**PC**), a Macintosh (**Mac**), an Atari, or a Sun workstation, the source file is independent of the computer. You may type the source file on a **Mac**, while your co-author may make improvements to that same file on a **PC**; and the journal publishing the article may use a DEC minicomputer.

- It is a tremendous appeal of the TEX language, from which $\mathcal{A}_{\mathcal{M}}S$-LATEX was developed, that the coded presentation, the source file, is *plain text*—an ASCII file. Therefore articles containing even the most complicated mathematical expressions can be readily *transmitted electronically*— to colleagues, co-authors, journals, and so on.

And we have barely scratched the surface of this truly universal system.

## 2. Is this the book for you?

This book is for you: the mathematician, engineer, or scientist who wants to write and typeset articles containing mathematical formulas without spending much time learning how to do it.

All you need is:

- Access to a computer.
- TEX software (which provides the foundation for $\mathcal{A}_{\mathcal{M}}S$-LATEX).
- $\mathcal{A}_{\mathcal{M}}S$-LATEX, available from the TEX software publisher or directly from the $\mathcal{A}_{\mathcal{M}}S$.
- It is useful to have AMSFonts (version 2.1 or later), which is an extended set of fonts, also available from the $\mathcal{A}_{\mathcal{M}}S$.

For a detailed description of what you need and how to set up the software, see Chapter 1.

We only assume that:

- You know how to operate the computer and the printer.
- If you are on a **PC**, you have a program (called an "Editor") with which you can perform editing functions, that is, create, open, close files; enter, insert, and delete characters. (If you know how to use any standard word processing program, you are well-prepared; use the word processing program in "text only" mode.)

## 3. For the novice

PART I: A SHORT COURSE, consisting of the first two chapters of this book, will help you get started quickly with $\mathcal{A}_{\mathcal{M}}S$-LATEX. If you read PART I carefully, you will certainly be ready to start typing your first article and tackle $\mathcal{A}_{\mathcal{M}}S$-LATEX in more depth.

Chapter 1 provides an overview of the *structure* of $\mathcal{A}_{\mathcal{M}}S$-LATEX and of the *installation process* on either a **PC** or a **Mac**.

Chapter 2 guides you through:

- Typing text.
- Typing math.
- The anatomy of an article.

• Step-by-step instructions on how to set up an article template.

There is quite a bit to learn about how to organize an article. In Chapter 2, to speed you along, we create an *article template* for you by **simply copying examples** from the book. We do not wish to become too technical and get you bogged down in terminology. You will learn how to choose the style of theorems, corollaries, lemmas, how to use the numbering schemes and the insertion of references by just copying the appropriate examples and formats that have been provided. And, to facilitate the copying procedure, we have provided, included with this book, a number of sample files on a diskette, which we shall call the DISK. (The diskette is in **PC** format with instructions on how to convert it to the **Mac** with an Apple system utility.)

## 4. For the experienced user

PART II introduces $\mathcal{AMS}$-LaTeX in more detail. It is difficult to say what you absolutely need from the vast amount of material in PART II. However, some topics are so basic that you **must** be familiar with them. They are marked in the margin with a double bar as shown here. While many of these topics are dealt with in PART I (typing text and typing math, for example), the same topics are treated in greater depth in PART II.

Sections marked in the margin with a single bar as shown here should, at least, be **skim-read**.

Chapters 3 and 4 introduce systematically the two most basic skills: *typing text* and *typing mathematics*. Read the "must" parts; you will be surprised how few there are. Then briefly look at the "skim-read" sections. Read the remaining sections at leisure. When the time comes to use some esoteric feature, you will probably know where to find it; and there is a detailed Index to help you along.

In Chapter 5, you learn about the structure of the source file of an article. The source file has three major parts: the "Preamble", the "Topmatter", and the "Body".

The *Preamble* consists of three parts:

• The Style section: the article style and options.
• The Declaration section: the style and numbering of theorems (and similar information).
• The Command section: the commands and macros.

The *Style section* is just one line.

The *Declaration section* is discussed in Section 5-2; there is no "must" in this section. Full examples to choose from have been presented in Section 2-7. We hope that one of the examples will do the job for you; just copy it from the DISK. If none of our examples will suit your needs, then copy the closest one, and make the necessary changes; the sections you may need *for the changes* are marked "skim-read".

The *Command section* is treated very briefly in Section 5-3; it is treated in depth in PART III.

In the section dealing with the *Topmatter*, only Section 5-4.5—the full example section—is a "must". Consult the sections you may need to make changes as necessary.

Chapters 6–9 discuss the *Body* of the article.

The structure of the article is dealt with in Chapter 6:

- Sectioning.
- Cross-referencing.
- Table of Contents.
- Figures and tables.

In Chapter 6, there are only two "must" topics: sectioning and cross-referencing.

In your first article, you may want to put the *Bibliography* right into the source file, as we did in the sample article (page xxix) and in PART I. This is simple enough, as explained in Section 7-1. You are shown models for the most common types of bibliographic items. Just *copy and edit* the ones you need.

However, if you write many articles, the "proper way" of doing the Bibliography is by building *reusable* bibliographic database files and then invoke the BibTeX program. This process is explained in the remaining sections of Chapter 7.

*Multiline math displays* are taken up in Chapter 8. $\mathcal{AMS}$-LaTeX really shines here with its ability to easily typeset a large variety of multiline displays.

There are many multiline math environments, but you do not have to learn them all at the beginning. As must-read, the three you will come across in PART I have been selected: the "simple align", the "double align", and the "cases". A few others are marked "skim-read". Later, look at the examples in the remaining sections, and come back to them as the need arises.

*Displayed text*, such as *lists and tables*, are treated in Chapter 9. None of them are on the "must-read" list. To learn the proof environment, mathematicians should consult Section 9-2.

### 5. Some more advanced topics

PART III takes up some topics that go slightly beyond $\mathcal{AMS}$-LaTeX.

Chapter 10 introduces you to *customizing* $\mathcal{AMS}$-LaTeX. If you have become somewhat impatient with $\mathcal{AMS}$-LaTeX's slowness in typesetting an article or with the amount of typing you have to do, then this is the chapter for you. $\mathcal{AMS}$-LaTeX really speeds up with user-defined commands, user-defined environments, and custom format files. For the beginner, we would recommend two topics as "must": user-defined commands as shorthand and custom format files.

Chapter 11 shows some useful examples of TeX *macros*, which are more powerful than $\mathcal{AMS}$-LaTeX commands. This chapter concludes with a sample macro file, and with a discussion of numbering in $\mathcal{AMS}$-LaTeX. There is no "must" reading in this chapter.

There are a number of appendices. In your work, you will probably turn most often to Appendix A: the *math symbol tables*. Appendix B lists the *text symbol tables*; in particular, accents.

Appendix C relates some *background* material on $\mathcal{A}_{\mathcal{M}}\mathcal{S}$-LaTeX: how it developed, and how does it work. Knowing the latter may sometimes help you to track down some errors.

Appendix D shows you how you can *obtain* $\mathcal{A}_{\mathcal{M}}\mathcal{S}$-LaTeX, and how you can keep it up-to-date by accessing the Internet network. A work session is reproduced (in part), getting the files from the $\mathcal{A}_{\mathcal{M}}\mathcal{S}$ using "anonymous ftp" (a file transfer protocol).

Appendix E is a brief illustration of how you can use *PostScript fonts* in $\mathcal{A}_{\mathcal{M}}\mathcal{S}$-LaTeX.

It is hoped that Appendix F will be of assistance to those who worked with TeX, LaTeX, or $\mathcal{A}_{\mathcal{M}}\mathcal{S}$-TeX, programs from which $\mathcal{A}_{\mathcal{M}}\mathcal{S}$-LaTeX developed. Some tips are given to *smooth their transition* to $\mathcal{A}_{\mathcal{M}}\mathcal{S}$-LaTeX.

Finally, Appendix G points the way for *further study* of $\mathcal{A}_{\mathcal{M}}\mathcal{S}$-LaTeX.

## 6. Acknowledgments

Thanks are due to a number of people who have helped me:

- Harry Lakser, who declined to co-author this book but nevertheless was extremely generous with his time.
- My colleagues, Michael Doob and Craig Platt who assisted me with TeX and UNIX; David Kelly and Arthur Gerhard, who read and commented on an early version of the manuscript.
- Michael Downes, Frank Mittelbach, and Ralph Freese, who read the Third Draft of the book for the Publisher, and offered lots of practical advise.
- Michael Downes, who also read the Fifth Draft of the book for the Publisher, and also offered a lot of help in-between the two drafts he read.
- Richard Ribstein, who read the Third and Fourth Drafts so conscientiously; he produced 35 pages of commentary on the first 30 pages of the Third Draft—somewhat discouraging at the time, but certainly resulting in great improvements in the manuscript.
- Edwin Beschler, who believed in the project when it was still in Draft One— with five more to come.

This book is written by a user from a user's point of view. Leaning the mysteries of the system has given me great respect for those who crafted it: Donald Knuth, Leslie Lamport, and Michael Spivak did the original work; Michael Downes, Romesh Kumar, Frank Mittelbach, and Rainer Schöpf built on it to create $\mathcal{A}_{\mathcal{M}}\mathcal{S}$-LaTeX.

Of course, the responsibility is mine for all the mistakes that remained in the book. Please send corrections—and suggestions for improvements and additions—to me at the following address:

Department of Mathematics
University of Manitoba
Winnipeg MB, R3T 2N2
Canada
email: George_Gratzer@umanitoba.ca

# SAMPLE ARTICLE

The typeset sample article is printed on the
following three pages (xviii-xx).

# A CONSTRUCTION OF COMPLETE-SIMPLE
# DISTRIBUTIVE LATTICES

G. A. MENUHIN

March 15, 1991

ABSTRACT. In this note we prove that there exist *complete-simple distributive lattices*, that is, complete distributive lattices in which there are only two complete congruences.

## 1. INTRODUCTION

In this note we prove the following result:

**Main Theorem.** *There exists an infinite complete distributive lattice $K$ with only the two trivial complete congruence relations.*

## 2. THE $D^{(2)}$ CONSTRUCTION

For the basic notation in lattice theory and universal algebra, see F. R. Richardson [5] and G. A. Menuhin [2].

We start with some definitions:

**Definition 1.** Let $V$ be a complete lattice, and let $\mathfrak{p} = [u, v]$ be an interval of $V$. Then $\mathfrak{p}$ is called *complete-prime* if the following three conditions are satisfied:

  (M) $u$ is meet-irreducible but $u$ is *not* completely meet-irreducible;

  (J) $v$ is join-irreducible but $v$ is *not* completely join-irreducible;

  (C) $[u, v]$ is a complete-simple lattice.

Now we prove

**Lemma 1.** *Let $D$ be a complete distributive lattice satisfying Conditions (M) and (J). Then $D^{(2)}$ is a sublattice of $D^2$, hence $D^{(2)}$ is a lattice, and $D^{(2)}$ is a complete distributive lattice satisfying Conditions (M) and (J).*

1991 *Mathematics Subject Classification.* Primary: 06B10; Secondary: 06D05.

*Key words and phrases.* Complete lattice, distributive lattice, complete congruence, congruence lattice.

Research supported by the NSF under grant number 23466.

2                                              G. A. MENUHIN

*Proof.* By Conditions (M) and (J), $D^{(2)}$ is a sublattice of $D^2$. Hence, $D^{(2)}$ is a lattice.

Since $D^{(2)}$ is a sublattice of a distributive lattice, $D^{(2)}$ is a distributive lattice. Using the characterization of standard ideals in E. T. Moynahan [3], obviously, $D^{(2)}$ has a zero and a unit element, namely, $\langle 0, 0 \rangle$ and $\langle 1, 1 \rangle$. To show that $D^{(2)}$ is complete, let $\varnothing \neq A \subseteq D^{(2)}$, and let $a = \bigvee A$ in $D^2$. If $a \in D^{(2)}$, then $a = \bigvee A$ in $D^{(2)}$. Otherwise, $a$ is of the form $\langle b, 1 \rangle$ for some $b \in D$, $b < 1$. Then $\bigvee A = \langle 1, 1 \rangle$ in $D^2$. The dual argument shows that $\bigwedge A$ also exists in $D^2$. Hence $D$ is complete. Conditions (M) and (J) are obvious for $D^{(2)}$. $\square$

**Corollary 1.** *If $D$ is complete-prime, then so is $D^{(2)}$.*

The motivation for the following result comes from S.-K. Foo [1].

**Lemma 2.** *Let $\Theta$ be a complete congruence relation of $D^{(2)}$ such that*

$$(2.1) \qquad\qquad\qquad \langle 1, d \rangle \equiv \langle 1, 1 \rangle \pmod{\Theta},$$

*for some $d \in D$, $d < 1$. Then $\Theta = \iota$.*

*Proof.* Let $\Theta$ be a complete congruence relation of $D^{(2)}$ satisfying (C). Then $\Theta = \iota$. $\square$

## 3. THE $\Pi^*$ CONSTRUCTION

The following construction is crucial in our proof of the Main Theorem:

**Definition 2.** Let $D_i$, $i \in I$, be complete distributive lattices satisfying Condition (J). Their $\Pi^*$ product is defined as follows:

$$\Pi^*(D_i \mid i \in I) = \Pi(D_i^- \mid i \in I) + 1;$$

that is, $\Pi^*(D_i \mid i \in I)$ is $\Pi(D_i^- \mid i \in I)$ with a new unit element.

*Notation.* If $i \in I$ and $d \in D_i^-$, then

$$\langle \ldots, 0, \ldots, \overset{i}{d}, \ldots, 0, \ldots \rangle$$

is the element of $\Pi^*(D_i \mid i \in I)$ whose $i$-th component is $d$ and all the other components are 0.

See also E. T. Moynahan [4].

Now we can prove:

**Theorem 1.** *Let $D_i$, $i \in I$, be complete distributive lattices satisfying Condition (J). Let $\Theta$ be a complete congruence relation on $\Pi^*(D_i \mid i \in I)$. If there exists an $i \in I$ and a $d \in D_i$ with $d < 1_i$ such that for all $d \leq c < 1_i$,*

$$(3.1) \qquad \langle \ldots, 0, \ldots, \overset{i}{d}, \ldots, 0, \ldots \rangle \equiv \langle \ldots, 0, \ldots, \overset{i}{c}, \ldots, 0, \ldots \rangle \pmod{\Theta},$$

*then $\Theta = \iota$.*

*Proof.* Since

$$(3.2) \qquad \langle \ldots, 0, \ldots, \overset{i}{d}, \ldots, 0, \ldots \rangle \equiv \langle \ldots, 0, \ldots, \overset{i}{c}, \ldots, 0, \ldots \rangle \ (\text{mod } \Theta),$$

and $\Theta$ is a complete congruence relation, it follows from Condition (C) that

$$(3.3)$$

$$\langle \ldots, \overset{i}{d}, \ldots, 0, \ldots \rangle \equiv$$

$$\bigvee (\langle \ldots, 0, \ldots, \overset{i}{c}, \ldots, 0, \ldots \rangle \mid d \leq c < 1) \equiv 1 \ (\text{mod } \Theta).$$

Let $j \in I$, $j \neq i$, and let $a \in D_j^-$. Meeting both sides of the congruence (3.2) with $\langle \ldots, 0, \ldots, \overset{j}{a}, \ldots, 0, \ldots \rangle$, we obtain

$$(3.4) \qquad 0 = \langle \ldots, 0, \ldots, \overset{i}{d}, \ldots, 0, \ldots \rangle \wedge \langle \ldots, 0, \ldots, \overset{j}{a}, \ldots, 0, \ldots \rangle \equiv$$

$$\langle \ldots, 0, \ldots, \overset{j}{a}, \ldots, 0, \ldots \rangle \ (\text{mod } \Theta),$$

Using the completeness of $\Theta$ and (3.4), we get:

$$0 \equiv \bigvee (\langle \ldots, 0, \ldots, \overset{j}{a}, \ldots, 0, \ldots \rangle \mid a \in D_j^-) = 1 \quad (\text{mod } \Theta),$$

hence $\Theta = \iota$. $\square$

**Theorem 2.** *Let $D_i$, $i \in I$, be complete distributive lattices satisfying Conditions (J) and (C). Then $\Pi^*(D_i \mid i \in I)$ also satisfies Conditions (J) and (C).*

*Proof.* Let $\Theta$ be a complete congruence on $\Pi^*(D_i \mid i \in I)$. Let $i \in I$. Define

$$\widehat{D}_i = \{ \langle \ldots, 0, \ldots, \overset{i}{d}, \ldots, 0, \ldots \rangle \mid d \in D_i^- \} \cup \{1\}.$$

Then $\widehat{D}_i$ is a complete sublattice of $\Pi^*(D_i \mid i \in I)$, and $\widehat{D}_i$ is isomorphic to $D_i$. Let $\Theta_i$ be the restriction of $\Theta$ to $\widehat{D}_i$. Since $D_i$ is complete-simple, so is $\widehat{D}_i$, hence $\Theta_i$ is $\omega$ or $\iota$. If $\Theta_i = \rho$ for all $i \in I$, then $\Theta = \omega$. If there is an $i \in I$, such that $\Theta_i = \iota$, then $0 \equiv 1 \ (\text{mod } \Theta)$, hence $\Theta = \iota$. $\square$

The Main Theorem easily follows from Theorems 1 and 2.

REFERENCES

1. S.-K. Foo, *Lattice constructions*, Ph.D. thesis, University of Winebago, Winebago MN, December 1990.
2. G. A. Menuhin, *Universal Algebra*, D. van Nostrand, Princeton-Toronto-London-Melbourne, 1968.
3. E. T. Moynahan, *On a problem of M. H. Stone*, Acta Math. Acad. Sci. Hungar. 8 (1957), 455–460.
4. ———, *Ideals and congruence relations in lattices. II*, Magyar Tud. Akad. Mat. Fiz. Oszt. Közl. 9 (1957), 417–434. (Hungarian)
5. F. R. Richardson, *General Lattice Theory*, MIR, Moscow, expanded and revised ed., 1982. (Russian)

COMPUTER SCIENCE DEPARTMENT, UNIVERSITY OF WINEBAGO, WINEBAGO, MINNESOTA 23714
*E-mail address*: menuhin@ccw.uwinebago.edu

The source file and the typeset version of the sample article
are shown together (pages xxii-xxix) so you can see how
the marked up source file (which is framed) is
turned into the typeset article.

```
%Sample file: article.tex
%Typeset with AMSLaTeX format file

%Preamble
%Style section
\documentstyle[amscd,amssymb,verbatim]{amsart}

%Declaration section
\theoremstyle{plain}
\newtheorem{Thm}{Theorem}
\newtheorem{Cor}{Corollary}
\newtheorem{Main}{Main Theorem}
\renewcommand{\theMain}{}
\newtheorem{Lem}{Lemma}
\newtheorem{Prop}{Proposition}

\theoremstyle{definition}
\newtheorem{Def}{Definition}

\theoremstyle{remark}
\newtheorem{notation}{Notation}
\renewcommand{\thenotation}{}

%Command section
\errorcontextlines=0
\numberwithin{equation}{section}
\renewcommand{\rm}{\normalshape}%
   % redefining \rm to mean: change to roman style


\begin{document}

%Topmatter
\title[Complete-simple distributive lattices]%
   {A construction of complete-simple\\
     distributive lattices}
\author{G. A. Menuhin}
\address{Computer Science Department \\
   University of Winebago \\
   Winebago, Minnesota 23714}
\email{menuhin@ccw.uwinebago.edu}
\thanks{Research supported by the NSF under grant number ~23466.}
\keywords{Complete lattice, distributive lattice, complete congruence,
     congruence lattice}
\subjclass{Primary: 06B10; Secondary: 06D05}
\date{March 15, 1991}

%End topmatter
\maketitle
\begin{abstract}
   In this note we prove that there exist {\em complete-simple distributive
   lattices}, that is, complete distributive lattices in which there are
   only two complete congruences.
\end{abstract}

\section{Introduction} \label{S:intro}
In this note we prove the following result:

\begin{Main}
   There exists an infinite complete distributive lattice \( K \) with only
   the two trivial complete congruence relations.
\end{Main}
```

# A CONSTRUCTION OF COMPLETE-SIMPLE
# DISTRIBUTIVE LATTICES

G. A. MENUHIN

March 15, 1991

ABSTRACT. In this note we prove that there exist *complete-simple distributive lattices*, that is, complete distributive lattices in which there are only two complete congruences.

## 1. INTRODUCTION

In this note we prove the following result:

**Main Theorem.** *There exists an infinite complete distributive lattice $K$ with only the two trivial complete congruence relations.*

1991 *Mathematics Subject Classification.* Primary: 06B10; Secondary: 06D05.

*Key words and phrases.* Complete lattice, distributive lattice, complete congruence, congruence lattice.

Research supported by the NSF under grant number 23466.

```
\section{The \( D^{\langle 2 \rangle} \) construction} \label{S:Ds}
For the basic notation in lattice theory and universal algebra, see F.~ R.~
Richardson \cite{fR82} and G.~ A.~ Menuhin \cite{gM68}.

We start with some definitions:

\begin{Def} \label{D:prime}
   Let \( V \) be a complete lattice, and let \( \frak p = [u, v] \) be an
   interval of \( V \).  Then \( \frak p \) is called {\em complete-prime\/}
   if the following three conditions are satisfied:

   (M) \( u \) is meet-irreducible but \( u \) is\/ {\em not} completely
       meet-irreducible;

   (J) \( v \) is join-irreducible but \( v \) is\/ {\em not} completely
       join-irreducible;

   (C) \( [u, v] \) is a complete-simple lattice.
\end{Def}

Now we prove

\begin{Lem} \label{L:ds}
   Let \( D \) be a complete distributive lattice satisfying Conditions
   {\rm (M)} and {\rm (J)}.  Then \( D^{\langle 2 \rangle} \) is a
   sublattice of \( D^{2} \), hence \( D^{\langle 2 \rangle} \) is a
   lattice, and \( D^{\langle 2 \rangle} \) is a complete distributive
   lattice satisfying Conditions {\rm (M)} and {\rm (J)}.
\end{Lem}
```

2                                   G. A. MENUHIN

## 2. THE $D^{(2)}$ CONSTRUCTION

For the basic notation in lattice theory and universal algebra, see F. R. Richardson [5] and G. A. Menuhin [2].

We start with some definitions:

**Definition 1.** Let $V$ be a complete lattice, and let $\mathfrak{p} = [u, v]$ be an interval of $V$. Then $\mathfrak{p}$ is called *complete-prime* if the following three conditions are satisfied:

  (M) $u$ is meet-irreducible but $u$ is *not* completely meet-irreducible;

  (J) $v$ is join-irreducible but $v$ is *not* completely join-irreducible;

  (C) $[u, v]$ is a complete-simple lattice.

Now we prove

**Lemma 1.** *Let $D$ be a complete distributive lattice satisfying Conditions (M) and (J). Then $D^{(2)}$ is a sublattice of $D^2$, hence $D^{(2)}$ is a lattice, and $D^{(2)}$ is a complete distributive lattice satisfying Conditions (M) and (J).*

```
\begin{pf}
   By Conditions (M) and (J), \( D^{\langle 2 \rangle} \) is a sublattice
   of \( D^{2} \).  Hence, \( D^{\langle 2 \rangle} \) is a lattice.

   Since \( D^{\langle 2 \rangle} \) is a sublattice of a distributive
   lattice, \( D^{\langle 2 \rangle} \) is a distributive lattice.  Using
   the characterization of standard ideals in E.~T.~Moynahan \cite{eM57},
   obviously, \( D^{\langle 2 \rangle} \) has a zero and a unit element,
   namely, \( \langle 0, 0 \rangle \) and \( \langle 1, 1 \rangle \).
   To show that \( D^{\langle 2 \rangle} \) is complete, let
   \( \varnothing \ne A \subseteq D^{\langle 2 \rangle} \), and let
   \( a = \bigvee A \) in \( D^{2} \).  If
   \( a \in D^{\langle 2 \rangle} \), then
   \( a = \bigvee A \) in \( D^{\langle 2 \rangle} \).  Otherwise, \( a \)
   is of the form \( \langle b, 1 \rangle \) for some
   \( b \in D \), \( b < 1 \).  Then \( \bigvee A = \langle 1, 1\rangle \)
   in \( D^{2} \).  The dual argument shows that \( \bigwedge A \) also
   exists in \( D^{2} \).  Hence \( D \) is complete. Conditions (M) and
   (J) are obvious for \( D^{\langle 2 \rangle} \).
\end{pf}

\begin{Cor} \label{C:prime}
   If \( D \) is complete-prime, then so is \( D^{\langle 2 \rangle} \).
\end{Cor}

The motivation for the following result comes from S.-K. Foo \cite{sF90}.

\begin{Lem} \label{L:ccr}
   Let \( \Theta \) be a complete congruence relation of
   \( D^{\langle 2 \rangle} \) such that
   \begin{equation} \label{E:rigid}
      \langle 1, d \rangle \equiv \langle 1, 1 \rangle \pmod{\Theta},
   \end{equation}
   for some \( d \in D \), \( d < 1 \). Then \( \Theta = \iota \).
\end{Lem}
```

COMPLETE-SIMPLE DISTRIBUTIVE LATTICES                                    3

*Proof.* By Conditions (M) and (J), $D^{\langle 2 \rangle}$ is a sublattice of $D^2$. Hence, $D^{\langle 2 \rangle}$ is a lattice.

Since $D^{\langle 2 \rangle}$ is a sublattice of a distributive lattice, $D^{\langle 2 \rangle}$ is a distributive lattice. Using the characterization of standard ideals in E. T. Moynahan [3], obviously, $D^{\langle 2 \rangle}$ has a zero and a unit element, namely, $\langle 0, 0 \rangle$ and $\langle 1, 1 \rangle$. To show that $D^{\langle 2 \rangle}$ is complete, let $\varnothing \ne A \subseteq D^{\langle 2 \rangle}$, and let $a = \bigvee A$ in $D^2$. If $a \in D^{\langle 2 \rangle}$, then $a = \bigvee A$ in $D^{\langle 2 \rangle}$. Otherwise, $a$ is of the form $\langle b, 1 \rangle$ for some $b \in D$, $b < 1$. Then $\bigvee A = \langle 1, 1 \rangle$ in $D^2$. The dual argument shows that $\bigwedge A$ also exists in $D^2$. Hence $D$ is complete. Conditions (M) and (J) are obvious for $D^{\langle 2 \rangle}$. $\square$

**Corollary 1.** *If $D$ is complete-prime, then so is $D^{\langle 2 \rangle}$.*

The motivation for the following result comes from S.-K. Foo [1].

**Lemma 2.** *Let $\Theta$ be a complete congruence relation of $D^{\langle 2 \rangle}$ such that*

$$(2.1) \qquad\qquad \langle 1, d \rangle \equiv \langle 1, 1 \rangle \pmod{\Theta},$$

*for some $d \in D$, $d < 1$. Then $\Theta = \iota$.*

```
\begin{pf}
    Let \( \Theta \) be a complete congruence relation of
    \( D^{\langle 2 \rangle} \) satisfying (C). Then \( \Theta = \iota \).
\end{pf}

\section{The \( \Pi^{*} \) construction} \label{S:P*}
The following construction is crucial in our proof of the Main Theorem:

\begin{Def} \label{D:P*}
    Let \( D_{i} \), \( i \in I \), be complete distributive lattices
    satisfying Condition (J).  Their \( \Pi^{*} \) product is defined as
    follows:
    \[
        \Pi^{*} ( D_{i} \mid i \in I ) = \Pi ( D_{i}^{-} \mid i \in I ) + 1;
    \]
    that is, \( \Pi^{*} ( D_{i} \mid i \in I ) \) is \( \Pi ( D_{i}^{-} \mid
    i \in I ) \) with a new unit element.
\end{Def}

\begin{notation}
    If \( i \in I \) and \( d \in D_{i}^{-} \), then
    \[
        \langle \dotsc, 0, \dotsc,\overset{i}{d}, \dotsc,0,\dotsc \rangle
    \]
    is the element of \( \Pi^{*} ( D_{i} \mid i \in I ) \) whose \( i \)-th
    component is \( d \) and all the other components are \( 0 \).
\end{notation}

See also E.~T.~Moynahan \cite{eM57a}.

Now we can prove:
```

G. A. MENUHIN

*Proof.* Let $\Theta$ be a complete congruence relation of $D^{(2)}$ satisfying (C). Then $\Theta = \iota$. $\square$

## 3. The $\Pi^*$ construction

The following construction is crucial in our proof of the Main Theorem:

**Definition 2.** Let $D_i$, $i \in I$, be complete distributive lattices satisfying Condition (J). Their $\Pi^*$ product is defined as follows:

$$\Pi^*(D_i \mid i \in I) = \Pi(D_i^- \mid i \in I) + 1;$$

that is, $\Pi^*(D_i \mid i \in I)$ is $\Pi(D_i^- \mid i \in I)$ with a new unit element.

*Notation.* If $i \in I$ and $d \in D_i^-$, then

$$\langle \ldots, 0, \ldots, \overset{i}{d}, \ldots, 0, \ldots \rangle$$

is the element of $\Pi^*(D_i \mid i \in I)$ whose $i$-th component is $d$ and all the other components are 0.

See also E. T. Moynahan [4].

Now we can prove:

```
\begin{Thm} \label{T:P*}
  Let \( D_{i} \), \( i \in I \), be complete distributive lattices
  satisfying Condition~{\rm(J)}. Let \( \Theta \) be a complete congruence
  relation on \( \Pi^{*} ( D_{i} \mid i \in I ) \). If there exists an
  \( i \in I \) and a \( d \in D_{i} \) with \( d < 1_{i} \) such that for
  all \( d \le c < 1_{i} \),
  \begin{equation} \label{E:cong1}
    \langle \dotsc, 0, \dotsc,\overset{i}{d},
    \dotsc, 0, \dotsc \rangle \equiv \langle \dotsc, 0, \dotsc,
    \overset{i}{c}, \dotsc, 0, \dotsc \rangle \pmod{\Theta},
  \end{equation}
  then \( \Theta = \iota \).
\end{Thm}

\begin{pf}
  Since
  \begin{equation} \label{E:cong2}
    \langle \dotsc, 0, \dotsc, \overset{i}{d}, \dotsc, 0,
      \dotsc \rangle \equiv \langle \dotsc, 0, \dotsc,
      \overset{i}{c}, \dotsc, 0, \dotsc \rangle \pmod{\Theta},
  \end{equation}
  and \( \Theta \) is a complete congruence relation, it follows from
  Condition (C) that
  \begin{align} \label{E:cong}
    & \langle \dotsc, \overset{i}{d}, \dotsc, 0,
      \dotsc \rangle \equiv \\
    &\qquad \qquad \quad \bigvee ( \langle \dotsc, 0, \dotsc,
      \overset{i}{c}, \dotsc, 0, \dotsc \rangle \mid d \le c < 1 )
      \equiv 1 \pmod{\Theta}. \notag
  \end{align}

  Let \( j \in I \), \( j \neq i \), and let \( a \in D_{j}^{-} \).
  Meeting both sides of the congruence \eqref{E:cong2} with
  \( \langle \dots, 0, \dots, \stackrel{j}{a}, \dots, 0, \dots \rangle \),
  we obtain
```

COMPLETE-SIMPLE DISTRIBUTIVE LATTICES                    5

**Theorem 1.** *Let $D_i$, $i \in I$, be complete distributive lattices satisfying Condition (J). Let $\Theta$ be a complete congruence relation on $\Pi^*(D_i \mid i \in I)$. If there exists an $i \in I$ and a $d \in D_i$ with $d < 1_i$ such that for all $d \le c < 1_i$,*

$$(3.1) \qquad \langle \dots, 0, \dots, \overset{i}{d}, \dots, 0, \dots \rangle \equiv \langle \dots, 0, \dots, \overset{i}{c}, \dots, 0, \dots \rangle \pmod{\Theta},$$

*then $\Theta = \iota$.*

*Proof.* Since

$$(3.2) \qquad \langle \dots, 0, \dots, \overset{i}{d}, \dots, 0, \dots \rangle \equiv \langle \dots, 0, \dots, \overset{i}{c}, \dots, 0, \dots \rangle \pmod{\Theta},$$

and $\Theta$ is a complete congruence relation, it follows from Condition (C) that

$$(3.3)$$
$$\langle \dots, \overset{i}{d}, \dots, 0, \dots \rangle \equiv$$
$$\bigvee (\langle \dots, 0, \dots, \overset{i}{c}, \dots, 0, \dots \rangle \mid d \le c < 1) \equiv 1 \pmod{\Theta}.$$

Let $j \in I$, $j \neq i$, and let $a \in D_j^-$. Meeting both sides of the congruence (3.2) with $\langle \dots, 0, \dots, \overset{j}{a}, \dots, 0, \dots \rangle$, we obtain

```
\begin{align} \label{E:comp}
   0 = & \langle \dotsc, 0, \dotsc, \overset{i}{d}, \dotsc, 0, \dotsc
      \rangle \wedge \langle \dotsc, 0, \dotsc, \overset{j}{a},\dotsc, 0,
      \dotsc \rangle \equiv \\
        &\langle \dotsc, 0, \dotsc,\overset{j}{a}, \dotsc, 0, \dotsc
      \rangle \pmod{\Theta}, \notag
\end{align}
Using the completeness of \( \Theta \) and \eqref{E:comp}, we get:
\[
    0 \equiv \bigvee ( \langle \dotsc, 0, \dotsc, \overset{j}{a},
    \dotsc, 0, \dotsc \rangle \mid a \in D_{j}^{-} ) = 1 \pmod{\Theta},
\]
hence \( \Theta = \iota \).
\end{pf}

\begin{Thm} \label{T:P*a}
   Let \( D_{i} \), \( i \in I \), be complete distributive lattices
   satisfying Conditions {\rm(J)} and {\rm(C)}.  Then
   \( \Pi^{*} ( D_{i} \mid i \in I ) \) also satisfies Conditions {\rm(J)}
   and {\rm(C)}.
\end{Thm}

\begin{pf}
   Let \( \Theta \) be a complete congruence on
   \( \Pi^{*} ( D_{i} \mid i \in I ) \). Let \( i \in I \).  Define
   \[
      \widehat{D}_{i} = \{ \langle \dotsc, 0, \dotsc, \overset{i}{d},
      \dotsc, 0, \dotsc \rangle \mid d \in D_{i}^{-} \} \cup \{ 1 \}.
   \]
   Then \( \widehat{D}_{i} \) is a complete sublattice of
   \( \Pi^{*} ( D_{i} \mid i \in I ) \), and \( \widehat{D}_{i} \) is
   isomorphic to \( D_{i} \).  Let \( \Theta_{i} \) be the restriction of
   \( \Theta \) to \( \widehat{D}_{i} \).
```

G. A. MENUHIN

$$(3.4) \qquad 0 = \langle \dots, 0, \dots, \overset{i}{d}, \dots, 0, \dots \rangle \wedge \langle \dots, 0, \dots, \overset{j}{a}, \dots, 0, \dots \rangle \equiv$$

$$\langle \dots, 0, \dots, \overset{j}{a}, \dots, 0, \dots \rangle \pmod{\Theta},$$

Using the completeness of $\Theta$ and (3.4), we get:

$$0 \equiv \bigvee (\langle \dots, 0, \dots, \overset{j}{a}, \dots, 0, \dots \rangle \mid a \in D_j^-) = 1 \pmod{\Theta},$$

hence $\Theta = \iota$. $\square$

**Theorem 2.** *Let $D_i$, $i \in I$, be complete distributive lattices satisfying Conditions (J) and (C). Then $\Pi^*(D_i \mid i \in I)$ also satisfies Conditions (J) and (C).*

*Proof.* Let $\Theta$ be a complete congruence on $\Pi^*(D_i \mid i \in I)$. Let $i \in I$. Define

$$\widehat{D}_i = \{\langle \dots, 0, \dots, \overset{i}{d}, \dots, 0, \dots \rangle \mid d \in D_i^-\} \cup \{1\}.$$

Then $\widehat{D}_i$ is a complete sublattice of $\Pi^*(D_i \mid i \in I)$, and $\widehat{D}_i$ is isomorphic to $D_i$. Let $\Theta_i$ be the restriction of $\Theta$ to $\widehat{D}_i$.

```
        Since \( D_{i}\) is complete-simple, so is \( \widehat{D}_{i} \), hence
    \( \Theta_{i} \) is \( \omega \) or \( \iota \).  If
    \( \Theta_{i} = \rho \) for all \( i \in I \), then
    \( \Theta = \omega \).  If there is an \( i \in I \), such that
    \( \Theta_{i} = \iota \), then \( 0 \equiv 1\pmod{\Theta} \), hence
    \( \Theta = \iota \).
\end{pf}

The Main Theorem easily follows from Theorems \ref{T:P*} and \ref{T:P*a}.

\begin{thebibliography}{9}

    \bibitem{sF90}
        S.-K. Foo, {\em Lattice constructions}, Ph.D. thesis, University of
        Winebago, Winebago MN, December 1990.

    \bibitem{gM68}
        G. A. Menuhin, {\em Universal Algebra}, D. van Nostrand,
        Princeton-Toronto-London-Melbourne, 1968.

    \bibitem{eM57}
        E. T. Moynahan, {\em On a problem of M. H. Stone}, Acta Math. Acad.
        Sci. Hungar. {\bf 8} (1957), 455--460.

    \bibitem{eM57a}
        \bysame, {\em Ideals and congruence relations in lattices. II}, Magyar
        Tud. Akad. Mat. Fiz. Oszt. K\"ozl. {\bf 9} (1957), 417--434.
        (Hungarian)

    \bibitem{fR82}
        F. R. Richardson, {\em General Lattice Theory}, MIR, Moscow, expanded
        and revised ed., 1982. (Russian)

\end{thebibliography}

\end{document}
```

COMPLETE-SIMPLE DISTRIBUTIVE LATTICES                    7

Since $D_i$ is complete-simple, so is $\widehat{D}_i$, hence $\Theta_i$ is $\omega$ or $\iota$. If $\Theta_i = \rho$ for all $i \in I$, then $\Theta = \omega$. If there is an $i \in I$, such that $\Theta_i = \iota$, then $0 \equiv 1 \pmod{\Theta}$, hence $\Theta = \iota$. $\square$

The Main Theorem easily follows from Theorems 1 and 2.

### REFERENCES

1. S.-K. Foo, *Lattice constructions*, Ph.D. thesis, University of Winebago, Winebago MN, December 1990.
2. G. A. Menuhin, *Universal Algebra*, D. van Nostrand, Princeton-Toronto-London-Melbourne, 1968.
3. E. T. Moynahan, *On a problem of M. H. Stone*, Acta Math. Acad. Sci. Hungar. 8 (1957), 455–460.
4. _____, *Ideals and congruence relations in lattices. II*, Magyar Tud. Akad. Mat. Fiz. Oszt. Közl. 9 (1957), 417–434. (Hungarian)
5. F. R. Richardson, *General Lattice Theory*, MIR, Moscow, expanded and revised ed., 1982. (Russian)

COMPUTER SCIENCE DEPARTMENT, UNIVERSITY OF WINEBAGO, WINEBAGO, MINNESOTA 23714
*E-mail address*: menuhin@ccw.uwinebago.ca

# PART I

# A SHORT COURSE

# CHAPTER 1

# The Structure of
# $\mathcal{AMS}$-L&TEX

### 1-1. Basic information

It is not absolutely necessary for you to know how $\mathcal{AMS}$-L&TEX is structured. However, familiarity with the structure may be useful for setting up the software, as well as for using $\mathcal{AMS}$-L&TEX. This topic is further discussed in Section C-2.

As we pointed out in the Introduction, at the core of $\mathcal{AMS}$-L&TEX is a *programming language* called TEX. It is a special purpose programming language containing instructions (commands or macros) for typesetting. TEX instructions are easy to recognize; they always start with a backslash \. Along with TEX comes a set of fonts called *Computer Modern* (CM). The CM fonts with TEX form the foundation of any TEX system.

TEX is easily expandable, that is, additional instructions can be defined in terms of the basic instructions. To the 300 basic instructions of TEX another 600 were added in Plain TEX—contained in the file plain.tex. All further expansions of TEX have been built on this enlarged platform. (L&TEX uses a modified version of Plain TEX called LPlain TEX—the file lplain.tex.) It is not surprising, therefore, that when reference is made to TEX in the literature, it usually means TEX with Plain TEX and the CM fonts. We shall use the same convention in PART III and in Appendix F.

Expansions of TEX are called "macro packages". Such packages consist of a set of macros to make using TEX easier. One of the best known macro packages is L&TEX, which introduced the idea of "environment", as an implementation of a *logical unit*. (More about this in Section 2-10.) Environments are easily recognized; they begin with:

\begin{name}

and end with

\end{name}

where name is the name of the environment. (Environments are defined in Section 3-3.)

For instance, in the sample article source file (on page xxii),

```
\begin{Main}

....

\end{Main}
```

contains the Main Theorem. Take a look at the first page of the typeset article (on page xxiii) to see how $\mathcal{A}_{\mathcal{M}}S$-L&#9500;TEX handles this environment.

The structure of $\mathcal{A}_{\mathcal{M}}S$-L&#9500;TEX is illustrated in the following diagram:

$\mathcal{A}_{\mathcal{M}}S$-L&#9500;TEX is a macro package built on top of L&#9500;TEX. By installing all these macro packages and specifying the document style amsart in the source file (page xxii, line 6 in the sample article), this macro package is added to L&#9500;TEX.

The diagram above suggests that, in order to have $\mathcal{A}_{\mathcal{M}}S$-L&#9500;TEX, we first install TEX and the CM fonts, then L&#9500;TEX. Moreover, AMSFonts are useful but not absolutely necessary.

Let us emphasize that in this book when we refer to $\mathcal{A}_{\mathcal{M}}S$-L&#9500;TEX, we mean the **whole structure**. In Section C-2.1 you can read some more about the parts that form $\mathcal{A}_{\mathcal{M}}S$-L&#9500;TEX.

Error messages refer to the antecedents of $\mathcal{A}_{\mathcal{M}}S$-L&#9500;TEX: TEX, L&#9500;TEX, and $\mathcal{A}_{\mathcal{M}}S$-TEX; you can safely ignore these references.

## 1-2. $\mathcal{A}_{\mathcal{M}}S$-L&#9500;TEX and your computer

If you work on a terminal connected to a mainframe or minicomputer, then the installation of the software will have to be done by local experts. In this chapter we shall concentrate on a typical $\mathcal{A}_{\mathcal{M}}S$-L&#9500;TEX setup on a personal computer, as, for example, on an IBM compatible personal computer (a **PC**) or a Macintosh personal computer (a **Mac**).

To make the discussion concrete, we choose PCTEX (Personal TEX, Inc., (415) 388-8853) as the TEX software to be installed on a **PC**, and TEXTURES (Blue Sky Research, (503) 222-9571) to be installed on a **Mac**.

## 1-3. Setting up $\mathcal{A}_{\mathcal{M}}\mathcal{S}$-LATEX on a PC

We assume a standard computer configuration: a **PC** with a hard drive C and a floppy drive A, and a VGA monitor. The hard drive has at least 15 megabytes (15,000,000 bytes) free. The printer is a (300 dpi) PostScript laser printer, plugged in the printer port LPT1.

You also have a program, called the "Editor", for standard editing functions. The Editor could be a word processor used in "text only" mode. When we say that you should "edit" a file or "open" a file, we mean that you use the open command of the Editor, then read the file and perform the usual editing functions in the Editor.

**1-3.1. Installation.** You have to install four programs:

- TEX;
- PTI View, the "screen previewer" (which allows you to view the typeset version on the screen);
- PTI Laser/PS, the Printer Driver (to print the typeset version);
- an Editor (for writing and editing the source file);

and a very large collection of data files, fonts, and document files:

- CM font files;
- AMSFonts font files;
- font metric files;
- LATEX files;
- $\mathcal{A}_{\mathcal{M}}\mathcal{S}$-LATEX files.

(Font files, metric files, and the role they play are discussed in Section C-2.)

When you order PCTEX, provide information about:

- the CPU (Central Processing Unit) of the computer: 8086, 80286, 80386, 80486 (or newer);
- what type of floppy disk is accepted by drive A;
- the printer.

If the CPU is an 80386 or 80486 (or newer) and the computer has at least two megabytes of memory, you can order PCTEX/386 or Big PCTEX/386, two more powerful versions of PCTEX. The installation instructions slightly differ with the version; to simplify the discussion here, we assume that you ordered Big PCTEX/386.

The printer will determine the printer driver required and the font sets you must obtain. The laser printer with PostScript needs the PTI Laser/PS Printer Driver, and it uses 300 dpi fonts (fonts that print 300 dots per inch).

No Editor comes with PCTEX. Buy a good Editor or use a word processor in the "text only" mode.

The program and data disks come with detailed installation instructions. We shall only outline the major steps so that you can obtain an overview. Please follow the installation instructions carefully.

**Step 1.** Set up PCTEX in the directory pctex. Make sure there is presently no such directory.

Place PCT$_{E}$X diskette #1 in drive A, and at the C:> prompt type:

```
C:>a:install a c
```

(Always press Return to terminate a command.)

You will be asked (in Steps 1, 2, and 5) to replace the floppy disk in drive A; do so when asked and press the spacebar to continue.

Every so often you will be asked to agree with what the installation program wants to do; it is advisable to agree. Press the spacebar whenever you see the message:

```
Press any key to continue...
```

Once you get the message:

```
Initializing the Plain format
```

press Ctrl-C (that is, hold down the Ctrl key, and press the C key). Then to

```
Terminate batch job (Y/N)?
```

respond by pressing Y.

The following is the directory structure created by the installation program of PCT$_{E}$X:

```
PCTEX
    TEXFMTS
    TEXBIB
    TEXDOC
    TEXINPUTS
    TEXTFMS
    LATEX
    AMSTEX
    AMSTFMS
```

At this stage, the T$_{E}$X font metric files (tfm files) are installed in textfms, and the AMS font metric files are installed in amstfms. The files necessary for running T$_{E}$X, L$^{A}$T$_{E}$X, and $\mathcal{A}_{\mathcal{M}}\mathcal{S}$-T$_{E}$X are split into three groups: by default, they go into texinputs; the L$^{A}$T$_{E}$X documents go into latex, and the $\mathcal{A}_{\mathcal{M}}\mathcal{S}$-T$_{E}$X documents into amstex. (We shall not use $\mathcal{A}_{\mathcal{M}}\mathcal{S}$-T$_{E}$X; it is, however, automatically installed.)

**Step 2.** The CM fonts (PCT$_{E}$X fonts) come on a number of floppy disks. Again, with the first floppy disk in drive A, type

```
C:>a:install a c
```

at the C:> prompt. The installation will create the pixel subdirectory of the pctex directory. In turn, pixel has a series of subdirectories: dpi300, ... , dpi746. Each will contain a large number of font files (pk files).

**Step 3.** To install PTI View, place the diskette in drive A, and type

```
C:>a:install a c
```

This will not add to the directory structure; it just adds a few files to the existing structure.

**Step 4.** Similarly, to install PTI Laser/PS, place the diskette in drive A, and type

```
C:>a:install a c
```

**Step 5.** To install AMSFonts (Version 2.1 or later), place the diskette in drive A, and type (note the difference!):

```
C:>a:
```

and at the `A:>` prompt:

```
A:>install
```

You have to answer a series of questions. Tell the program you want to install on drive C; in the `\pctex\pixel` subdirectory (option 1); install all magnifications (option 1), and all AMSFonts (option 1). Confirm the choices by pressing the spacebar. This step does not add any new subdirectories, but it adds a large number of files to the subdirectories of pixel.

If you are low on space on the hard disk, you may wish to omit the installation of AMSFonts, except for the few tfm files recommended in the $\mathcal{A}_{\mathcal{M}}S$-LATEX installation instructions; see [6].

(If you do not choose to install AMSFonts, you will still be able to do everything in this book, except that some symbols listed in the tables of Appendix A will not be available; in particular, many bold math symbols will be missing. You will also lack some math fonts, such as Fraktur and Euler script.)

**Step 6.** Now, install $\mathcal{A}_{\mathcal{M}}S$-LATEX. Place the $\mathcal{A}_{\mathcal{M}}S$-LATEX disk in drive A, and in the pctex directory create a new subdirectory:

```
C:>cd \pctex
C:>mkdir amslatex.doc
C:>cd amslatex.doc
```

This creates the subdirectory: amslatex.doc of pctex. We are currently in the subdirectory `C:\pctex\amslatex.doc` and issue the command:

```
C:>copy a:\doc *.*
```

This will copy all the $\mathcal{A}_{\mathcal{M}}S$-LATEX documents into amslatex.doc. Now we move over to the texinputs subdirectory, and copy everything else from A into it:

```
C:>cd ..
C:>cd texinputs
C:>copy a:\fontsel *.*
C:>copy a:\inputs *.*
```

**Step 7.** Finally, we now place the DISK (supplied with this book) in drive A, and create under pctex the appropriate subdirectories:

```
C:>cd ..
C:>mkdir disk
C:>cd disk
C:>mkdir parti
C:>mkdir partii
```

```
C:>mkdir partiii
C:>cd parti
C:>copy a:\parti *.*
C:>cd ..
C:>cd partii
C:>copy a:\partii *.*
C:>cd ..
C:>cd partiii
C:>copy a:\partiii *.*
C:>cd ..
C:>mkdir work
```

(If you do not have the DISK, you will be instructed on how to type in the source files as necessary.)

This ends the installation procedure, and creates the subdirectory work for our experimentations.

**1-3.2. Adjustments.** The config.sys and autoexec.bat files must be set up properly. config.sys must contain the lines:

```
files=20
buffers=20
```

(or higher numbers). Check if they are there; if not, add them. If these lines are there with smaller numbers, edit them. The autoexec.bat file has to contain

```
path=c:\pctex
```

as a rule, as part of a longer path such as:

```
path=c:dos; ...; c:\pctex;...
```

and the line:

```
set texfmts=c:\pctex\texfmts
```

**1-3.3. Format file.** Now we shall make the format file: amslatex.fmt to be used in the rest of the book. This format file will contain all the $\mathcal{A}\mathcal{M}\mathcal{S}$-LaTeX software in a "precompiled" form that will run faster.

**Step 1.** The setup procedure placed the file lfonts.tex in the latex subdirectory; this file contains the LaTeX font selection scheme. In order to teach LaTeX the $\mathcal{A}\mathcal{M}\mathcal{S}$-LaTeX font selection scheme, we need the file lfonts.new. First we get lfonts.tex out of the way by renaming it olfonts.tex:

```
C:>ren \pctex\latex\lfonts.tex olfonts.tex
```

**Step 2.** Rename tex386b.exe to tex.exe:

```
C:>ren \pctex\tex386b.exe tex.exe
```

**Step 3.** Issue the command:

```
C:>tex lplain "\dump" /i/pi=c:\pctex\latex;c:/pt=c:\pctex\amstfms;c:
```

Copy this command carefully; the " in the command is the double quote symbol, **not** two single quotes: '  '. T$_\mathrm{E}$X will inform you that it cannot find the file lfonts.tex; in response to the prompt:

```
Please type another input file name:
```

type

```
lfonts.new
```

This dialog repeats three more times: T$_\mathrm{E}$X cannot find a file and you have to type in the name of the replacement. The file names are shown in the following table:

| File cannot be found: | Replace by: |
|---|---|
| fontdef.tex | fontdef.max |
| preload.tex | preload.ori |
| xxxlfont.sty | basefont.tex |

This will create a file lplain.fmt in the texfmts subdirectory. Rename this file amslatex.fmt:

```
C:>ren \pctex\texfmts\lplain.fmt amslatex.fmt
```

**1-3.4. Testing.** The following diagram illustrates some of the steps when using PCTᴇX.

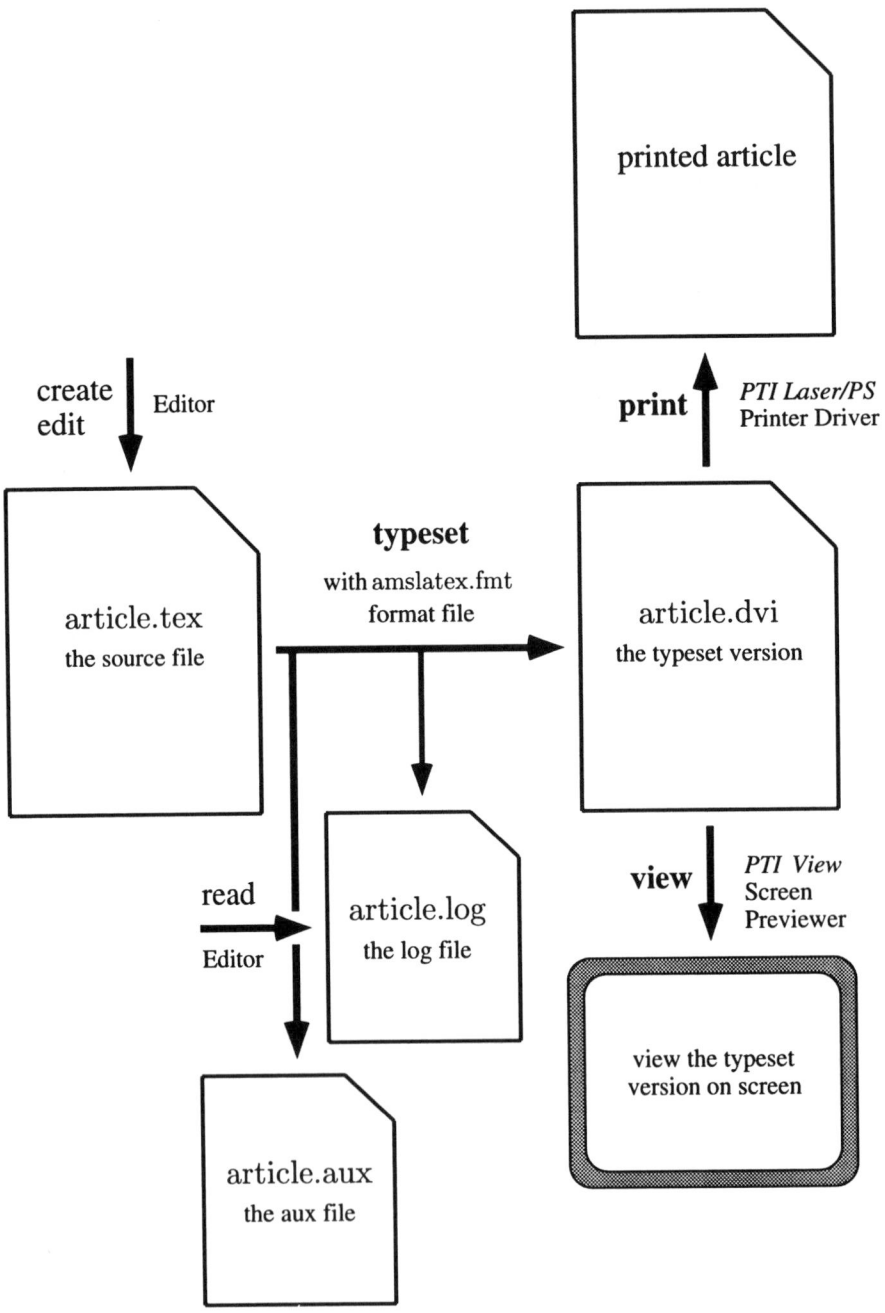

The first step is the creation of the source file in the Editor. In the Editor, create a new file in the subdirectory pctex\disk\work, and type in the source file of article.tex as shown on pages xxii–xxix. Alternatively, copy article.tex over from the subdirectory pctex\disk\parti.

Make sure you are in the subdirectory c:\pctex\disk\work, and at the prompt, issue the command:

```
C:>tex &amslatex article
```

Repeat this command. This should create two new files: article.dvi and article.log. (In fact, it also creates the auxiliary file article.aux; see Section C-2.4.)

article.dvi is the typeset version of the article. We shall use it to view and print the article.

Open the article.log file with the Editor; it contains the same information that was scrolling on the screen when the command was executed, and informs you of what was accomplished and what errors (if any) were found.

The next step is to view the result. With the Editor, create a file called font.sub and place it in the directory pctex. This is a text file containing the single line:

```
sub cmcsc8 for cmcsc10 at 8pt
```

Edit the file v.bat to read:

```
ptiview %1 -a=VGA -f=c:\pctex\font.sub -%3 -%4 -%5 -%6 -%7 -%8 -%9
```

Move back to parti:

```
C:>cd parti
```

Now you can view the test article with

```
v article
```

(PTI View knows to add the extension .dvi to the name to find the typeset version.)

Then print the typeset article with the printer driver obtained with PCT$_E$X. Remember to use the font substitution option:

```
C:>ptips article -f=c:\pctex\font.sub -ou=prn
```

when invoking the printer driver.

**Tip.** If the new format file does not work, check if there is enough free disk space (at least two megabytes); less disk space may corrupt the file. Note that if the hard disk is partitioned, then the *partition you work in* must contain the two free megabytes.

**Tip.** Did you touch any of the text files used in the compilation of the format file? If the Editor wrapped a line, a commented out line (see Section 3-5) may have partly crept in, corrupting the format file. Start again with newly-copied text files.

**Tip.** For convenience, create the files p.bat for printing and t.bat for typesetting. The file p.bat contains the one line:

```
ptips %1 -f=c:\pctex\font.sub -ou=prn
```

Place the file in the directory pctex. Then in the subdirectory work, you can print article with

```
p article
```

The file t.bat contains the one line:

```
tex &amslatex %1
```

Place the file t.bat in the directory pctex. Then in the subdirectory work, you can typeset article.tex with

```
t article
```

**1-3.5. Files.** A number of files are created on the disk when article.tex is typeset. The main one is article.dvi, the typeset version. When the typesetting takes place, messages from $\mathcal{A}_{\mathcal{M}}\mathcal{S}$-L#TEX are shown on the screen; these are collected in the file article.log, the log file. $\mathcal{A}_{\mathcal{M}}\mathcal{S}$-L#TEX also writes one or more auxiliary files, as necessary. The most important one is article.aux, the aux file; see Section C-2.4.

**1-3.6. Interactive $\mathcal{A}_{\mathcal{M}}\mathcal{S}$-L#TEX.** $\mathcal{A}_{\mathcal{M}}\mathcal{S}$-L#TEX is interactive: you give it an instruction, and $\mathcal{A}_{\mathcal{M}}\mathcal{S}$-L#TEX does its best to carry it out; if it cannot, it will ask for your intervention. $\mathcal{A}_{\mathcal{M}}\mathcal{S}$-L#TEX will inform you of the error found, and ask for help by displaying a prompt.

The ** prompt means that $\mathcal{A}_{\mathcal{M}}\mathcal{S}$-L#TEX wants to know the name of the source file to typeset. Probably, you misspelled the name, or you are in the wrong subdirectory.

The ? prompt asks "What should I do about the error I found?" Press Return to continue; most of the time $\mathcal{A}_{\mathcal{M}}\mathcal{S}$-L#TEX recovers from the error, and completes the typesetting. If $\mathcal{A}_{\mathcal{M}}\mathcal{S}$-L#TEX cannot recover from the error, at the ? prompt, press x to exit.

The * prompt is the real $\mathcal{A}_{\mathcal{M}}\mathcal{S}$-L#TEX interactive mode; $\mathcal{A}_{\mathcal{M}}\mathcal{S}$-L#TEX is waiting for an instruction. \end{document} exits $\mathcal{A}_{\mathcal{M}}\mathcal{S}$-L#TEX. Interactive instructions (such as \show; see Section 10-1.2) must be given at the * prompt.

To get a * prompt, delete (comment out) the

```
\end{document}
```

line in a source file, and typeset.

**1-3.7. Discussion.** The installation of a standard $\mathcal{A}_{\mathcal{M}}\mathcal{S}$-L#TEX system on any personal computer should be very similar to what was described in this section. Of course, if no installation program is given, you have to copy the files into the appropriate subdirectories yourself.

PCTEX is slightly non standard.

- It splits up the input files into several subdirectories. As a rule, most implementations have only one textfms subdirectory and only one texinputs subdirectory (all the input files, including the L#TEX files, have to be placed in this directory).
- When $\mathcal{A}_{\mathcal{M}}\mathcal{S}$-L#TEX is looking for a file, it will first look in the current subdirectory, and then in the texinputs directory. PCTEX (as we set it up) will do the same except that it will look, additionally, in the latex subdirectory.

- TeX looks for metric files in the textfms subdirectory. PCTeX will do the same except that it will look, additionally, in the amstfms subdirectory. PCTeX does this because of the clause

  `/pi=c:\pctex\latex;c:/pt=c:\pctex\amstfms;c:`

  in the command that set up the format file.

- Most TeX implementations have only the texfmts subdirectory; PCTeX also has texfmts.386 so that PCTeX and PCTeX.386 can be run together without conflict.

- When making the format file, in Step 3, most TeXs ask you to invoke the program `initex` (in PCTeX, `tex /i` invokes `initex`). So the command to make the format file will be:

  `C:>initex lplain`

  or some variant thereof.

- The name of the subdirectory pixel—containing the font files— changes with the implementation; the way this subdirectory is organized (by font sizes) does not.

For a **PC**, three commercial programs are best established: PCTeX (which we used as the example), $\mu$TeX (ArborText Inc. (313) 996-3566), and TurboTeX (Kinch Computer Company, (607) 273-0222). Make sure that the version you buy can typeset $\mathcal{A}_{\mathcal{M}}\mathcal{S}$-LaTeX articles.

There are also a number of public domain TeX implementations. These can be obtained from a variety of sources; inquire from TUG; see Section D-5. Commercial packages give technical support, not available for public domain programs; for a novice, this may be an important consideration.

As compared with the **Mac** implementation, TEXTURES, the **PC** implementations differ in that you have to use a number of different programs: TeX itself, the Editor, the printer driver, and the screen previewer; switching programs is time consuming and inconvenient. This setup is changing. Windows 3.1 on the **PC** now provides a framework for the introduction of integrated TeX environments. The first "Windows" screen previewer has already appeared: DVIWindow (Y&Y, (508) 371-3286). Both PCTeX and TurboTeX now have Windows versions. Soon it should be as convenient to run $\mathcal{A}_{\mathcal{M}}\mathcal{S}$-LaTeX under Windows as it is to run it with TEXTURES on a **Mac**.

## 1-4. Setting up $\mathcal{A}_{\mathcal{M}}\mathcal{S}$-LaTeX on a Mac

We assume a standard computer configuration: you have a **Mac** with a hard drive and a floppy drive. The hard drive must have at least 15 megabytes (15,000,000 bytes) free, and the computer must have at least 4 megabytes of memory.

We now install TEXTURES.

**1-4.1. Installation.** Create the following folders:

```
TeXtures
    TeX fonts
    Tex formats
    Tex inputs
    disk
```

The names TeX formats, TeX fonts, and TeX inputs must be typed exactly as shown; spaces and capitalization matter. From the Textures disks, drag the Textures application into the TeXtures folder, the VirTeX format file (it is a cylinder with the Textures logo) into the TeX formats folder, and the file hyphen.tex into the TeX inputs folder. From the Textures font disks, drag all the font files (they look like small suitcases), the metrics file, and the file called "dummy" into the TeX fonts folder.

The $\mathcal{AMS}$-L̸ᴬTᴇX distribution disk has three folders of interest to us: inputs, latex, and fontsel. From all three folders drag all files (except the "read me" files) into the TeX inputs folder.

From Disk 1 of AMSFonts, drag the metrics file into the TeX fonts folder. Disk 2 contains CM-MS.sit and Disk 3 contains Euler.sit; these are compressed files. With both, proceed as follows: double click on the icon; a file saving box appears, select the TeX fonts folder, and click on the "Install" button. (If AMSFonts Version 2.1 is not installed, some symbols listed in the tables of Appendix A will not be available; in particular, many bold math symbols will be missing. You will also lack some fonts, such as Fraktur and Euler script.)

Finally, drag the contents of the DISK into the disk folder.

**1-4.2. Format file.** Now we shall make the format file AMSLaTeX; we shall use it in the rest of the book.

**Step 1.** If you previously had L̸ᴬTᴇX installed in your system, you may have a file lfonts.tex which is in the TeX inputs folder. Rename this file olfonts.tex.

**Step 2.** Start Textures, in the File menu choose Open, and in the file opening box select lplain.tex in the TeX inputs folder; click on Open.

In the Typeset menu find the item VirTeX; select it. Now again in the Typeset menu choose Typeset.

A dialog box appears which informs you that

```
I can't read ''lfonts'' (not found)
Shall I try another file?
```

Click on the Yes button. The file opening box appears, choose the file lfonts.new in the TeX inputs folder; click on Open.

This dialog repeats three more times: TeX cannot find a file and you have to type in the name of the replacement. The file names are shown in the following table:

| File cannot be read: | Replace by: |
| --- | --- |
| fontdef.tex | fontdef.max |
| preload.tex | preload.ori |
| xxxlfont.sty | basefont.tex |

After some processing, you are prompted with

```
(please type a command or say '\end')
*
```

The * is a prompt (more about it in Section 1-4.4); following it type

```
* \dump
```

and press Return. A file saving box appears. Locate it in the TeX formats folder, and name the file AMSLaTeX. Click on Save. Quit TEXTURES.

**1-4.3. Testing.** The following diagram illustrates some of the steps you take when using TEXTURES.

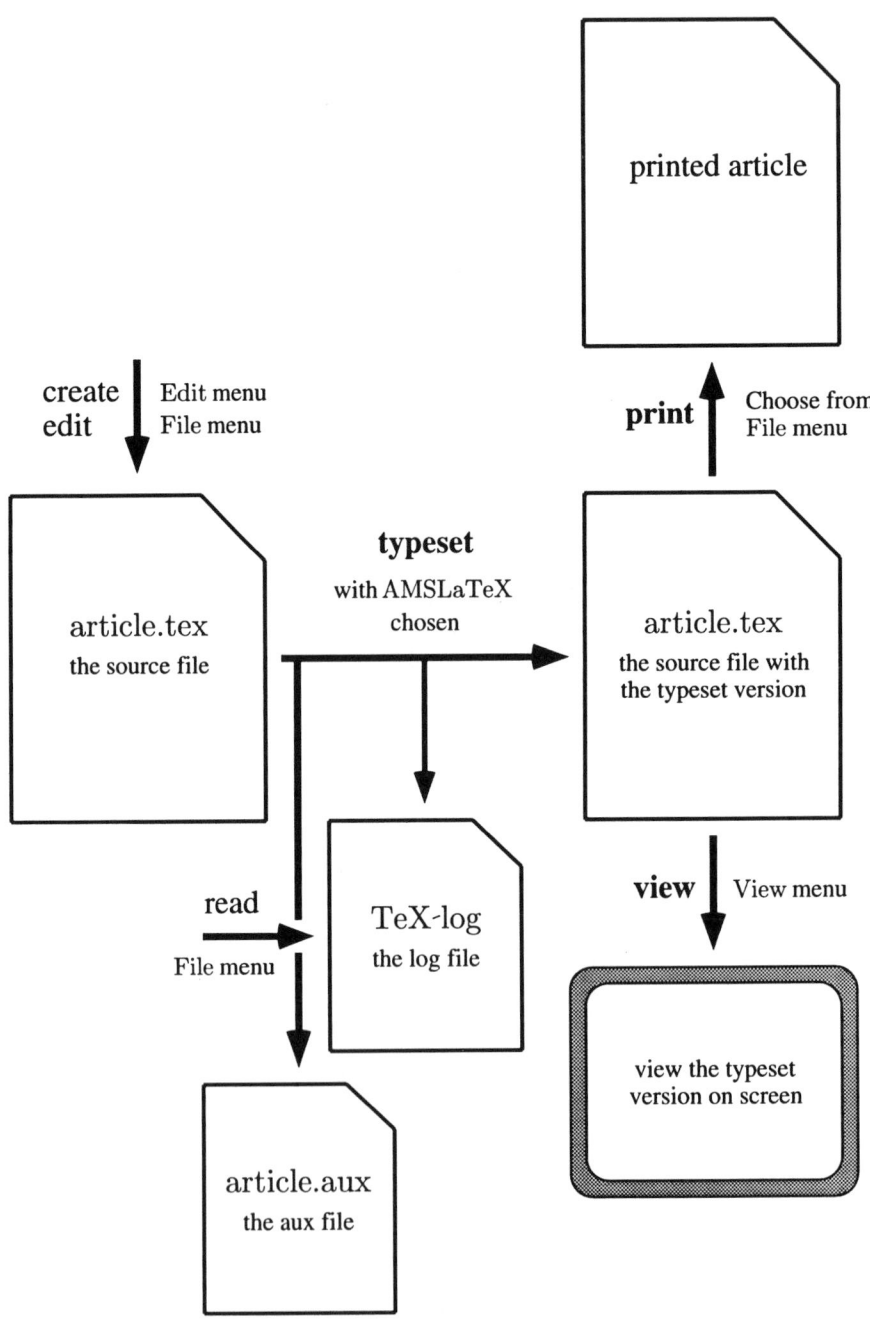

The first step is the creation of the source file. Start TEXTURES; in the File menu choose New, type in the source file article.tex as shown on pages xxii–xxix, and save it in the folder work. Alternatively, copy article.tex over from the folder parti.

In the Typeset menu you find a new item, AMSLaTeX; select it. Then in the Typeset menu choose Typeset. The typeset version of the article will appear in a new window, and a file, article.aux, is created on the disk containing numbering, cross-referencing, and bibliographic information. When the typesetting is finished, do it again: in the Typeset menu choose Typeset. The second typesetting utilizes article.aux to insert the numbers in the article. When the typesetting is finished the second time, the typeset article should look identical to the typeset sample article; see pages xviii–xx. Typesetting also creates the TEX log file; see Section C-2.4.

The TEXTURES setup is much more convenient to use than PCTEX (of 1992) since TEX, the Editor, and the screen previewer form one integrated package. You do not have to be bothered with dvi files. The typeset article appears immediately on the screen. (However, the TEXTURES Editor is rather weak compared to typical stand-alone editors.) TEXTURES also displays the TEX log file as the typesetting proceeds. It really pays to have a large monitor (or two) so you can view all these files with minimal overlap.

The source file remembers the format file you last used to typeset it, so **you** do not have to remember. The format file last used in the session stays in memory, so future typesettings start up much faster.

To print, make sure the window showing the typeset version is selected. Choose Print from the File menu, and click OK. (If you forget to choose the view window, the source file or the log file will be printed.)

**Tip.** The name of an $\mathcal{A}_{\mathcal{M}}S$-L𝐀T𝐄X file must be one word (no space) ending with .tex. If the name contains two words, e.g., first test.tex, $\mathcal{A}_{\mathcal{M}}S$-L𝐀T𝐄X will get confused and send the message

```
LaTeX error.  See LaTeX manual for explanation.
            Type  H <return>  for immediate help.
! Missing \begin{document}.
\@latexerr ....}\errmessage {#1}


...

1.23 \begin{document}
```

On the other hand, `first_test.tex` is an acceptable name.

**Tip.** If the new format file does not work, check that there is enough free disk space (at least two megabytes); less disk space may corrupt the file. Note that if the hard disk is partitioned, then the *partition you work in* must contain the two free megabytes.

**Tip.** Did you touch any of the text files used in the creation of the format file? If TEXTURES wrapped a line, a commented out line (see Section 3-5) may have partly crept in, corrupting the format file. Start again with newly copied text files.

**1-4.4. Interactive** $\mathcal{A}_{\mathcal{M}}S$-$\mathbb{L}^{A}T_{E}X$**.** $\mathcal{A}_{\mathcal{M}}S$-$\mathbb{L}^{A}T_{E}X$ is interactive: give $\mathcal{A}_{\mathcal{M}}S$-$\mathbb{L}^{A}T_{E}X$ an instruction, and it does its best to carry it out; if it cannot, it will ask for your intervention. $\mathcal{A}_{\mathcal{M}}S$-$\mathbb{L}^{A}T_{E}X$ will inform you of the error found, and ask for help by displaying a prompt.

In the log window, the ? prompt asks "What should I do about the error I found?" Press Return or click on the "Continue" button to continue; most of the time $\mathcal{A}_{\mathcal{M}}S$-$\mathbb{L}^{A}T_{E}X$ recovers from the error, and completes the typesetting. If $\mathcal{A}_{\mathcal{M}}S$-$\mathbb{L}^{A}T_{E}X$ cannot recover from the error, at the ? prompt, click on the "Quit" button to exit. Clicking on the "Help" button may occasionally yield useful advice.

The * prompt is the real $\mathcal{A}_{\mathcal{M}}S$-$\mathbb{L}^{A}T_{E}X$ interactive mode; $\mathcal{A}_{\mathcal{M}}S$-$\mathbb{L}^{A}T_{E}X$ is waiting for an instruction. To get to such a prompt, delete (comment out) the

```
\end{document}
```

line in the source file and typeset. Interactive instructions (such as \show; see Section 10-1.2) must be given at the * prompt.

```
\end{document}
```

exits $\mathcal{A}_{\mathcal{M}}S$-$\mathbb{L}^{A}T_{E}X$, as does clicking on the "Quit" button.

**1-4.5. Files.** A number of files are created on the disk when article.tex is typeset. When the typesetting takes place, the file TeX log appears on the screen, containing messages from $\mathcal{A}_{\mathcal{M}}S$-$\mathbb{L}^{A}T_{E}X$; TeX log is the log file, it is stored on the disk. $\mathcal{A}_{\mathcal{M}}S$-$\mathbb{L}^{A}T_{E}X$ also writes one or more auxiliary files, as necessary. The most important one is article.aux, the aux file; see Section C-2.4.

## 1-5. Version numbers and creation dates

All components of $\mathcal{A}_{\mathcal{M}}S$-$\mathbb{L}^{A}T_{E}X$ interact. Since all of them have dozens of versions, make sure that they are up-to-date and compatible. The version numbers and dates listed here are the ones we are currently using. Make sure that in your system all of them are as listed here, or newer.

$T_{E}X$ is an implementation of Version 3.0. PCTEX is Version 3.14 (earlier versions could not run $\mathcal{A}_{\mathcal{M}}S$-$\mathbb{L}^{A}T_{E}X$). TEXTURES is Lightning TEXTURES Version 1.5. You can check the version numbers and dates of the text files used in setting up the system by reading the first few lines in the Editor. latex.tex is dated 14 January 1991. lplain.tex is dated March 15, 1990. hyphen.tex has no date.

AMSFonts is version 2.1, and $\mathcal{A}_{\mathcal{M}}S$-$\mathbb{L}^{A}T_{E}X$ is Version 1.1. See Appendix D on how to get updated versions of $\mathcal{A}_{\mathcal{M}}S$-$\mathbb{L}^{A}T_{E}X$ and AMSFonts.

# CHAPTER 2

# Typing Your First Article

## 2-1. Outline

The goal of this chapter is to produce a printed article. You type in the (electronic) *source file*; $\mathcal{A}_{\mathcal{M}}\mathcal{S}$-LaTeX does the rest.

The source file is made up of *text*, *math*, and *instructions to $\mathcal{A}_{\mathcal{M}}\mathcal{S}$-LaTeX*. For instance,

"The source file you type" is text,

"$\sqrt{5}$" (typed as "\( \sqrt{5} \)") is math, and

"\em" is a command (an instruction).

(Remember: all commands start with a backslash \ and are meant to instruct $\mathcal{A}_{\mathcal{M}}\mathcal{S}$-LaTeX; this particular command: \em emphasizes the text that follows.) Another kind of instruction comes in pairs; they bracket an *environment*. For instance,

\begin{flushright}

and

\end{flushright}

bracket the `flushright` environment. What is typed in this environment will come out flush right.

In practice, text, math, and instructions are intertwined:

{\em My first integral\/} \( \int \zeta^{2}(x) \, dx \)

(which produces *My first integral* $\int \zeta^2(x)\,dx$ ) is a mixture of all three.

Nevertheless, to some extent we try to introduce the three topics: typing text, typing math, and giving instructions to $\mathcal{A}_{\mathcal{M}}\mathcal{S}$-LaTeX (commands, macros, and environments) as if they were separate topics.

In this chapter we explain the first two, and teach the third by copying and emulation. In PART II, instructions to $\mathcal{A}_{\mathcal{M}}\mathcal{S}$-LaTeX assume their proper role and, in PART III, they are discussed in yet more depth.

## 2-2. Typing a note

First we will have an overview of how to use the keyboard in $\mathcal{A}_{\mathcal{M}}S$-LaTeX; then we type a simple note containing only text.

**2-2.1. The keyboard.** In $\mathcal{A}_{\mathcal{M}}S$-LaTeX, to type text, use only the following keys:

```
a-z
A-Z
0-9
+  =  *  /  (  )  [  ]
```

the punctuation marks:

```
,  ;  .  ?  !  :  '  '  -
```

the space key (the spacebar or the tab key) and the Return (or Enter).

There are thirteen special keys:

```
#  $  %  &  ~  _  ^  \  {  }  @  "  |
```

used mostly in instructing $\mathcal{A}_{\mathcal{M}}S$-LaTeX. There are special rules on how to type these characters as well as composite characters (such as accented characters) if you need them in text. For instance, @ is typed as @@ (as in note2.tex), _ is typed as \_, and % is typed as \%. See Section 3-4.4 for details.

Every other key is prohibited! Do not use the computer's modifier keys (**PC**: Alt, Ctrl; **Mac**: Command, Option, Ctrl) to produce special characters. $\mathcal{A}_{\mathcal{M}}S$-LaTeX will either reject or misunderstand them. When trying to typeset a source file that contains a *prohibited character*, the log file (see Sections 1-3.5 and 1-4.5) will show the error message:

```
! Text line contains an invalid character.
1.222 completely irreducible^^?
                              ^^?
```

In this message 1.222 means line 222 of your source file. Try deleting and retyping lines until the error goes away.

**2-2.2. The first note.** We start our discussion of how to type a note in $\mathcal{A}_{\mathcal{M}}S$-LaTeX with a simple example. We want to use $\mathcal{A}_{\mathcal{M}}S$-LaTeX to produce the following:

It is of some concern to me that the terminology used in multi-section math courses is not uniform.

The term "hamiltonian-reduced" is used in several sections of the course on advanced matrix theory. I, personally, would rather call these "hyper-simple". I would like to invite others to comment on this problem.

In my new course "mathematical database concepts", the terminology is of special concern to me. Since this field is new, there is no accepted terminology. It is imperative that we arrive at a satisfactory solution.

Now create a new file with the Editor in the work subdirectory/folder of the disk subdirectory/folder under the name note1.tex and type in the following (if you do

not feel like typing it, copy it over from the parti subdirectory/folder of the disk
subdirectory/folder):

```
%Sample file: note1.tex
%Typeset with AMSLaTeX format
\documentstyle[amscd,amssymb,verbatim]{amsart}
\errorcontextlines=0 \textwidth=29pc


\begin{document}


It is of some concern to me    that
the terminology used in  multi-section
 math courses is not uniform.


The term
 ''hamiltonian-reduced'' is used in several sections of the course
 on advanced matrix theory.
    I, personally, would rather call these ''hyper-simple''.    I
would like  to invite others to comment on this  problem.


In my new course ''mathematical database concepts'',
 the terminology is of special concern to me.
Since this field is new, there is
 no accepted
terminology.   It is imperative
that we arrive at a satisfactory solution.


\end{document}
```

The first two lines start with %; they are *comments* ignored by $\mathcal{A}_{\mathcal{M}}\mathcal{S}$-LATEX. (The
% character is very useful. If, for example, while typing in the source file you wish
to want to make a comment, but do not want that comment to appear in the typeset
version, start the line with %. All text in that line will be ignored at the typesetting
stage.)

The next two lines set the "style" and instruct $\mathcal{A}_{\mathcal{M}}\mathcal{S}$-LATEX to format the error
messages and the typeset version as shown in the book. Ignore these lines. Note that
we typed the left double quote " as '' (two left single quotes) and the right double
quote " as '' (two right single quotes).

The text of the note is typed in the "document environment", that is, between the
two lines

```
\begin{document}
\end{document}
```

In the subsequent examples, we shall assume that you type the first four lines as in
this example (except that in the first line you give the appropriate name for the note),

and you type the two lines bracketing the document environment. Henceforth, we shall reproduce only the lines of the source file within the document environment.

From this example you can see that $\mathcal{AMS}$-LaTeX is somewhat different from most word processors. It ignores the way you formatted the text. $\mathcal{AMS}$-LaTeX takes note of whether you put a space in the text, but it ignores *how many spaces* have been inserted. For $\mathcal{AMS}$-LaTeX, one (or more) blank line(s) marks the end of a paragraph. Tabs are treated as spaces.

**2-2.3. Lines too wide.** $\mathcal{AMS}$-LaTeX reads the text in the source file one paragraph at a time, typesets it, then reads the next paragraph, and so on; see Section C-2 for a more detailed discussion. Most of the time, there is no need for corrective action. Occasionally, however, $\mathcal{AMS}$-LaTeX gets into trouble splitting the paragraph into lines. In note1.tex, rewrite the second sentence as follows:

```
In several sections of the course on
advanced matrix theory,  the term
  ''hamiltonian-reduced'' is used.
```

and the fifth sentence as follows:

```
Of special concern, is the terminology in my new course
  ''mathematical database concepts''.
```

and save it under the name note1B.tex in the work subdirectory/folder of the disk subdirectory/folder. (You can find note1B.tex in the parti subdirectory/folder of the disk subdirectory/folder; just copy it over.)

Typesetting the edited note, we get:

It is of some concern to me that the terminology used in multi-section math courses is not uniform.

In several sections of the course on advanced matrix theory, the term "hamiltonian-reduced" is used. I, personally, would rather call these "hyper-simple". I would like to invite others to comment on this problem.

Of special concern, is the terminology in my new course "mathematical database concepts". Since this field is new, there is no accepted terminology. It is imperative that we arrive at a satisfactory solution.

The first line of paragraph two is about 1/4 inch too wide. The first line of paragraph three is also slightly too wide. Open the log file (see Sections 1-3.5 and 1-4.5):

```
Overfull \hbox (17.9173pt too wide) in paragraph at lines 11--16
[]\cmr/m/n/10 In sev-eral sec-tions of the course on ad-vance
d ma-trix the-ory, the term ''hamiltonian-

\hbox(6.94444+1.94444)x348.0, glue set - 1.0
.\hbox(0.0+0.0)x12.0
.\cmr/m/n/10 I
.\cmr/m/n/10 n
.\glue 3.33333 plus 1.66666 minus 1.11111
```

```
.\cmr/m/n/10 s
.etc.
```

```
Overfull \hbox (6.47284pt too wide) in paragraph at lines 17--23
[]\cmr/m/n/10 Of spe-cial con-cern, is the ter-mi-nol-ogy in
my new course ``math-e-mat-i-cal database
```

```
\hbox(6.94444+1.94444)x348.0, glue set - 1.0
.\hbox(0.0+0.0)x12.0
.\cmr/m/n/10 O
.\cmr/m/n/10 f
.\glue 3.33333 plus 1.66666 minus 1.11111
.\cmr/m/n/10 s
.etc.
```

The reference:

```
Overfull \hbox (17.9173pt too wide) in paragraph at lines 11--16
```

is to paragraph two; the typeset version has a line (line number unspecified within the paragraph) which is 17.9173pt too wide. $\mathcal{AMS}$-LaTeX uses points (pt) to measure distance; 72 points make an inch. The next two lines:

```
[]\cmr/m/n/10 In sev-eral sec-tions of the course on ad-vance
d ma-trix the-ory, the term ``hamiltonian-
```

identify the source of the problem: $\mathcal{AMS}$-LaTeX would not hyphenate "hamiltonian" because it hyphenates a hyphenated word (hamiltonian-reduced) only at the hyphen.

The second reference:

```
Overfull \hbox (6.47284pt too wide) in paragraph at lines 17--23
```

is to paragraph three (line number unspecified within the paragraph); the trouble is with the word "database"; the hyphenation routine of $\mathcal{AMS}$-LaTeX cannot hyphenate it.

If you encounter such problems, try to rephrase the sentence (for instance, as it was phrased in the previous version). Or add optional hyphens, \-, to help $\mathcal{AMS}$-LaTeX: rewrite database as data\-base and the problem goes away.

**2-2.4. Some more text features.** Next we will produce in $\mathcal{AMS}$-LaTeX the following note:

January 19, 1991

February 7–21 *please use* my temporary email address:
George_Gratzer@umanitoba.ca

G. Grätzer

Type in the following source file, save it as note2.tex in the work subdirectory/folder of the disk subdirectory/folder. (You can find note2.tex in the parti subdirectory/folder of the disk subdirectory/folder; you can copy it over.) Remember that we show here only the lines in the document environment.

```
\begin{flushright}
    January 19, 1991
\end{flushright}
February 7--21 {\em please use\/} my temporary email address:
\begin{center}
    George\_Gratzer@@umanitoba.ca
\end{center}


\vspace{.7 in}


\noindent G. Gr\"atzer
```

This note introduces several additional features of $\mathcal{A}\mathcal{M}\mathcal{S}$-LaTeX:

- Use environments to *flush right* or to *center* text. Use the command \em to *emphasize text*; the text to be emphasized is surrounded by { and \/}. (We shall explain the \/ part later.) There is also \bf for *bold text*, as in **bold**. Bold requires the { and } to delimit it, but it does not require \/ as \em does.

- Commands to $\mathcal{A}\mathcal{M}\mathcal{S}$-LaTeX always start with \ and are terminated by the first non alphabetical character. Be careful to leave a space after \em, \bf, and other like commands. Command names are case sensitive; do not type \EM or \Em for \em.

- Use double hyphens for number ranges (en dash): 7--21 prints: 7–21; use triple hyphens (---) for the "em dash" punctuation mark—such as this.

- If you have to skip lines (as in the last note for the signature), use the command \vspace{.7 in} with the appropriate distance. The distance may be given in points, centimeters (cm), or in inches, as in this example.

- There are special rules for *accented characters* and *foreign characters*. For instance, ä is typed as \"a. Accents are explained in Section 3-4.6; see also the table in Section B-2.

You will seldom need to know more about typing text. For more detail, however, see Chapters 3 and 9. Text symbol tables are presented in Appendix B.

### 2-3. Typing math

Now we start mixing text with math formulas.

**2-3.1. The keyboard.** There are five additional keys to use when typing math:

$$+ \quad = \quad | \quad < \quad >$$

(| is the shifted \ on most keyboards.)

**2-3.2. A note with math.** We start learning about typesetting math with the following note:

In our first year Calculus, we define intervals such as $(u, v)$ and $[u, \infty)$. Such an interval is a *neighborhood* of $a$ if $a$ is in the interval. The students should understand that $\infty$ is only a symbol, not a real number. This is important since we soon introduce concepts such as $\lim_{x \to \infty} f(x)$.

When we introduce the derivative:

$$\lim_{x \to a} \frac{f(x) - f(a)}{x - a}$$

we assume that the function is defined in a neighborhood of $a$.

To create the source file for this mixed math and text note, create a new document in the Editor. Name it math.tex, place it in the work subdirectory/folder, and type in the following source file—or copy over math.tex from the parti subdirectory/folder (remember that we show here only the lines in the document environment):

```
In our first year Calculus, we    define intervals   such as
\( (u, v) \) and \( [u, \infty) \).  Such an interval is a
{\em neighborhood\/} of   \( a \)
if  \( a \) is in the interval.  The students should
understand that  \( \infty \) is only a
symbol, not a real number.  This is important since
 we soon introduce concepts
such as \(\lim_{x \to \infty} f(x) \).

When we introduce the derivative:
\[
   \lim_{x \to a} \frac{f(x) - f(a)}{x - a}
\]
we assume that the function is defined in a
neighborhood of  \( a \).
```

Observe:

- There are two kinds of math formulas and corresponding environments: *inline* and *displayed*.
- The *inline* math environment opens with \( and closes with \). You can also type $ both for opening and closing the inline math environment. This is the first exception to the general rule that an environment must be bracketed by

  \begin{name}

  and

  \end{name}

- The *displayed* math environment opens with \[ and closes with \]. This is the second (and last) exception to the general rule governing how environments must be bracketed.

- $\mathcal{A}\mathcal{M}\mathcal{S}$-LaTeX ignores the spaces you insert in math environments with two exceptions: spaces that delimit commands (see Section 3-3) and spaces in the argument of the command \text (which temporarily reverts into text mode). Spacing in math is important only for readability. To put it in another way: **in text mode, many spaces equal one space; in math mode, the spaces you type are ignored.**

- The same formula may be typeset differently depending on which math environment it is in. $x \to a$ is typed as a subscript to lim (_ starts the subscript). But notice how  \lim_{x \to a} f(x)  is typeset in an inline formula: $\lim_{x\to a} f(x)$, and how different it looks as a displayed formula:

$$\lim_{x \to a} f(x)$$

typed as

```
\[
   \lim_{x \to a} f(x)
\]
```

- A special math symbol is invoked by its name which always begins with \. Examples: the name of $\infty$ is \infty and the name of $\to$ is \to. All math symbols are listed in Appendix A.

- Some commands such as \sqrt need *arguments*; they are enclosed in { and }. To get $\sqrt{5}$, you have to type \( \sqrt{5} \), where \sqrt is the command and 5 is the argument. Some commands need more than one argument. To get $\frac{3}{5}$ you have to type \( \frac{3}{5} \); \frac is the command, 3 and 5 are the arguments.

There are many mistakes we can make even in such a simple note. We will now insert mistakes in math.tex, and insert and delete % signs to make the mistakes visible to $\mathcal{A}\mathcal{M}\mathcal{S}$-LaTeX one at a time. (Recall that lines starting with % are ignored by $\mathcal{A}\mathcal{M}\mathcal{S}$-LaTeX.)

To facilitate this, type the following source file, and save it under the name mathB.tex in the work subdirectory/folder (or copy over the file mathB.tex from the parti directory/folder).

```
In our first year Calculus, we   define intervals   such as
%\( (u, v) \) and \( [u, \infty) \).  Such an interval is a
 \( (u, v) \) and    [u, \infty) \).  Such an interval is a
 {\em neighborhood\/} of \( a \)
if \( a \) is in the interval.  The students should
understand that  \( \infty \) is only a
symbol, not a real number.  This is important since
we soon introduce concepts
 such as \(\lim_{x \to \infty} f(x) \).
%such as \(\lim_{x \to \infty  f(x) \).
```

When we introduce the derivative:
```
\[
    \lim_{x \to a} \frac{f(x) - f(a)} {x - a}
  %\lim_{x \to a} \frac{f(x) - f(a)    x - a}
\]
```
we assume that the function is defined in a
neighborhood of \( a \).

Note that in line 3 of the text (line 9 of the file), we neglected to type the second \(. When typesetting mathB.tex, in the log file you find the error message:

```
! Missing $ inserted.
<inserted text>
                $
. . .
1.9 ..., v) \) and      [u, \infty
                             ) \).  Such an interval is a
```

By omitting \(, $\mathcal{AMS}$-LATEX reads [u, \infty) in the text mode; but the command \infty instructs $\mathcal{AMS}$-LATEX to typeset a math symbol; this can only be done in math mode. So $\mathcal{AMS}$-LATEX offers to put a $ in front of \infty; remember that $ substitutes for \(. $\mathcal{AMS}$-LATEX suggests a cure, but do not follow this suggestion. The math mode must start before [u.

In the next example, we demonstrate another error by moving some % signs. In the Editor open the file mathB.tex which is in the work subdirectory/folder. Delete % at the beginning of line 2 (of the text) and insert a % at the beginning of line 3 (this eliminates the previous error); delete % at the beginning of line 10 and insert a % at the beginning of line 9 (this introduces the new error: the closing brace of the subscript is missing). Save the changes, and typeset the note. In the log file you get the error message:

```
! Missing }
inserted. <inserted text>
                    }
. . .
1.16 ...im_{x \to \infty f(x) \)
```

$\mathcal{AMS}$-LATEX is telling us that a closing brace } is missing, but it is not sure where. $\mathcal{AMS}$-LATEX noticed that the subscript started with { and it reached the end of the math formula before finding }. You have to look in the formula for a { that is not closed, and close it with }.

As a final exercise with this note, delete % at the beginning of line 9 and insert a % at the beginning of line 10 (removing the last error), and delete % at the beginning of line 15 (of the text) and insert a % at the beginning of line 14 (introducing the final error: deleting the closing brace of the first argument of \frac). Save and typeset it. In the log file you find the error message:

```
LaTeX error.  See LaTeX manual for explanation.
               Type  H <return>  for immediate help.
! Bad math environment delimiter.
\@latexerr ....}\errmessage {#1}


...

1.22 \]
```

The log file tells you that there is a bad math environment delimiter in line 22 of the file. This is the line:

```
\]
```

So the reference to

```
! Bad math environment delimiter.
```

is to the displayed formula. Since the environment delimiter is correct, the message tells us that something went wrong in the displayed formula. This is what happened: $\mathcal{A}_{\mathcal{M}}S$-LaTeX was trying to typeset

```
\lim_{x \to a} \frac{f(x) - f(a)   x - a}
```

but \frac needs two arguments. $\mathcal{A}_{\mathcal{M}}S$-LaTeX found f(x) - f(a)   x - a as the first argument. While looking for the second, it found \] which is obviously an error.

**2-3.3. Some building blocks of a formula.** A formula is built up from various types of components:

> **Arithmetic:** The arithmetic operations $a + b$, $a - b$, $-a$, $a/b$, $ab$ are typed as expected:
>
> ```
> \( a + b \), \( a - b\), \( -a \), \( a / b \), \( a b \).
> ```
>
> If you wish the $\cdot$ for multiplication, as in $a \cdot b$, use the command \cdot: `\(a \cdot b\)`. Fractions, such as
>
> $$\frac{1 + 2x}{x + y + xy}$$
>
> are typed with \frac:
>
> ```
> \[
>     \frac{1 + 2x}{x + y + xy}
> \]
> ```
>
> **Subscripts and superscripts:** Subscripts are typed with _ and superscripts with ^. Remember to enclose them in { and }. To get $a_1$:
>
> | | |
> |---|---|
> | Go into inline math mode: | \( |
> | type the letter a: | a |
> | subscript command: | _ |
> | bracket the subscripted 1: | {1} |
> | exit inline math mode: | \) |

that is, type \( a_{1} \). Note that the spaces are in the formula only
for readability. Further examples: $a_{i_1}$, $a^2$, $a^{i_1}$, typed as

\( a_{i_{1}} \), \( a^{2} \), \( a^{i_{1}} \)

**Accents:** The four most often used math accents are:

| | | |
|---|---|---|
| $\bar{a}$ | typed as | \( \bar{a} \) |
| $\hat{a}$ | typed as | \( \hat{a} \) |
| $\tilde{a}$ | typed as | \( \tilde{a} \) |
| $\vec{a}$ | typed as | \( \vec{a} \) |

**Binomials:** The command for binomials is \binom.
Examples: (inline) $\binom{a}{b+c}$ typed as

\( \binom{a}{b + c} \)

and (displayed)

$$\binom{a}{b+c}\binom{\frac{n^2-1}{2}}{n+1}$$

typed as

\[
    \binom{a}{b + c} \binom{\frac{n^{2} - 1}{2}}{n + 1}
\]

**Congruences:** The two most important forms:

| | | |
|---|---|---|
| $a \equiv v \pmod{\theta}$ | typed as | a \equiv v \pmod{ \theta } |
| $a \equiv v \ (\theta)$ | typed as | a \equiv v \pod{ \theta } |

**Delimiters:** These are parentheses-like symbols that expand to bracket a
formula, for example: $(a)$, typed as \( (a) \), and

$$\left(\frac{1}{2}\right)$$

typed as

\[
    \left( \frac{1}{2} \right)
\]

Further examples:

$$\left|\frac{a+b}{2}\right|, \quad \|A^2\|$$

typed as:

\[
    \left| \frac{a + b}{2} \right|,
    \quad \left\| A^{2} \right\|
\]

(\quad is a spacing command.)

**Operators:** To typeset the sine function: $\sin x$, type: \( \sin x \). Note that \( sin x \) prints: $sinx$; the type of $sin$ is wrong, as is the spacing. $\mathcal{AMS}$-LaTeX calls \sin an *operator*; there are a number of operators listed in Sections 4-7 and A-10. Some are just like \sin; others can produce a more complex display:

$$\lim_{x \to 0} f(x) = 0$$

which is typed as

```
\[
    \lim_{x \to 0} f(x)= 0
\]
```

**Ellipses:** \dots produces the ellipsis. In $F(x_1, x_2, \ldots, x_n)$, it prints low dots (this is typed as \( F(x_{1}, x_{2}, \dots , x_{n}) \)). While in $x_1 + x_2 + \cdots + x_n$, it prints centered dots; this is typed as

```
\( x_{1} + x_{2} +  \dots  + x_{n} \)
```

A comma after \dots tells $\mathcal{AMS}$-LaTeX to prints low dots.

**Integrals:** The command for integrals is \int; the lower limit is a subscript and the upper limit is a superscript. Example: $\int_0^\pi \sin x \, dx = 2$ is typed as \( \int_{0}^{\pi} \sin x \, dx = 2 \). (Notice the use of the spacing command \,; see Sections 4-4.2 and B-6.)

**Matrices:** A matrix:

$$
\begin{matrix}
a+b+c & uv & x-y & 27 \\
a+b & u+v & z & 134
\end{matrix}
$$

is typed as follows:

```
\[
    \begin{matrix}
    a + b + c & uv & x - y & 27 \\
    a + b & u + v & z & 134
    \end{matrix}
\]
```

The matrix elements are separated by &; the rows are separated by \\. This form gives no parentheses. If you want parentheses, use the environment name pmatrix; for brackets, bmatrix; for determinant, vmatrix. Example:

$$
\begin{pmatrix}
a+b+c & uv & x-y & 27 \\
a+b & u+v & z & 134
\end{pmatrix}
$$

is typed as follows:

```
\[
    \begin{pmatrix}
    a + b + c & uv & x - y & 27 \\
    a + b & u + v & z & 134
```

```
    \end{pmatrix}
\]
```

**Roots:** \sqrt produces the square root; for instance, $\sqrt{5}$ is typed as

```
\( \sqrt{5} \),
```

and $\sqrt{a + 2b}$ is typed as

```
\( \sqrt{a + 2b} \)
```

The $n$-th root, for instance, $\sqrt[n]{5}$, is done with two arguments:

```
\( \sqrt[n]{5} \)
```

Note that the first argument is in brackets [ ].

**Sums and products:** The command for sum is \sum and for products is \prod. Examples:

$$\sum_{i=1}^{n} x_i^2 \quad \prod_{i=1}^{n} x_i^2$$

typed as

```
\[
    \sum_{i=1}^{n}{x_{i}^{2}} \quad
        \prod_{i=1}^{n}{x_{i}^{2}}
\]
```

(We used the spacing command \quad to separate the two formulas.)
Such operators are called *large operators*; all of them are listed in Sections 4-9 and A-10. They display in a different style (and size) in an inline formula: $\sum_{i=1}^{n} x_i^2 \quad \prod_{i=1}^{n} x_i^2$.

**Text:** Place text in a formula with the \text command. For instance,

$$a = b \quad \text{by assumption}$$

is typed as

```
\[
    a = b \text{\quad by assumption}
\]
```

Note the space command \quad in the argument of \text before "by".

**2-3.4. Building a formula step-by-step.** It is simple to build up complicated formulas from the components described in Section 2-3.3. Take the formula:

$$\sum_{i=1}^{\left[\frac{n}{2}\right]} \binom{x_{i,i+1}^{i^2}}{\left[\frac{i+3}{3}\right]} \frac{\sqrt{\mu(i)^{\frac{3}{2}}(i^2-1)}}{\sqrt[3]{\rho(i)-2} + \sqrt[3]{\rho(i)-1}}$$

We build this up in several steps. Create a new file in the Editor in the work subdirectory/folder. Call it formula.tex, and type in the lines:

```
%File: formula.tex
%Typeset with AMSLaTeX format
\documentstyle[amscd,amssymb,verbatim]{amsart}
\errorcontextlines=0 \textwidth=29pc

\begin{document}
\end{document}
```

and save it. At present, this has an empty document environment. (The quickest way to create this file is to open mathb.tex, save it under the name formula.tex, and edit out the lines in the document environment.) We shall type each part of the formula as an inline or a displayed formula so that we can typeset the document and check for errors.

**Step 1.** Let us start with $\left[ \frac{n}{2} \right]$: \( \left[ \frac{n}{2} \right] \). Type this in formula.tex, and test it by typesetting it.

**Step 2.** Now we can do the sum; for the superscript, we can cut and paste the formula we created in Step 1 (without the inline math environment delimiters):

$$\sum_{i=1}^{\left[ \frac{n}{2} \right]}$$

we type it as

```
\[
    \sum_{i = 1}^{ \left[ \frac{n}{2} \right] }
\]
```

**Step 3.** Next, we do the two formulas in the binomial:

$$x_{i,i+1}^{i^2} \qquad \left[ \frac{i+3}{3} \right],$$

type them as separate formulas in formula.tex:

```
\[
    x_{i, i + 1}^{i^{2}}  \left[ \frac{i + 3}{3} \right]
\]
```

**Step 4.** Now it is easy to do the binomial. Type the following formula by cutting and pasting from the previous formulas:

```
\[
    \binom{ x_{i,i + 1}^{i^{2}} }{ \left[ \frac{i + 3}{3} \right] }
\]
```

and it prints:

$$\binom{x_{i,i+1}^{i^2}}{\left[\frac{i+3}{3}\right]}$$

**Step 5.** Next we do the formula under the square root: $\mu(i)^{\frac{3}{2}}(i^2 - 1)$, typed as

\( \mu(i)^{ \frac{3}{2} } (i^{2} - 1) \)

and we type the square root, $\sqrt{\mu(i)^{\frac{3}{2}}(i^2 - 1)}$, as:

\( \sqrt{ \mu(i)^{ \frac{3}{2} } (i^{2} - 1) } \)

**Step 6.** The two cubic roots, $\sqrt[3]{\rho(i) - 2}$ and $\sqrt[3]{\rho(i) - 1}$, are easy to type:

\( \sqrt[3]{ \rho(i) - 2 } \)    \( \sqrt[3]{ \rho(i) -1 } \)

**Step 7.** So now we get the fraction:

$$\frac{\sqrt{\mu(i)^{\frac{3}{2}}(i^2 - 1)}}{\sqrt[3]{\rho(i) - 2} + \sqrt[3]{\rho(i) - 1}}$$

typed, cut, and pasted as

\[
    \frac{  \sqrt{ \mu(i)^{ \frac{3}{2}} (i^{2} -1) }  }
    {  \sqrt[3]{\rho(i) - 2} + \sqrt[3]{\rho(i) - 1}  }
\]

**Step 8.** Finally, we get the formula

$$\sum_{i=1}^{\left[\frac{n}{2}\right]} \binom{x_{i,i+1}^{i^2}}{\left[\frac{i+3}{3}\right]} \frac{\sqrt{\mu(i)^{\frac{3}{2}}(i^2 - 1)}}{\sqrt[3]{\rho(i) - 2} + \sqrt[3]{\rho(i) - 1}}$$

by cutting and pasting the pieces together, leaving only one pair of display math delimiters:

\[
    \sum_{i = 1}^{ \left[ \frac{n}{2} \right] }
    \binom{ x_{i, i + 1}^{i^{2}} }
    { \left[ \frac{i + 3}{3} \right] }
    \frac{  \sqrt{ \mu(i)^{ \frac{3}{2}} (i^{2} - 1) }  }
    {  \sqrt[3]{\rho(i) - 2} + \sqrt[3]{\rho(i) - 1}  }
\]

Notice the use of spacing to help distinguish the braces. New lines for the various pieces, indentation for the second argument of \frac. **Keep the source file readable.** Of course, this is for your benefit, $\mathcal{A}\mathcal{M}\mathcal{S}$-LATEX does not care; it would also accept

\[\sum_{i=1}^{\left[\frac{n}{2}\right]}\binom{x_{i',i+1}^{i^{2}}}
{\left[\frac{i+3}{3}\right]}\frac{\sqrt{\mu(i)^{\f'rac{3}
{2}}(i^{2}-1)}}{\sqrt[3]{\rho(i)-2}+\sqrt[3]{\r'ho(i)-1}}\]

Problems arise with this style (or lack thereof) when you make a mistake. Try to find the error in the next version:

\[\sum_{i=1}^{\left[\frac{n}{2}\right]}\binom{x_{i',i+1}^{i^{2}}}
{\left[\frac{i+3}{3}\right]}\frac{\sqrt{\mu(i)^{\f'rac{3}
{2}}}(i^{2}-1)}}{\sqrt[3]{\rho(i)-2}+\sqrt[3]{\'rho(i)-1}}\]

( \frac{3}{2} should be followed by } and not by }}.)

## 2-4. Formula gallery

In this section, we present the "Formula gallery" (gallery.tex on the DISK). This is a collection of formulas, some simple, some complex, to illustrate the power of $\mathcal{A}\mathcal{M}\mathcal{S}$-LaTeX. Most of the commands in these examples have not yet been discussed but comparing the source file with the typeset version should clear up most questions. Occasionally, we give you a helping hand with some comments.

Many of these formulas are from text books and research articles. The last six are reproduced from the document testart.tex distributed by the $\mathcal{A}\mathcal{M}\mathcal{S}$ with $\mathcal{A}\mathcal{M}\mathcal{S}$-LaTeX.

**1.** \left| and \right| print | symbols whose size is adjusted to the size of the other math symbols in the formula. \frak gives the *Fraktur font*:

$$\left| \bigcup (I_j \mid j \in J) \right| < \mathfrak{m}$$

typed as

```
\[
    \left| \bigcup ( I_{j} \mid j \in J  ) \right|  < \frak m
\]
```

Notice that both | and \mid print |; the difference is that \mid also provides the extra spacing we need.

**2.** Note that we need a space both before and after "for some" in the next example. The argument of \text is in text mode, so a single space is recognized.

$$A = \{ x \in X \mid x \in X_i \text{ for some } i \in I \}$$

```
\[
    A = \{ x \in X \mid x \in X_{i} \text{ for some } i \in I \}
\]
```

**3.**

$$x \mapsto \{ c \in C \mid c \leq x \}$$

```
\[
    x \mapsto \{ c \in C \mid c \leq x \}
\]
```

**4.**

$$\langle a_1, a_2 \rangle \leq \langle a_1', a_2' \rangle \text{ iff } a_1 < a_1', \text{ or } a_1 = a_1' \text{ and } a_2 \leq a_2'$$

```
\[
    \langle a_{1}, a_{2} \rangle \le
    \langle a_{1}',a_{2}' \rangle \text{  if{f} }
    a_{1} < a_{1}' \text{, or } a_{1} = a_{1}'
    \text{ and } a_{2} \le a_{2}'
\]
```

Note that there are two spaces before "if{f}" in the argument of \text; since the argument is in text mode, two spaces are the same as a single space. Moreover, we put the second f in braces to avoid the use of the ligature (the merging of the two f's; see Section 3-4.5).

**5.** Here are some examples of Greek letters:

$$\Gamma_{u'} = \{\gamma \mid \gamma < 2\chi,\ B_\alpha \nsubseteq u',\ B_\gamma \subseteq u'\}$$

```
\[
   \Gamma_{u'} = \{ \gamma \mid \gamma < 2\chi,
    \ B_{\alpha} \nsubseteq u', \ B_{\gamma} \subseteq u' \}
\]
```

See Section A-1 for a complete listing of Greek letters.

**6.** \Bbb gives the *Blackboard bold font* (available only in upper case):

$$A = B^2 \times \mathbb{Z}$$

```
\[
   A = B^{2} \times {\Bbb Z}
\]
```

**7.** \left( and \right) tell $\mathcal{A}\mathcal{M}\mathcal{S}$-LATEX to size the parentheses correctly (relative to the size of the symbols in the parentheses).

$$\left(\bigvee(s_i \mid i \in I)\right)^c = \bigvee(s_i^c \mid i \in I)$$

```
\[
   \left( \bigvee ( s_{i} \mid i \in I ) \right)^{c} =
   \bigvee ( s_{i}^{c} \mid i \in I )
\]
```

Notice how the superscript is placed right on top of the subscript in $s_i^c$.

**8.** We use \textstyle so that the large operator is displayed in the inline style:

$$f(\mathbf{x}) = \bigvee_{\mathfrak{m}}(\bigwedge_{\mathfrak{m}}(x_j \mid j \in I_i) \mid i < \aleph_\alpha)$$

```
\[
   \textstyle
   f(\bold{x}) = \bigvee_{\frak m} ( \bigwedge_{\frak m}
      (x_{j} \mid j \in I_{i}) \mid i < \aleph_{\alpha})
\]
```

**9.**

$$y \vee \bigvee([B_\gamma] \mid \gamma \in \Gamma) \equiv z \vee \bigvee([B_\gamma] \mid \gamma \in \Gamma) \pmod{\Phi^x}$$

```
\[
   y \vee \bigvee ( [B_{\gamma}] \mid \gamma )
    \in \Gamma \equiv z \vee \bigvee ( [B_{\gamma}]
    \mid \gamma \in \Gamma ) \pmod{ \Phi^{x} }
\]
```

**10.** \left. is the blank left delimiter.

$$F(x)\big|_a^b$$

```
\[
  \left. F(x) \right|_{a}^{b}
\]
```

**11.**

$$\overset{\alpha}{a} \quad \underset{\alpha}{X}$$

```
\[
  \overset{\alpha}{a} \quad \underset{\alpha}{X}
\]
```

**12.**

$$f(x) \overset{\text{def}}{=} x^2 - 1$$

```
\[
  f(x) \overset{ \text{def} }{=} x^{2} - 1
\]
```

**13.**

$$\overbrace{a + b + \cdots + z}$$

```
\[
  \overbrace{a + b + \dots + z}
\]
```

**14.**

$$\begin{vmatrix} a + b + c & uv \\ a + b & c + d \end{vmatrix}$$

```
\[
  \begin{vmatrix}
    a + b + c & uv \\
    a + b & c + d
  \end{vmatrix}
\]
```

$$\begin{Vmatrix} a + b + c & uv \\ a + b & c + d \end{Vmatrix}$$

```
\[
  \begin{Vmatrix}
    a + b + c & uv \\
    a + b & c + d
  \end{Vmatrix}
\]
```

**15.**

$$\sum_{j \in \mathbf{n}} b_{ij} \hat{y}_j = \sum_{j \in \mathbf{n}} b_{ij}^{(\lambda)} \hat{y}_j + (b_{ii} - \lambda_i)\hat{y}_i\hat{y}$$

\[
    \sum_{j \in \bold n} b_{ij} \hat{y}_{j} =
    \sum_{j \in \bold n} b^{ (\lambda) }_{ij} \hat{y}_{j} +
    (b_{ii} - \lambda_{i}) \hat{y}_{i} \hat{y}
\]

**16.** We may try to type the formula:

$$\left( \prod_{j=1}^{n} \hat{x}_j \right) H_c = \frac{1}{2}\hat{k}_{ij} \det \widehat{\mathbf{K}}(i|i)$$

as

\[
    \left( \prod^n_{\, j = 1} \hat x_{j} \right) H_{c} =
    \frac{1}{2} \hat k_{ij} \det \hat{ \bold{K} }(i|i)
\]

However, this produces:

$$\left( \prod_{j=1}^{n} \hat{x}_j \right) H_c = \frac{1}{2}\hat{k}_{ij} \det \hat{\mathbf{K}}(i|i)$$

We correct the parentheses that are too large by using \biggl and \biggr in place of \left( and \right), respectively; and the hat over $K$ that is too small by using \widehat:

\[
    \biggl( \prod^n_{\, j = 1} \hat x_{j} \biggr) H_{c} =
    \frac{1}{2} \hat{k}_{ij} \det \widehat{ \bold{K} }(i|i)
\]

**17.** In this formula we use \overline{I} to get $\overline{I}$; it seems to me that \bar{I} (which prints $\bar{I}$) is less pleasing:

$$\det \mathbf{K}(t = 1, t_1, \ldots, t_n) = \sum_{I \in \mathbf{n}}(-1)^{|I|} \prod_{i \in I} t_i \prod_{j \in I}(D_j + \lambda_j t_j) \det \mathbf{A}^{(\lambda)}(\overline{I}|\overline{I}) = 0$$

\[
    \det \bold{K} K (t = 1, t_{1}, \dots, t_{n}) =
    \sum_{I \in \bold{n} }(-1)^{|I|}
    \prod_{i \in I} t_{i}
    \prod_{j \in I} (D_{j} + \lambda_{j} t_{j})
    \det \bold{A}^{(\lambda)} (\overline{I} | \overline{I}) = 0
\]

Observe that, in math, the command \bold (**not** the command \bf) produces a boldface letter.

**18.** \; is a spacing command.

$$D_l = \sum_{I_l \subseteq \mathbf{n}} D(t_1, \ldots, t_n) \Bigg|_{t_i = \begin{cases} 0, & \text{if } i \in I_l \\ 1, & \text{otherwise} \end{cases}}, \quad i=1,\ldots,n$$

```
\[
  D_{1} =
   \left. %matches \right|
      \sum_{I_{1}} \subseteq \bold{n} } D(t_{1}, \dots, t_{n})
   \right|_{t_{i} = %beginning of subscript
   \left\{% the large curly bracket, matches  \right.
      \begin{smallmatrix}
         0,& \text{if } i \in I_{1} \quad \\
         % \quad added for centering
         1,& \text{otherwise}
      \end{smallmatrix}
   \right.
   \; , \; \; i=1, \dots, n} %end of subscript
\]
```

Observe that we do not use the cases subsidiary math environment in the subscript (see Section 8-3.4) but emulate it with \left{, \right., and the smallmatrix subsidiary math environment.

**19.** \| gives the ‖ in this formula:

$$\lim_{(v,v')\to(0,0)} \frac{H(z+v) - H(z+v') - BH(z)(v-v')}{\|v - v'\|} = 0$$

```
\[
  \lim_{(v, v') \to (0, 0)}
   \frac{H(z + v) - H(z + v') - BH(z)(v - v')}
   {\| v - v' \|}  = 0
\]
```

**20.**

$$\int_{\mathcal{D}} |\overline{\partial u}|^2 \Phi_0(z) e^{\alpha|z|^2} \geq c_4 \alpha \int_{\mathcal{D}} |u|^2 \Phi_0 e^{\alpha|z|^2} + c_5 \delta^{-2} \int_A |u|^2 \Phi_0 e^{\alpha|z|^2}$$

```
\[
  \int_{\cal D} | \overline{\partial u} |^{2}
   \Phi_{0}(z) e^{\alpha |z|^2} \geq c_{4} \alpha
   \int_{\cal D} |u|^{2} \Phi_{0} e^{\alpha |z|^{2}}
   + c_{5} \delta^{-2} \int_ {A} |u|^{2} \Phi_{0}
   e^{\alpha |z|^{2}}
```

\]

You may prefer to use the Euler Script D instead of the Calligraphic D in this formula:

$$\int_{\mathcal{D}} |\overline{\partial u}|^2 \Phi_0(z) e^{\alpha|z|^2} \geq c_4 \alpha \int_{\mathcal{D}} |u|^2 \Phi_0 e^{\alpha|z|^2} + c_5 \delta^{-2} \int_A |u|^2 \Phi_0 e^{\alpha|z|^2}$$

See Sections 4-13.1 and 11-2 on how to use Euler Script.

**21.** \hdotsfor places dots spanning multiple columns in the matrix:

$$\begin{Vmatrix} \dfrac{\varphi}{(\varphi_1, \varepsilon_1)} & 0 & \cdots & & 0 \\ \dfrac{\varphi k_{n2}}{(\varphi_2, \varepsilon_1)} & \dfrac{\varphi}{(\varphi_2, \varepsilon_2)} & \cdots & & 0 \\ \hdotsfor{5} \\ \dfrac{\varphi k_{n1}}{(\varphi_n, \varepsilon_1)} & \dfrac{\varphi k_{n2}}{(\varphi_n, \varepsilon_2)} & \cdots & \dfrac{\varphi k_{n\,n-1}}{(\varphi_n, \varepsilon_{n-1})} & \dfrac{\varphi}{(\varphi_n, \varepsilon_n)} \end{Vmatrix}$$

```
\[
  \begin{Vmatrix}
    \dfrac{\varphi} {(\varphi_{1},\varepsilon_{1})}
    & 0 & \cdots & 0 \\
    \dfrac{\varphi k_{n2}}{(\varphi_{2},\varepsilon_{1})} &
    \dfrac\varphi{(\varphi_{2},\varepsilon_{2})}
    & \cdots & 0 \\
    \hdotsfor{5} \\
    \dfrac{\varphi k_{n1}}{(\varphi_{n},\varepsilon_{1})} &
    \dfrac{\varphi k_{n2}}{(\varphi_{n},\varepsilon_{2})} &
    \cdots & \dfrac{\varphi k_{n\,n-1}}{(\varphi_{n},
    \varepsilon_{n-1})} & \dfrac{\varphi}{(\varphi_{n},
    \varepsilon_{n})}
  \end{Vmatrix}
\]
```

## 2-5. Typing equations and displayed formulas

**2-5.1. Equations.** The equation environment creates displayed math with a formula number automatically generated and displayed by $\mathcal{A}\mathcal{M}\mathcal{S}$-L&#8202;AT&#8202;E&#8202;X. The equation

$$(1) \qquad \int_0^\pi \sin x\, dx = 2.$$

is typed as

```
\begin{equation} \label{E:firstInt}
   \int_{0}^{\pi} \sin x \, dx = 2.
\end{equation}
```

Of course, the number generated depends on how many equations precede the given one.

Give each equation a name as the argument of the command \label. In this section, let us call the first equation "firstInt" (first integral). We use the convention that the name (label) of an equation starts with "E:".

The number generated by the command \label{E:firstInt} can be referenced with the command \ref. Example: typing

```
see \ref{E:firstInt}
```

produces: see 1. Alternatively, you can use the command \eqref; for instance,

```
see \eqref{E:firstInt}
```

produces: see (1). The great virtue of this system is that if a new equation is introduced or the existing ones are rearranged, the numbering will automatically adjust to reflect the changes. **For the renumbering to work, you do have to typeset the source file twice** (that is, for the **PC**, give the

```
tex &amslatex article
```

command twice, where article is the name of the source file; for the **Mac**, from the Typeset menu, choose Typeset twice).

An equation will be numbered whether or not there is a \label command attached to it. Of course, if there is no \label command, the number generated by $\mathcal{AMS}$-LaTeX for the equation cannot be referenced. As a rule, if $\mathcal{AMS}$-LaTeX generates a number, there should be a label so that the number can be referenced.

The system we have described here could be called *symbolic numbering*. The argument of \label is the "symbol" for the number, and \ref provides the symbolic referencing. $\mathcal{AMS}$-LaTeX uses the same mechanism for all numberings it automatically generates, whether they are for equations, theorems, lemmas, or bibliographic references (except that for bibliographic references the commands are \bibitem and \cite; see Sections 2-7 and 2-8.3).

At the end of the typesetting, $\mathcal{AMS}$-LaTeX stores the symbols in the aux file. For every symbol, it stores the number the symbol corresponds to (and also the page number on which the symbol occurs in the typeset version).

Equations can also be *tagged* by attaching the name to the formula with the command \tag; the tag replaces the number.

Example:

$$\text{(Int)} \qquad\qquad \int_0^\pi \sin x \, dx = 2.$$

is typed as

```
\begin{equation}
    \int_{0}^{\pi} \sin x \, dx = 2. \tag{Int}
\end{equation}
```

Tags are **absolute**; this equation is always ref.
are **relative**; they can change as equations are adde
we need a symbol and the \ref command to refer .

**2-5.2. Aligned formulas.** $\mathcal{A}\mathcal{M}\mathcal{S}$-L^AT_EX has many w
las. Right now we shall discuss only three: *simple align*
Chapter 8 for a discussion of the others.

The environment align is used for simple align, and th
used for double align. Each line in these environments is .
automatically numbers them.

**Simple align.** Simple align is used to align two or more fo
formula with the "=" signs aligned (again, \\ is the line separat.

• In each i
• Plac
42

(2) $$x = y + z,$$

(3) $$u = v + w.$$

type
```
\begin{align}
   x &= y + z, \label{E:equ1} \\
   u &= v + w. \label{E:equ2}
\end{align}
```
(These equations are numbered (2) and (3) because they are preceded by a single numbered equation in the text.)

This environment can also be used to break a long formula into two. Since numbering both lines is undesirable, we prevent it with the \notag command.

(4) $$h(x) = \int \left( \frac{f(x) + g(x)}{1 + f^2(x)} + \frac{1 + f(x)g(x)}{\sqrt{1 - \sin x}} \right) dx$$
$$= \int \frac{1 + f(x)}{1 + g(x)} \, dx - 2 \tan^{-1}(x - 2)$$

may be typed as
```
\begin{align} \label{E:longInt}
   h(x) &= \int \left( \frac{ f(x) + g(x) }{ 1+ f^{2}(x) } +
   \frac{1+ f(x)g(x) }{ \sqrt{1 - \sin x} } \right) \, dx \\
   &= \int \frac{ 1 + f(x) }{ 1 + g(x) } \, dx - 2 \tan^{-1}
   (x-2) \notag
\end{align}
```
(See the \split environment in Section 8-2.1 for a better way to split a long formula; see also Section 8-2 on how to center the formula number (4) between the two lines.)

The rules are easy for the align environment:

   • Separate the lines with \\.

...ne, indicate the alignment point with &.

...e a \notag in each line which you do not wish numbered.

In each numbered line place a \label, so you can reference the line with \ref or \eqref.

**Doubly aligned formulas.** *Double align* will align the formulas, and align the explanatory text as in:

$$
\begin{aligned}
(5) \qquad x &= x \wedge (y \vee z) && \text{(by distributivity)} \\
&= (x \wedge y) \vee (x \wedge z) && \text{(by Condition (M))} \\
&= y \vee z
\end{aligned}
$$

This is typed as:

```
\begin{alignat}{2} \label{E:DoAlign}
  x &= x \wedge (y \vee z)
                    &&\text{\quad (by distributivity)} \\
  &= (x \wedge y) \vee (x \wedge z)
                    &&\text{\quad (by Condition (M))} \notag \\
  &= y \vee z \notag
\end{alignat}
```

The rules are the same as for `align`; in addition, we have a second alignment point in each line, marked by &&. Note the first line of the environment:

```
\begin{alignat}{2}
```

the number 2 (in braces) specifies the number of alignments.

The `alignat` environment can do much more than double align; see Section 8-1.2.

**Cases.** Finally, the `cases` environment is a *subsidiary math environment*; it must be used in a displayed math environment or in the `equation` environment (more precisely, in one of the equation environments: `equation`, `align`, `alignat`, `split`; see Chapter 8). Here is a typical example:

$$
f(x) = \begin{cases}
-x^2, & \text{if } x \le 0; \\
0 + x, & \text{if } 0 \le x \le 1; \\
x^2, & \text{otherwise.}
\end{cases}
$$

which may be typed as follows:

```
\[
  f(x)=
  \begin{cases}
    -x^{2},  &\text{if \( x \leq 0 \);} \\
    0 + x,   &\text{if \( 0 \leq x \leq 1 \);} \\
    x^{2},   &\text{otherwise.}
  \end{cases}
\]
```

The rules for cases are the simplest.

- Separate the lines with \\.
- In each line, indicate the alignment point for the text with &.

### 2-6. The anatomy of an article

The source file of an article consists of four parts: the *Preamble*, the *Topmatter*, the *Body*, and the *Bibliography*. In this section, we briefly review what the four parts do.

Our sample article is article.tex on the DISK; you can find the typeset version on pages xviii–xx. The printed source file and the typeset version of the sample article are shown together on pages xxii–xxix. Use the sample article to follow the discussion.

**2-6.1. The Preamble.** The *Preamble* (on page xxii of the sample article) is the beginning of the source file up to the line

```
\begin{document}
```

The Preamble contains instructions for the whole article. It is also where (using commented out lines, that is, lines that start with %) you may describe the topic/title of the article, with which format file to typeset it, and so on.

The Preamble contains the *Style section*, the *Declaration section*, and the *Command section*.

The Style section names the document style (and its options) for the article.

A *declaration* is a theorem, definition, corollary, note, and so on. The Declaration section defines the attributes of the declarations for the article: their names, styles, and form of numbering; there are seven declarations defined in the sample article. The actual declarations are in the Body of the article.

The Command section names the macro files (if any), and defines the commands/macros for the article. The sample article article.tex has a very small Command section. You can find a more typical Command section in article2.tex; see the DISK and Section 11-3.

**2-6.2. The Topmatter and the Body.** The Topmatter (on page xxii for the sample article) contains the "titlepage" information; it is placed between the lines:

```
\begin{document}
```

and

```
\maketitle
```

The Body of an article is between the line

```
\maketitle
```

and the Bibliography (see the Body of the sample article on pages xxii–xxix). The Body starts (with the optional) abstract, which is between the lines

```
\begin{abstract}
```

and

```
\end{abstract}
```

**2-6.3. The Bibliography.** Finally, the Bibliography (on page xxix for the sample article) is between the lines

```
\begin{thebibliography}{9}
```

and

```
\end{thebibliography}
```

The line

```
\end{document}
```

indicates the end of the source file.

In the typeset article, the Bibliography is titled "References".

## 2-7. Setting up your article template

In this section, we shall create a "template" for your articles, containing customized Preamble and Topmatter, and models for the bibliographic items. By a template, we mean a file which is on the disk as a "read-only" file; with the Editor, open the file, save it under a new name (say, in the work subdirectory/folder), and proceed to write the new article—without having to learn the rules governing the Preamble and the Topmatter.

By way of an example, we create a template.

**Step 1.** In the Editor, open the document article.tpl in the parti subdirectory/folder of the disk subdirectory/folder (alternatively, type in the lines as shown in this section), and save it in the work subdirectory/folder of the disk subdirectory/folder under the name gg.tpl (of course, use your own initials). The first few lines read:

```
%Sample file: article.tpl
%Typeset with AMSLaTeX format file

%Preamble
%Style section
\documentstyle[amscd,amssymb,verbatim]{amsart}

%Declaration section
```

We use commented out lines (lines that start with %) for comments and for grouping.

Rewrite line 1 to read:

```
%This is the article template, gg.tpl
```

The line

```
\documentstyle[amscd,amssymb,verbatim]{amsart}
```

specifies the document style amsart.sty, the $\mathcal{AMS}$ article document style, and some options; see Section 5-1.

**Step 2.** Following the line:

```
%Declaration section
```

five options are presented for the declaration, style, and numbering of constructs such as theorems, definitions, lemmas, and so on.

*Option 1*: The article has Theorems, Lemmas, and Definitions; they are all in the most emphatic (plain) style. Each is separately numbered, so that you may have Definition 1, Definition 2, Theorem 1, Lemma 1, Lemma 2, Theorem 2, and so on.

If you choose Option 1, delete all the lines relating to the other options, so you are left with the lines:

```
%Declaration section
%Theorems, Lemmas, Definitions in the most
%emphatic style (plain), each numbered consecutively

\theoremstyle{plain}
\newtheorem{Thm}{Theorem}
\newtheorem{Lem}{Lemma}
\newtheorem{Def}{Definition}
```

We use commented out lines (lines that start with %) to describe the option.

A typical declaration is

```
\theoremstyle{plain}
\newtheorem{Thm}{Theorem}
```

This defines a new environment Thm which is used to invoke the Theorem; see Section 2-8.2. The second argument, Theorem, is the name that will be typeset. For a detailed explanation of the form of a declaration, see Section 5-2.2.

*Option 2*: The article has Theorems, Lemmas, Definitions, and Corollaries; they are all in the most emphatic (plain) style. They are all jointly numbered, so that you may have Definition 1, Definition 2, Theorem 3, Corollary 4, Lemma 5, Lemma 6, Theorem 7, and so on.

If you choose Option 2, delete all the lines relating to the other options, so you are left with the lines:

```
%Declaration section
%Theorems, Lemmas, Definitions, and Corollaries in the plain
%style, all jointly numbered

\theoremstyle{plain}
\newtheorem{Thm}{Theorem}
\newtheorem{Lem}[Thm]{Lemma}
\newtheorem{Def}[Thm]{Definition}
\newtheorem{Cor}[Thm]{Corollary}
```

The declaration

```
\newtheorem{Lem}[Thm]{Lemma}
```

shows a command with an *optional argument*; see Section 3-3.

*Option 3*: The article has Theorems, Propositions, Lemmas, and Definitions in the plain style and Notations in the less emphatic definition style. The Notations are not numbered. Propositions and Lemmas are jointly numbered and they are *numbered within sections*, so that you may have Definition 1, Definition 2, Theorem 1, Lemma 1.1, Lemma 1.2, Proposition 1.3, Theorem 2, Lemma 2.1, and so on.

If you choose Option 3, delete all the lines relating to the other options, so you are left with the lines:

```
%Declaration section
%Theorems, Propositions, Lemmas, and Definitions
%in the plain style
%Propositions and Lemmas are jointly numbered within sections
%Notations in the less emphatic (definition)
%style; the Notations are not numbered

\theoremstyle{plain}
\newtheorem{Thm}{Theorem}
\newtheorem{Prop}{Proposition}[section]
\newtheorem{Lem}[Prop]{Lemma}
\newtheorem{Def}{Definition}

\theoremstyle{definition}
\newtheorem{notation}{Notation}
\renewcommand{\thenotation}{}
```

*Option 4*: The article has Theorems, Definitions, and Lemmas in the plain style and Rules in the less emphatic (definition) style. Definitions and Lemmas are jointly numbered, and they are numbered within sections. There is also an unnumbered Main Theorem. So you may have Definition 1.1, Definition 1.2, Main Theorem, Rule, Lemma 1.3, Lemma 2.1, Theorem 1, and so on.

If you choose Option 4, delete all the lines relating to the other options, so you are left with the lines:

```
%Declaration section
%Theorems, Definitions, and Lemmas in the plain style
%Definitions and Lemmas are jointly numbered within sections
%There is a Main Theorem in the plain
%style, unnumbered.
%There are Rules, in the definition style, unnumbered

\theoremstyle{plain}
\newtheorem{Thm}{Theorem}
\newtheorem{Main}{Main Theorem}
\renewcommand{\theMain}{}
\newtheorem{Def}{Definition}[section]
```

```
\newtheorem{Lem}[Def]{Lemma}

\theoremstyle{definition}
\newtheorem{rule}{Rule}
\renewcommand{\therule}{}
```

*Option 5*: The article has Theorems, Corollaries, Lemmas, and Propositions in the plain style and an unnumbered Main Theorem. It has Definitions in the less emphatic (definition) style. All are separately numbered. So that you may have Definition 1, Definition 2, Main Theorem, Lemma 1, Proposition 1, Lemma 2, Theorem 1, Corollary 1, and so on. Notations are in the least emphatic (remark) style, unnumbered.

If you choose Option 5, delete all the lines relating to the other options, so you are left with the lines:

```
%Declaration section
%Theorems, Corollaries, Lemmas, and Propositions, in the plain
%style; all are numbered separately
%There is a Main Theorem in the plain
%style, unnumbered
%There are Definitions, in the definition style
%There are Notations, in the remark style, unnumbered

\theoremstyle{plain}
\newtheorem{Thm}{Theorem}
\newtheorem{Cor}{Corollary}
\newtheorem{Main}{Main Theorem}
\renewcommand{\theMain}{}
\newtheorem{Lem}{Lemma}
\newtheorem{Prop}{Proposition}

\theoremstyle{definition}
\newtheorem{Def}{Definition}

\theoremstyle{remark}
\newtheorem{notation}{Notation}
\renewcommand{\thenotation}{}
```

For gg.tpl, choose Option 5.

Next comes the Command section:

```
%Command section
\errorcontextlines=0
\renewcommand{\rm}{\normalshape}
    %redefining \rm to mean: change to roman style
```

The first command

```
\errorcontextlines=0
```

instructs $\mathcal{AMS}$-LaTeX to display error messages as shown in this book. The second command defines \rm to have the meaning: change to roman style; see Section 3-6.2.

**Step 3.** Then come the lines:

```
\begin{document}
%Topmatter
```

and two choices are presented: One author or two authors (for more complicated situations; see Section 5-4). For this template, gg.tpl, choose one author, so delete the line

```
%One author
```

and delete everything between the lines (inclusive)

```
%End One author
```

and

```
%End Two authors
```

We are left with:

```
\begin{document}
%Topmatter
\title[<short title>]{<title line 1> \\
   <title line 2>}
\author{<name>}
\address{<line 1> \\
   <line 2> \\
   <line3>}
\email{<name>@@<address>}
\thanks{<thanks>}

\keywords{<keywords>}
\subjclass{Primary: <subject>; Secondary: <subject>}
\date{<date>}

%End Topmatter

\maketitle
\begin{abstract}
   <abstract>
\end{abstract}

%Bibliography
\begin{thebibliography}{99}

\end{thebibliography}
\end{document}
```

In the Topmatter section, there are a number of items of information to provide, basically, personal information. So edit

```
\author{<name>}
```

to read

```
\author{G.~Gr\"atzer}
```

and similarly edit \address, \email, and \thanks (of course, using your personal information). Parts that must be edited are enclosed between the carats (angle brackets) < and >; make sure that all the carats are edited out before typesetting the article.

After editing we get:

```
%Topmatter
\title[<short title>]{<title line 1> \\
   <title line 2>}
\author{G. Gr\"atzer}
\address{University of Manitoba \\
   Department of Mathematics \\
   Winnipeg, Man. R3T 2N2 \\
   Canada}
\email{George\_Gratzer@@umanitoba.ca}
\thanks{Research supported by the NSERC of Canada.}

\keywords{<keywords>}
\subjclass{Primary: <subject>; Secondary: <subject>}
\date{<date>}

%End Topmatter

\maketitle
\begin{abstract}
   <abstract>
\end{abstract}

%Bibliography
\begin{thebibliography}{99}

\end{thebibliography}
\end{document}
```

This is a template for future articles, so do not edit the lines (\title, \keyword, and so on) that change from article to article; leave them generic.

Note that the short title is for "running heads" ("headers", that is, for the title shown at the top of every odd page other than the title page); if the title is only one line long, delete the separation mark \\ and the second line. If the title is short, delete [<short title>].

Now save gg.tpl. We can also have a second version, gg2.tpl, with two authors, to be used as a template for joint articles. Note that at the end of the template, just before the line \end{document}, there are two lines:

```
\begin{thebibliography}{99}
```

```
\end{thebibliography}
```

The argument of \begin{thebibliography} should be 99 if there are more than 9 references (see Section 2-8.3); otherwise, it should be 9. In the next section we discuss how to insert the bibliographic items. The templates for the bibliographic items are listed after the line \end{document} as shown in Section 2-8.3.

To make sure that you do not overwrite your template, make it "read only". On the **PC**, you accomplish this with the command:

```
attrib +r gg.tpl
```

On the **Mac**, select the icon for gg.tpl and press Command and I. The information box for the article appears; check "locked" and close the box.

## 2-8. Typing your first $\mathcal{AMS}$-LaTeX article

To start your first article, open the template in the Editor, and save it under the name of the article. Remember that for the **PC** the name should end with .tex; for the **Mac**, the name must be **one word** (no spaces) ending with .tex. Edit the lines of the Topmatter to contain the article information (title, and so on). Make sure there are no carats (angle brackets) left. Then start writing the article after the line

```
\maketitle
```

**2-8.1. Sectioning.** If you wish to divide the article into sections, type the first line (after \maketitle) as follows:

```
\section{Introduction} \label{S:intro}
```

"Introduction" is the title of the section, "S:intro" is the label. We use the convention that the label for a section starts with "S:". The number for the section is automatically assigned by $\mathcal{AMS}$-LaTeX, and you can refer to this section by \ref{S:intro}, as in

```
In Section \ref{S:intro}, we introduced ...
```

For instance, the section title of this section is as follows:

```
\section{Sectioning} \label{S:sectioning}
```

You can refer to the section number by

```
\ref{S:sectioning}
```

**2-8.2. Invoking declarations.** Assuming that we choose Option 5 of the Declaration section, we can declare theorems, corollaries, lemmas, propositions, definitions, notations, and a main theorem. All these take the same form: an environment.

You type a theorem in a Thm environment; the source of the theorem (that is, the part of the source file that produces the theorem) is between the two lines:

`\begin{Thm} \label{T:xxx}`

and

`\end{Thm}`

where T:xxx is the label for the theorem. Of course, xxx should be somewhat descriptive of the contents of the theorem. The theorem number is automatically assigned by $\mathcal{A}_{\mathcal{M}}\mathcal{S}$-LᴬTᴇX, and it can be referenced by \ref{T:xxx} as in

`it follows from Theorem \ref{T:xxx}.`

We use the convention that the label for a theorem starts with "T:".

The environments for corollaries, lemmas, propositions, definitions, notations, and the main theorem follow.

Corollaries:

`\begin{Cor} \label{C:xxx}`
`\end{Cor}`

Lemmas:

`\begin{Lem} \label{L:xxx}`
`\end{Lem}`

Propositions:

`\begin{Prop} \label{P:xxx}`
`\end{Prop}`

Definitions:

`\begin{Def} \label{D:xxx}`
`\end{Def}`

Notations:

`\begin{notation}`
`\end{notation}`

(There is no label for notations because they are unnumbered, by choice.)

And the Main Theorem:

`\begin{Main}`
`\end{Main}`

There is one more environment of importance we should mention here: the environment pf where pf stands for "proof". Place a proof between the lines:

`\begin{pf}`

and

`\end{pf}`

$\mathcal{A}\mathcal{M}\mathcal{S}$-LaTeX will preface your proof with *Proof.*, end it with an end-of-proof symbol, and add a little space after the last line.

Example. To obtain

*Proof.* This is a short proof.   □

type

```
\begin{pf}
This is a short proof.
\end{pf}
```

**2-8.3. Inserting references.** Finally, the Bibliography. Here are the models for the most often used types of references; an article in a journal, a book, an article in a conference proceedings, an article in a book, a Ph.D. thesis, and a technical report:

```
\bibitem{eM57}
    E. T. Moynahan, {\em On a problem of M. H. Stone},
    Acta Math. Acad. Sci.  Hungar. {\bf 8} (1957), 455--460.


\bibitem{gM68}
    G. A. Menuhin, {\em Universal algebra}, D.~ van ~Nostrand,
    Princeton-Toronto-London-Melbourne, 1968.


\bibitem{pK69}
    P. Konig, {\em Composition of functions}, Proceedings of
    the Conference on  Universal Algebra (Kingston, 1969).


\bibitem{hA70}
    H. H. Albert, {\em Free torsoids}, Current Trends in Lattice
    Theory, D. ~Van~  Nostrand, 1970.


\bibitem{sF90}
    S.-K. Foo, {\em Lattice constructions}, Ph.D. thesis,
    University of Winebago,  1990.


\bibitem{gF86}
    G. H. Foster, {\em Computational complexity in lattice
    theory}, Tech. report,  Carnegie Mellon University, 1986.
```

We use the convention that the label for the `\bibitem` is made up from the initials of the author and the year of publication (the second publication by A. B. Reich in 1987 would have the label: aR87a); of course, you can use any label you choose.

Suppose you want to include as the fifth item in the Bibliography the following article:

A. B. Reich, *Duplexes in posets*, Proc. Amer. Math. Soc. **112** (1987), 115–125.

Modeling it after Moynahan's article, we type it as:

```
\bibitem{aR87}
   A. B. Reich, {\em Duplexes in poset},
   Proc. Amer. Math. Soc. {\bf 112} (1987), 115--125.
```

Then a reference to this article can be made with \cite, for instance (if this article is assigned the number 5 by $\mathcal{A}_{\mathcal{M}}\mathcal{S}$-LATEX):

this result was first published in [5].

typed as

```
this result was first published in \cite{aR87}.
```

Note that you have to arrange the references in the order you wish to see them. $\mathcal{A}_{\mathcal{M}}\mathcal{S}$-LATEX will only take care of the numbering and the citations in the text.

## 2-9. More on $\mathcal{A}_{\mathcal{M}}\mathcal{S}$-LATEX error messages

There will probably be a number of mistakes in your first article which you will have to correct. The mistakes come in various flavors:

- Typographical errors. $\mathcal{A}_{\mathcal{M}}\mathcal{S}$-LATEX will just blindly typeset whatever you typed. When you view the typeset version, find these errors, and correct the source file.
- Errors in mathematical formulas or in formatting the text.
- Errors in your instructions to $\mathcal{A}_{\mathcal{M}}\mathcal{S}$-LATEX.

Let us look at some examples. We shall introduce a number of errors in the source file of the sample article article.tex (see pages xxii–xxix), and see what error messages we get.

Type in the source file of the sample article article.tex, or copy it from the parti subdirectory/folder of the disk subdirectory/folder. Make a copy of article.tex in the work subdirectory/folder of the disk subdirectory/folder.

**1.** Go to line 48 (you do not have to count lines; most Editors have a "GO to Line" command) and remove the closing brace } so it reads:

```
\begin{abstract
```

Now typesetting article.tex, $\mathcal{A}_{\mathcal{M}}\mathcal{S}$-LATEX informs you of a mistake:

```
Runaway argument?
{abstract In this note we prove that there exist {\em \ETC.
! Paragraph ended before \begin was complete.
<to be read again>
                   \par
l. 53
```

Line 53 of the file is the line after \end{abstract}. From the error message you can tell that something went wrong with the abstract environment.

**2.** Now correct line 48, and go to line 109, change it from

```
\end{pf}
```

to

```
\end{proof}
```

and typeset again. $\mathcal{A}_{\mathcal{M}}\mathcal{S}$-LaTeX will inform us of another mistake:

```
LaTeX error.  See LaTeX manual for explanation.
               Type  H <return>  for immediate help.
! \begin{pf} ended by \end{proof}.
\@latexerr ....}\errmessage {#1}
```

```
...
```

```
1.109 \end{proof}
```

This is clear. We made the mistake of typing \end{proof} instead of \end{pf}. Pressing Return, $\mathcal{A}_{\mathcal{M}}\mathcal{S}$-LaTeX recovers nicely; only the end-of-proof symbol will be missing.

**3.** Instead of correcting the error in line 109, comment it out:

```
%\end{proof}
```

and introduce an additional error in line 123. This line presently reads:

```
for some \( d \in D \), \( d < 1 \). Then \( \Theta = \iota \).
```

Change \Theta to \Teta:

```
for some \( d \in D \), \( d < 1 \). Then \( \Teta = \iota \).
```

Typesetting the article now, the message is:

```
! Undefined control sequence.
1.123 ...d < 1 \). Then \( \Teta
                                 = \iota \).
```

and pressing Return will give the message:

```
! \begin{pf} ended by \end{document}.
\@latexerr ....}\errmessage {#1}
```

```
...
```

```
1.254 \end{document}
```

These two mistakes are easy to identify. \Teta is a typo for \Theta. Observe how $\mathcal{A}_{\mathcal{M}}\mathcal{S}$-LaTeX tries to match

```
\begin{pf}
```

with

```
\end{document}
```

Undo the two changes (lines 109 and 123).

**4.** The next example shows what happens if the special character @ is not properly handled. Go to line 39:

`\email{menuhin@@ccw.uwinebago.edu}`

and change it to:

`\email{menuhin@ccw.uwinebago.edu}`

When typesetting the article, you get the error message:

```
AmS-TeX error:
! Invalid use of @.
\err@ ...error:}\errmessage {#1}
                                \fi
...
l.254 \end{document}
```

The mistake is at the beginning of the article, and the line number indicated is the very last line. Nevertheless, a search for @ will reveal the error.

**5.** Now correct line 39, and in line 182 omit one \ of the double \ in the formula, that is, change

        `\dotsc \, \rangle \equiv \\`

to

        `\dotsc \, \rangle \equiv \`

Typeset it, and the error message is:

```
AmS-TeX error:
! Extra & on this line.
\err@ ...error:}\errmessage {#1}
                                \fi
...
l.186 \end{align}
```

Line 186 is the line

`\end{align}`

so $\mathcal{AMS}$-LATEX tells you that there is something wrong with the `align` environment. Probably it is best to go to Section 8-1.1 and look up the rules which tell you that \\ marks the end of the line, and that in every line there must be only one &. Since we deleted (part of) the end-of-line symbol \\, $\mathcal{AMS}$-LATEX found two & symbols in the same line, hence the message:

`! Extra & on this line.`

**6.** Now correct the error in line 182, and in the same formula, change line 181 from

        `& \langle \dotsc, 0, \dotsc, \overset{i}{d}, \dotsc, 0,`

to

        `& \langle \dotsc, 0, \dotsc, \overset{i}{d, \dotsc, 0,`

This results in the message:

```
Runaway argument?
 \label {E:cong} & \langle \dotsc , \overset {i}{d, \dotsc \ETC.
! Paragraph ended before \align was complete.
<to be read again>
                     \par
1.205
```

Line 205 is a blank line following \end{pf}. $\mathcal{A}_{\mathcal{M}}\mathcal{S}$-LaTeX skipped over the construct \overset, the uncompleted align environment, the next align environment, a whole displayed formula, and indicates the error past the end of the pf environment. The error message indicates that the error may have been caused by the new paragraph (\par). Of course, the second argument of \overset, the align environments, and the displayed formula share that there can be no new paragraph therein. The solution does not come easily except by isolating all of the last paragraph, and investigating it as described below.

Error messages from $\mathcal{A}_{\mathcal{M}}\mathcal{S}$-LaTeX are sometimes misleading; but there is always some information you may glean from them. As a rule, the error message should at least inform you of the line number (or the paragraph or the formula) where the error was caught. Try to identify the structure that caused the error: a command, an environment, and so on. Read the section of this book that describes the command or environment; it should help in correcting the error.

The best defense is to isolate your problems. Create a file current.tex which is the same as your present article, except that there is only one paragraph between

\begin{document}

and

\end{document}

When this paragraph is typeset correctly, cut and paste it into your source file. If there is only one paragraph in the document, the error is easier to find. If the error is of the type as in the last example,

```
! Paragraph ended before \align was complete.
<to be read again>
                     \par
```

split the paragraph into smaller paragraphs. See also Section 3-5 on how to use the comment environment for finding errors.

## 2-10. Article design

This book attempts to teach how to typeset an article, **not** how to write it. Nevertheless, it seems appropriate to point out some approaches to article design.

The typeset version of our sample article article.tex (pages xviii–xx) looks impressive. To produce an article like this, we have to realize that there are two aspects of article design: the *visual* and *logical*. Let us borrow an example from the sample article to illustrate this: a lemma in an article. We tell $\mathcal{A}_{\mathcal{M}}\mathcal{S}$-LaTeX to make a lemma and number it. There is an equation in the lemma; $\mathcal{A}_{\mathcal{M}}\mathcal{S}$-LaTeX takes care of its numbering and formatting. Here is how to type the lemma (see page xxv):

```
\begin{Lem} \label{L:ccr}
   Let \( \Theta \) be a complete congruence relation of
   \( D^{\langle 2 \rangle} \) such that
   \begin{equation} \label{E:rigid}
      \langle 1, d \rangle \equiv \langle 1, 1 \rangle
      \pmod{\Theta},
   \end{equation}
   for some \( d \in D \), \( d < 1 \). Then \( \Theta = \iota \).
\end{Lem}
```

and this is its typeset form (see page xxv):

**Lemma 2.** *Let $\Theta$ be a complete congruence relation of $D^{\langle 2 \rangle}$ such that*

$$(2.1) \qquad \langle 1, d \rangle \equiv \langle 1, 1 \rangle \pmod{\Theta},$$

*for some $d \in D$, $d < 1$. Then $\Theta = \iota$.*

Notice that $\mathcal{A}_{\mathcal{M}}\mathcal{S}$-LaTeX makes literally hundreds of decisions in typesetting the lemma: from the vertical space before and after the lemma; from the bold **Lemma** to the numbering; the vertical space before and after the equation, and its numbering; the spacing of all the math symbols—inline and displayed formulas are spaced differently; the emphasized text of the lemma, and so on.

The visual decisions were made by professional designers, whose expertise is hidden in TeX itself and in $\mathcal{A}_{\mathcal{M}}\mathcal{S}$-LaTeX. Could we have composed this typeset lemma ourselves? Probably not. A number of aesthetic decisions are difficult for lay persons to make. But even if we could have guessed at the correct spacing, we would have faced the problem of consistency (how do we guarantee that the next lemma will look the same); and just as importantly, we would have spent a great deal of time and energy on the *visual design* of the lemma, as opposed to the *logical design*. With $\mathcal{A}_{\mathcal{M}}\mathcal{S}$-LaTeX, *you can concentrate on the logical design*, and let $\mathcal{A}_{\mathcal{M}}\mathcal{S}$-LaTeX take care of the visual design.

This approach has the great advantage that by changing the document style, the design can be changed. If you code the design into the article ("hard coding" it, a programmer would say), it is very difficult to change it.

$\mathcal{A}_{\mathcal{M}}\mathcal{S}$-LaTeX uses four major tools to separate the logical and visual designs of an article:

> **Commands:** Information can be given to $\mathcal{A}_{\mathcal{M}}\mathcal{S}$-LaTeX as arguments of commands; then it is up to $\mathcal{A}_{\mathcal{M}}\mathcal{S}$-LaTeX to handle the information. For instance, the title page information is given in this form; the organization of the title page is completely up to the document style.
>
> A more subtle example is the use of a command for distinguishing a term or for a notation. For instance, we may use the command \fn for file names. We may define \fn as follows (as explained in Section 10-1):

```
\newcommand{\fn}[1]{ {\tt #1} }
```

which typesets all file names in typewriter style (see Section 3-6.2). Now logically, we have decided that a file name be so designated. Visually, we may change the decision any time. By changing the definition to

```
\newcommand{\fn}[1]{ {\bf #1} }
```

all file names will be typeset in bold; see Section 3-6.2.

A more mathematical example is from article2.tex (slightly simplified here); see Section 11-3 and the DISK. We define the construct $D^{(2)}$ with the command

```
\newcommand{\Ds}{ D^{\langle 2 \rangle} }
```

If the referee (or co-author) suggests a different notation, changing this one line will carry out the change.

**Environments:** Important logical structures are placed in environments. For instance, we can give a list as an environment by saying that this is a list and these are the items; see Section 9-3. Again, how this is typeset is up to $\mathcal{A}\!\mathcal{M}\!\mathcal{S}$-LaTeX; we can even switch from one type of list to another by just changing the name of the environment.

**Declarations:** These are like (numbered) environments except that in the Declaration section we can further specify which one of the three styles is to be used for the typesetting. Any time, we can change the style and the numbering scheme in the Declaration section.

**Cross-referencing:** Since a theorem or a section is written as a logical design, it, or a whole section, or part of a section, can be freely moved around. This gives us tremendous freedom in reorganizing the source file to improve the logical design.

We write articles to communicate. The closer we get to a separation of logical and visual design, the more we can concentrate on communicating our ideas. Of course, we can never quite reach the ideal. For instance, "line too wide" (see Section 3-7.1) is a problem of visual design. When the journal changes the name of the document style, unless the new document style uses the same pagesize as amsart.sty, new "line too wide" problems arise. However, $\mathcal{A}\!\mathcal{M}\!\mathcal{S}$-LaTeX is successful in well over 95% of the time in solving the visual design problems without our intervention. This is getting fairly close to the ideal.

## 2-11. What's next?

You probably know enough about $\mathcal{A}\!\mathcal{M}\!\mathcal{S}$-LaTeX to start writing your first article. The best way to learn $\mathcal{A}\!\mathcal{M}\!\mathcal{S}$-LaTeX is by experimentation. Later, you can start reading PART II.

If you look at the source file of our sample article, your first impression may be how very verbose $\mathcal{A}\!\mathcal{M}\!\mathcal{S}$-LaTeX is. In actual practice, $\mathcal{A}\!\mathcal{M}\!\mathcal{S}$-LaTeX is fairly fast to type. There are two basic tools to make you more efficient.

First, you should have a good Editor with "macro" capability. For instance, you can write a macro so that a single keystroke may produce the text:

```
\begin{Thm} \label{T:}
```

```
\end{Thm}
```

with the cursor in the position following ":" (where you will type the label).

Secondly, customizing $\mathcal{A}_{\mathcal{M}}\mathcal{S}$-LaTeX, will make repetitious structures such as

```
\begin{equation}
    \langle \dotsc, 0, \dotsc, \overset{i}{d}, \dotsc, 0,
    \dotsc \rangle \equiv \langle
    \dotsc, 0, \dotsc, \overset{i}{c}, \dotsc, 0, \dotsc
    \rangle \pmod{\Theta},
\end{equation}
```

(see page xxvii) become much briefer and (with practice) much more readable. In article2.tex (on the DISK and in Section 11-3), using the macros \con (for congruence), \vct (for vector), and \gQ (for Greek theta), this long formula becomes

```
\begin{equation}
    \con{ \vct{i}{d} } = { \vct{i}{c} }(\gQ),
\end{equation}
```

The topic of $\mathcal{A}_{\mathcal{M}}\mathcal{S}$-LaTeX macros is taken up in PART III. The speed is yet to come.

# PART II

# A LEISURELY COURSE

# CHAPTER 3

# Typing Text

### 3-1. The keyboard

Most of the keys on the computer's keyboard produce characters as expected.

**3-1.1. The basic keys.** We group the basic keys as follows:

**Letters:** The 52 letter keys:

a    b    ...    z    A    B    ...    Z

**Digits:** The ten digits:

1    2    ...    9    0

**Punctuation marks:** There are nine:

,    ;    .    ?    !    :    '    '    –

' is the *left single quote*; ' is the *right single quote* and *apostrophe*; see Section 3-4.1. – is the dash or hyphen; see Sections 3-4.2 and 3-4.8.

**Parentheses:** There are four:

(    )    [    ]

( and ) are the *parentheses*; [ and ] are called *brackets*.

**Math symbols:** There are seven:

/    *    +    =    −    <    >

Minus: − is typed as - (hyphen) in math mode; see Section 4-5.1. The last three can only be displayed in math mode. There is also a version of colon (:) for math formulas; see Section 4-4.2.

**Space keys:** Pressing the spacebar (or the tab key), you get the *space character*; pressing the *Return* (or *Enter*) key gives the *end-of-line character*. These keys produce *invisible characters* and do not paint a symbol on the screen.

Sometimes it is important to know whether a space is required. In such cases, we will use the symbol ␣ to indicate a space, for instance, \in␣ut and \␣.

There is also a *visible space key*: ˜ the *nonbreakable space*, discussed in Section 3-4.3.

Of these keys, the period and the space keys require some discussion; see Sections 3-2 and 3-2.1.

**3-1.2. Special keys.** There are thirteen special keys:

     #    \$    %    &    ˜    _    ^    \    {    }    @    "    |

They are mostly used to give instructions to $\mathcal{AMS}$-LaTeX; some are used in math mode (see Chapter 4), and some others in BibTeX (see Chapter 7). See Section 3-4.4 on how to print these characters.

**Tip**. Some email "nodes" do not properly read all the special characters. Send a document with the special characters, and have it checked as to whether it is properly received. A typical line of this document:

```
tilde ˜
```

**3-1.3. Prohibited keys.** Every other key is prohibited! Do not use the computer's modifier keys (**PC**: Alt, Ctrl; **Mac**: Command, Option, Ctrl) to produce special characters. $\mathcal{AMS}$-LaTeX will either reject or misunderstand them.

TeX 3.0 provides the possibility of using some modified keys. Ignore this feature until standards are developed to ensure the portability of the source file.

**Tip**. If there is a prohibited character, you may receive the error message:

```
! Text line contains an invalid character.
1.222 completely irreducible^^?
                          ^^?
```

The line number may be off by one or two. Quite often, it is difficult to get rid of the "invalid character". Try deleting the lines until the error goes away, and retype them.

### 3-2. Words, sentences, and paragraphs

Text is made up of words, sentences, and paragraphs. In text, *words* are separated by spaces. A group of words terminated by the period, the exclamation mark, or the question mark makes a *sentence*. A group of sentences terminated by a blank line makes a *paragraph*.

Here are the most important rules of $\mathcal{AMS}$-LaTeX about spaces in text, sentences, and paragraphs:

**Rule 1**. Two or more spaces in text are the same as one.

**Rule 2**. A space, a tab, and an end-of-line character are regarded in the same way by $\mathcal{AMS}$-LaTeX in text.

**Rule 3**. Two end-of-line characters (that is, a blank line) indicate the end of a paragraph. (\par indicates the same.)

**Rule 4**. Spaces at the beginning of a line are ignored.

Rules **1** and **2** make typing and copying very convenient. In the source file, you do not have to worry about the line length or about the number of spaces separating words, as long as there is one space or end-of-line character separating any two words. So

```
You    do not have to    worry
 about the number of    spaces
separating words,
as long as there is    one space or end-of-line separating
any two words.
```

produces the same sentence as

```
You  do not have to worry about the number of  spaces separating
words, as long as there is one space or end-of-line separating
any two words.
```

However,

```
 the number of    spaces
separating words,
as long
```

and

```
 the number of    spaces
separating words
, as long
```

produce different outputs:

the number of spaces separating words, as long

and

the number of spaces separating words , as long

Observe the space between "words" and the comma in the second version. Of course, that space is produced by the end-of-line character by Rule **2**.

Note, however, the importance of the readability of the source file. $\mathcal{AMS}$-LaTeX may not care about the number of spaces or line length, but you may.

Rule **3** slightly contradicts Rules **1** and **2**; consider it an exception. Sometimes it is more convenient to indicate the end of a paragraph with \par.

There are also some other exceptions to these rules: BibTeX uses slightly different rules (see Section 7-2); delimited macros ignore Rules **1** and **2** (see Section 11-1.4). But these are not very important at this point.

Some environments use slightly different rules for blank lines; see Chapters 8 and 9.

**Tip.** Some email "nodes" cut the text lines off at character position 72. So if you want to email the document, keep the line length at 72 or less.

You may also change these rules. The command \obeyspaces tells $\mathcal{A}_{\mathcal{M}}$S-LᴬTEX to typeset all spaces as is. So

```
{\obeyspaces You    do not have to      worry
 about the number of    spaces
separating words,
as long as there is    one space or end-of-line separating
any two words.   }
```

is typeset

> You   do not have to    worry  about the number of   spaces separating words, as long as there is   one space or end-of-line separating any two words.

See also the related command \obeylines in Section 3-7.1.

**3-2.1. The period.** $\mathcal{A}_{\mathcal{M}}$S-LᴬTEX uses Rules **1** to **4** to decide where to put a space when typesetting a paragraph. It places a certain size space between words—the *interword space*—and a somewhat larger space between sentences —the *intersentence space*. So $\mathcal{A}_{\mathcal{M}}$S-LᴬTEX has to decide whether or not a period indicates the end of a sentence.

**Rule 5**. A period after a capital letter (for instance, A.) signifies an initial in someone's name. Every other period signifies the end of a sentence.

This rule works most of the time. When it does not, you have to inform $\mathcal{A}_{\mathcal{M}}$S-LᴬTEX.

**Rule 6**. If an abbreviation is not a single capital letter (for instance, "etc."), follow it by \␣.

Recall that ␣ is the space character. Example:

```
introduce␣␣the␣second␣variable,␣␣␣etc.\␣␣␣as␣␣required.␣Also,
```

will print:

introduce the second variable, etc. as required. Also,

Notice that "etc." is followed by a regular interword space. The intersentence space following "required." is longer.

**Rule 7**. If a capital letter followed by a period is the end of a sentence, precede the period with \@.

Example:

```
This follows from Condition A\@.  Therefore, we can proceed\\
This follows from Condition A.  Therefore, we can proceed
```

will print:

This follows from Condition A. Therefore, we can proceed
This follows from Condition A. Therefore, we can proceed

Notice that there is not enough space after "A." in the second line.

To make the intersentence space equal to the interword space, use the command \frenchspacing. To restore the spaces of different sizes, give the command \nonfrenchspacing.

### 3-3. Instructing $\mathcal{AMS}$-LaTeX: commands and environments

How do we instruct $\mathcal{AMS}$-LaTeX to do something special for us, such as starting a new line, changing the emphasis, or displaying the next theorem? We accomplish this with commands and environments. For example, the *command* \em instructs $\mathcal{AMS}$-LaTeX to emphasize text; in Section 3-2.1, we introduced the commands \@ and \␣ to instruct $\mathcal{AMS}$-LaTeX what space to use after a period.

The *environment* flushright instructs $\mathcal{AMS}$-LaTeX to typeset the text between the two commands

\begin{flushright}
\end{flushright}

flush right. The environment document contains the Topmatter and the Body of the article, and the environment abstract contains the abstract.

**Tip**. If \end{document} is missing, you get the ∗ prompt (see Sections 1-3.6 and 1-4.4):

(Please type a command or say '\end')
∗

Type \end{document}, and press Return.

**Rule 1**. An environment called name starts with the command

\begin{name}

and ends with

\end{name}

It affects the text between these two commands.

**Rule 2**. All commands to $\mathcal{AMS}$-LaTeX start with the backslash symbol: \. The symbol \ is followed either by a *single character* or by a *string of letters* (one or more letters).

So \# and \' are correct instructions (they are used in Sections 3-4.4 and 3-4.6), and so are \input and \date. However, \input3, \in#ut, and \in␣ut are not correct (3, #, or ␣ should not occur in a string).

$\mathcal{AMS}$-LaTeX finds the end of a command as follows:

**Rule 3**. If the first character of the string is not a letter, the command is terminated after the first character; if the first character of the command is a letter, the command is terminated by the first non-letter.

So \input3 is not really an incorrect command; it is the command \input terminated by 3, which is part of the following text.

$\mathcal{AMS}$-LATEX commands are referred to by many names: *command, control sequence, macro, control symbol and multiletter control sequence*; we shall use *command*. Commands in TEX (as opposed to $\mathcal{AMS}$-LATEX) we shall call *macros*; see Section 11-1.1.

**Rule 4**. Commands and environment names are *case sensitive*:

\ShowLabels

is not the same as

\showlabels

Commands (macros) may have *arguments*, typed in braces when you invoke the command; the argument(s) are used in processing the command. Accents provide very simple examples. For instance, \'{o} (printing ó) consists of the command \' and the argument o; see Section 3-4.6. Another example:

\bibliography{article1}

The command is

\bibliography

and the argument is

article1

see Section 7-3.1.

A few environments also have arguments; see Section 8-1.2 for the environment alignat which is invoked by the lines:

\begin{alignat}{2}

and

\end{alignat}

A command may have more than one arguments. The command \frac (Section 4-5.1) has two; \con (Section 11-1.4) has three.

Some commands (and a few environments) have an *optional argument*, an argument that may or may not be present.

**Rule 5**. An optional argument is enclosed in brackets [].

The command \sqrt (Section 4-5.3) has an optional argument for roots other than the square root: \sqrt[3]{25} prints: $\sqrt[3]{25}$. The \documentstyle command (Section 5-1) has an argument and an optional argument.

See also Section 11-1.4 for special macros with special termination rules.

In Chapters 1 to 8, we use only commands defined by $\mathcal{AMS}$-LATEX.

**Tip**. If you get an error using an $\mathcal{A}_{\mathcal{M}}S$-LATEX command, check:

(1) the spelling of the command, including the use of uppercase and lowercase characters;
(2) if the arguments are provided;
(3) whether the optional argument is in brackets, not braces;
(4) whether the command is properly terminated.

Most errors in the use of commands come from the termination rule. Let us, first, illustrate this with the command \em that produces emphasized text; see Section 3-6.1. The correct use is:

```
{\em␣this␣is␣␣emphasized\/}
```

which prints

*this is emphasized*

\em was terminated by the space. If the space is not there

```
{\emthis␣is␣emphasized\/}
```

you get the error message:

```
! Undefined control sequence.
1.66 \emthis
              is emphasized\/}
```

$\mathcal{A}_{\mathcal{M}}S$-LATEX thinks that \emthis is the command, and of course, does not recognize it.

Secondly, we illustrate the termination rule with the command \TeX that prints TEX ; see Section 3-4.7. Consider the line:

```
We use \TeX  for typesetting math.
```

and would expect to get:

We use TEX for typesetting math.

Instead, we get

We use TEXfor typesetting math.

The spaces after \TeX are regarded as one by Rule **1**. This space terminates the command \TeX, that is why we got: TEXfor. To put a space after TEX, type

```
We use \TeX\ for typesetting math.
```

See "Separating words" in Section 11-1.4 on how to avoid such errors.

**3-3.1. Scope.** A command issued between a pair of braces { } limits the effect of the command; the command has no effect beyond the right brace }.

You can have any number of *nonoverlapping* pairs of braces:

```
{ ... { ... { ... } ... } ... }
```

The innermost pair containing a command is the *scope* of the command; the command has no effect outside its scope; see however Section 11-4.3.

The commands, \begin{name} and \end{name}, bracketing an environment (including inline and display math modes; see Section 4-1), also act as a pair of braces.

Remember the following two obvious but very important rules about braces:

**Rule 6.** Braces must be balanced: an opening brace has to be closed, and a closing brace must have a matching opening brace.

**Rule 7.** Braces cannot overlap.

Violating Rule **6** generates warnings and error messages. If there is one more { opened than closed, the article is typeset, but we get a warning in the log file:

```
(\end occurred inside a group at level 1)
```

For two more { opened than closed, we are warned being inside a group of level 2, and so on. There is a tendency to disregard such warning since

- The article is typeset.
- The error may be difficult to find.

However, the error may have strange consequences. At one point in the writing of this book, there were two more { opened than closed in Chapter 2. As a result, the title of Chapter 7 was placed on a page by itself. So it is best not to disregard such warnings.

If there is one more closing brace }, we get an error message of the type:

```
! Too many }'s
```

Of course, if a special brace does not balance, we shall get an error message as discussed in Section 3-3.

Here are two simple examples of overlapping braces, violating Rule 7:

```
{\em some text \begin{Lem} more text \/} final text \end{Lem}
{some \bf text, then math: $\sqrt{2} }, \sqrt{3}$
```

The following, third, example of overlapping braces you may easily run into:

```
\begin{together}
\begin{Lem}
Statement of lemma.
\end{Lem}
\begin{pf}
Beginning of proof.

\end{together}
Rest of proof.
\end{pf}
```

In this example, we want to keep a lemma (see Section 5-2.3) and the first few lines of the proof (see the pf environment in Section 9-2) on the same page, with the user-defined environment `together` (see Section 11-2). To accomplish this, we place `\begin{together}` before the lemma and `\end{together}` after the first few lines of the proof. In this example, the special braces of `together` overlap the special braces of pf.

The first example (`\em` overlapping with the Lem environment) is easy to correct:

```
{\em ... \/}
\begin{Lem}
{\em ... \/}

 ...
\end{Lem}
```

The third example runs into a real limitation of $\mathcal{AMS}$-LaTeX, and would require more work to overcome it.

If the braces do overlap, and the braces are all { and }, $\mathcal{AMS}$-LaTeX will simply misunderstand the instructions: the closing brace of the first pair will be regarded as the closing brace of the second pair. Real conflicts develop only by using special braces. For instance,

```
{\em some text
\begin{Lem}
more text \/} final text
\end{Lem}
```

will give the error message:

```
! Extra }, or forgotten \endgroup.
1.35 more text \/}
                  final text
```

### 3-4. Symbols not on the keyboard

A typeset article contains a large number of symbols that cannot be typed. Some may be available on the keyboard, but you are prohibited from using them; see Section 3-1.3. In this section, we discuss how to type some of these symbols.

**3-4.1. Quotes.** We can produce single quotes and double quotes.

'subdirectly irreducible' and "subdirectly irreducible"

typed as

```
`subdirectly irreducible' and ``subdirectly irreducible''
```

Here ` is the left single quote, and ' is the right single quote. We get the double quote by doubling the single quotes, and **not** by using ". If you need both together, as in "He said, 'Hi.'", separate them with `\,`:

```
``He said, `Hi.'\,''
```

**3-4.2. Dashes.** Dashes come in three sizes. The shortest (called a *hyphen*) is used to connect words:

Mean-Value Theorem

this is typed as a single dash:

```
Mean-Value Theorem
```

The medium sized variant (called *en dash*) is typed as `--`; it is used for number ranges; for instance, see pages 23–45, typed as `see pages 23--45`.

The longest dash is a punctuation mark—called *em dash*—used to mark an abrupt change in thought or to add emphasis to a parenthetical clause, as in this sentence. We type the two em dashes in the last sentence as follows:

```
punctuation mark---called {\em em dash\/}---used
```

In math mode, the dash becomes the minus sign ($-$); see Section 4-5.1.

**3-4.3. Blue space.** A *blue space* (or *nonbreakable space*, or *tie*) is an interword space between two words where the line cannot be broken; for instance, when referencing P. Neukomm in an article, you do not want P. at the end of a line and Neukomm at the beginning of the next: to ensure this, type P.~Neukomm. Actually, ~ absorbs spaces, so P.~ Neukomm is just as good; this is very convenient when you have to add the ~ during editing. Consider using ~ as shown in the following examples:

```
Theorem ~1,
Donald~E. Knuth,
assume that \( f(x) \) is (a)~ continuous, (b)~ bounded.
```

Of course, if you add too many ~ symbols; for instance,

```
Peter ~ G.~ Neukomm
```

$\mathcal{A}_{\mathcal{M}}S$-LaTeX may send you a message that the line is too wide; see Section 3-7.1.

**3-4.4. Special keys.** Of the thirteen special keys (see Section 3-1.2), nine are produced by typing \ and then the key:

| Type: | Print: | Type: | Print: | Type: | Print: |
|-------|--------|-------|--------|-------|--------|
| \#    | #      | \$    | $      | \%    | %      |
| \&    | &      | \~{}  | ~      | \_    | _      |
| \^{}  | ^      | \{    | {      | \}    | }      |
| @@    | @      | \( \backslash \) | \ | \( * \) | * |

Printing special keys

@ follows a special rule: type `@@` to print @. The symbol @ is mostly used in email addresses (Section 5-4.2).

If for some reason you want to print the backslash, \, see Section 11-1.3 or type

```
\( \backslash \)
```

The key | is never used in text; if you need to print the math symbol |, type \( | \).

The key " should never be used in text for double quotes; see Section 3-4.1 on how to print double quotes.

Finally, * prints * (and in math, it prints ∗).

We can also print special characters with the \char command. For instance, \char 94 prints ̂ and \char 126 prints ˜.

**Tip.** Be careful when typing \{ to print { and \} to print }. Typing { instead of \{—or } instead of \}—you end up with unbalanced braces, in violation of Rule 6 of Section 3-3.1. See that section for the consequences.

**3-4.5. Ligatures.** Certain group of characters, when typeset, are joined together; such compound characters are called *ligatures*. There are five in $\mathcal{AMS}$-LaTeX: ff, fi, fl, ffi, and ffl. $\mathcal{AMS}$-LaTeX automatically does the ligatures, you do not have to do anything. On the other hand, if you want to prevent ligature, put the second character of the group in braces. Compare: iff, iff, typed as `iff`, `if{f}` (as in formula 4 in the Formula galery; see Section 2-4).

**3-4.6. Accents and symbols.** $\mathcal{AMS}$-LaTeX provides 14 foreign accents. You have to type the command for the accent (\ and the symbol) and follow it by the letter (in braces) on which you want the accent placed:

| Type: | Print: | Type: | Print: | Type: | Print: | Type: | Print: |
|-------|--------|-------|--------|-------|--------|-------|--------|
| \`{o} | ò | \'{o} | ó | \"{o} | ö | \H{o} | ő |
| \^{o} | ô | \~{o} | õ | \v{o} | ǒ | \u{o} | uo |
| \={o} | ō | \b{o} | o̩ | \.{o} | ȯ | \d{o} | o̩ |
| \c{o} | o̧ | \t{oo} | o͡o | | | | |

Accents

Examples: To get Grätzer György, type

`Gr\"{a}tzer Gy\"{o}rgy`

or simply

`Gr\"atzer Gy\"orgy`

and for Erdős Pál, type

`Erd\H os P\'al`

To place an accent on top of 'i' or 'j', you must use the *dotless* 'i' and 'j', obtained by \i and \j. Examples: `\'{\i}` prints í, and `\v{\j}` prints ǰ.

Finally, the following two tables list some extra symbols used in text and the list of foreign characters available in TeX.

| Type: | Print: | Type: | Print: | Type: | Print |
|-------|--------|-------|--------|-------|-------|
| \dag | † | \ddag | ‡ | \S | § |
| \P | ¶ | \copyright | © | \pounds | £ |

Extra text symbols

| Type: | Print: | Type: | Print: | Type: | Print: | Type: | Print: | Type: | Print: |
|-------|--------|-------|--------|-------|--------|-------|--------|-------|--------|
| \aa | å | \AA | Å | \ae | æ | \AE | Æ | \o | ø |
| \O | Ø | \oe | œ | \OE | Œ | \l | ł | \L | Ł |
| \ss | ß | ?` | ¿ | !` | ¡ | | | | |

Foreign characters

**3-4.7. Special strings and numbers.** \TeX prints TEX and \LaTeX prints LATEX. Remember to type \TeX\␣ if you need a space after TEX. Of more interest is the command \today which prints today's date in the form: March 15, 1991 (you may want to use this as the argument of \date; see Section 5-4.1).

Remember the termination rule (Rule 3 in Section 3-3).

```
today's date in the form: \today (you may want
```

prints:

today's date in the form: April 19, 1992(you may want

To get the desired line, type \␣ after the date:

today's␣date␣in␣the␣form:␣\today␣(you␣may␣want

One can also view the ellipsis ... , typed as \dots, as a special string; it has more variants in math mode; see Section 4-5.6.

AMS-LATEX also stores some useful numbers:

- \time is the time of the day in minutes since midnight.
- \day is the day of the month.
- \month is the month of the year.
- \year is the current year.

Display a number with the command \the. Example:

```
The year: \the \year, month: \the \month, day: \the \day
```

prints:

The year: 1992, month: 4, day: 12

**3-4.8. Hyphenation.** AMS-LATEX reads the source file a paragraph at a time, and tries to come up with balanced lines; see Section C-2. To achieve this, AMS-LATEX hyphenates long words, using a built-in hyphenation algorithm and the database in the hyphen.tex document. You can help AMS-LATEX to do a better job:

**Rule 1.** Put *optional hyphens* in the text; and optional hyphen is typed as \-; this will encourage AMS-LATEX to hyphenate the word at this point if the need arises.

Example: data\-base

**Rule 2.** List the words that often need help in a command

\hyphenation{data-base Birkh-h\"auser}

Please, note that in the \hyphenation command the hyphens are designated by "-" and not by "\-", and the words are separated by spaces (not by commas).

**Rule 3.** To *prevent* hyphenation, put the offending word in a \text command. |

Example: type the word "database" as \text{database} if you do not want the word hyphenated.

**Tip.** $\mathcal{A}_{\mathcal{M}}$S-LaTeX does not hyphenate a word with a hyphen except at the hyphen; nor does it hyphenate a word followed by an em dash; see Section 3-4.2. Such words often need help.

**Rule 4.** Use the *unbreakable hyphen*, @-, for a hyphen where the word cannot be |
broken.

Example: "m-complete lattice" should not be broken after m; so type it as

\( \frak{m} \)@-complete lattice

(See Section 4-13.1 for \frak.)

**Tip.** Editors have a tendency to wrap lines in the source file by breaking them at a hyphen, as in this example:

It follows from Theorems \ref{T:Mn} and \ref{T:Ap} that complete-
simple lattices are very large.

This is typeset by $\mathcal{A}_{\mathcal{M}}$S-LaTeX as follows

It follows from Theorems 2 and 5 that complete- simple lattices are very large.

As you can see, there is a space between the hyphen and "simple". Indeed, by Rule 2 of Section 3-2, the end-of-line character following the hyphen (which was placed there by the Editor to break the line) was interpreted by $\mathcal{A}_{\mathcal{M}}$S-LaTeX as a space. To correct the error, make sure that there is no such line break, or comment out (see Section 3-5) the end-of-line character:

It follows from Theorems \ref{T:Mn} and \ref{T:Ap} that complete-%
simple lattices are very large.

Alternatively, rearrange the two lines:

It follows from Theorems 2 and 5 that
complete-simple lattices are very large.

### 3-5. Commenting out

The % symbol makes $\mathcal{A}_{\mathcal{M}}$S-LaTeX ignore the rest of the line. Typical use: |

therefore, a reference to Theorem 1%check this!

a comment to yourself.

% has many uses. For instance, a typical document style command (see Section 5-1):

\documentstyle[amscd,amssymb,verbatim]{amsart}

may be typed, with explanations, as

```
\documentstyle[%
            amscd,%option for commutative diagrams
            amssymb,%symbol names defined
                   verbatim%verbatim and comment envs
                   ]{amsart}
```

and the undesired options may be commented out:

```
\documentstyle[%
            %amscd,%option for commutative diagrams
            amssymb,%symbol names defined
                   %verbatim%verbatim and comment envs
                   ]{amsart}
```

Notice that the first line is terminated with [% to comment out the end-of-line character. It is useful to start an article with a comment identifying it, and identifying the format file to be used:

```
%This is article.tex
%Typeset with AMSLaTeX format file
```

**Tip**. If the comment is too long, split it; otherwise, it may wrap to the next line and corrupt the file.

**Tip**. Some command definitions do not allow spaces; if you want to split the line with the definition, terminate the line with % as in the above example.

See also the example at the end of Section 3-4.8.

Other uses of % include marking parts of the article for the author; for instance, marking the various parts of the Preamble (e.g., as in the sample article, see page xxii); commenting commands (see macros02.tex, in Section 11-2 and on the DISK, for examples).

Note that % works slightly differently in BibTEX; see Section 7-3.4.

Since multiline math displays (see Chapter 8), as a rule, do not tell you what went wrong, try commenting out all but one line, until each line works separately.

**Tip**. The 25% rule: if you use the % symbol, make sure you type it as \%. Otherwise, % just comments out to the end of the line. There is no warning.

Commenting out larger numbers of lines is too tedious with %. Use instead:

```
\begin{comment}
    ...the commented out text...
\end{comment}
```

**Rule 1**. \end{comment} must be on a line by itself.

There can be no comment within a comment. In other words,

```
\begin{comment}
   commented out text...
   \begin{comment}
      some more commented out text...
   \end{comment}
   and some more commented out text...
\end{comment}
```

is not allowed. The error message is:

```
! Bad space factor (0).
<recently read> \@savsf
```

```
...
1.175 \end{comment}
```

The comment environment is very useful when working on a larger document: comment out large parts you are not working on—this should speed up the typesetting.

**Tip**. The comment environment is also very useful in locating errors. Suppose that you have unbalanced braces in the source file; see Section 3-3.1. Work with a **copy** of the source file; comment out the first half, typeset. If you still get the error message, the error is in the second half; delete the first half of the source file (of the copy). If there is no error message, the error is in the first half; delete the second half of the source file (of the copy). Proceed like this until you are down to a paragraph, and visually inspect it.

### 3-6. Special styles

Although $\mathcal{A}_{\mathcal{M}}\mathcal{S}$-LaTeX chooses the style of the typeset characters, there are occasions when you want to emphasize a word by changing its shape or size.

**3-6.1. Emphasizing.**  In ordinary text, you may want to *emphasize* a phrase, for instance the name of a new concept. Do this with the command \em:

```
you may want to {\em emphasize\/} a phrase
```

and the phrase appears in a slanted type (chosen by the document style designer). Note that

**Rule 1.**  \em appears in a pair of braces, { }; the emphasis stops at the closing brace }.

See "scope" in Section 3-3.1.

Example: to obtain

this function is *continuous*! As a result

type

```
{this function is \em continuous\/}! As a result
```

**Tip**. The opening brace of the scope of \em may be placed anywhere before the command.

The command \/ before the closing brace is called the *italic correction*. Look at the emphasized M in the next example: *M* M; "*M*" is leaning over the "M". To prevent this, add the italic correction. So "*M* M" should be typed as

{\em M\/} M

**Rule 2**.  If the emphasized text is closed with a period or comma, the italic correction should not be used.

You can emphasize in an emphasized sentence. For instance, in the statement of a theorem:

*the space satisfies all three conditions, a so called* Rubin space *that*

the emphasis changed the style from slanted to upright. This is typed as

{\em  the space satisfies all three conditions,
a so called\/ {\em Rubin space} that

You may be inclined to type the command \em with the italic correction as

{\em  the space satisfies all three conditions, a so
called\/ {\em Rubin space\/} that

This is good practice. If the change is to the upright style, the italic correction will be ignored.

**Tip**. It is a good idea to type {\em \/} and then the emphasized text so that you will not forget the closing brace.

**3-6.2. Style changes.** $\mathcal{A}_{\mathcal{M}}S$-LATEX chooses *roman* style for normal text such as this sentence. Some other styles are provided:

| Type: | Print: |
|---|---|
| {\rm This is roman.} | This is roman. |
| {\bf This is bold.} | **This is bold.** |
| {\sf This is sans serif.} | This is sans serif. |
| {\sl This is slanted.} | *This is slanted.* |
| {\em This is emphasized.} | *This is emphasized.* |
| {\it This is italic.} | *This is italic.* |
| {\sc This is Small Caps.} | THIS IS SMALL CAPS. |
| {\tt This is the typewriter.} | This is the typewriter. |

Of these, you will most often use \em or \bf for emphasis. You may want to use small caps for the name of an important theorem, such as MAIN THEOREM. Most other style choices are made for you by $\mathcal{A}_{\mathcal{M}}S$-LATEX (or, to be more precise, by the document style amsart.sty; see Section C-2.1).

**Tip**. In math mode, \bold forces the next letter to be bold. The command \bf is ignored.

Actually, in the present version of $\mathcal{A}_{\mathcal{M}}\mathcal{S}$-LaTeX, \rm does not work as claimed above. Test this:

{\em Emphasized \rm text}

is typeset

*Emphasized text*

While in TeX, $\mathcal{A}_{\mathcal{M}}\mathcal{S}$-TeX, and LaTeX, this would have been typeset as

*Emphasized* text

The reason is that in $\mathcal{A}_{\mathcal{M}}\mathcal{S}$-LaTeX, \rm is defined as the command that switches to the Computer Modern font family. If you wish to change \rm back to its original meaning, define

\renewcommand{\rm}{\normalshape}

This definition of \rm is included in the sample article(s) (see page xxii, the DISK, and Section 11-3) which contain some examples of its use, and in the sample macro file, macros02.tex (see the DISK and Section 11-2).

In order to preserve the functionality of \rm, you could also define

\newcommand{\Rm}{\fontfamily{\rmdefault}\selectfont}

This is a useful command if you use fonts other than Computer Modern; see Appendix E.

**3-6.3. Size changes.** This book is typeset in 10 point size (Times font); if you need uniformly larger type (for transparencies, use 12 point size), see Sections 5-1 and 10-3. The sizes of titles, subscripts, superscripts are automatically changed by the document style. If you still insist on changing the size, the following are provided:

| Type: | Print: |
|---|---|
| {\tiny This is tiny.} | This is tiny. |
| {\scriptsize This is scriptsize.} | This is scriptsize. |
| {\small This is small.} | This is small. |
| {\normalsize This is normalsize.} | This is normalsize. |
| {\large This is large.} | This is large. |

**3-6.4. Boxed text.** A rarer way of emphasizing is by boxing. This is very emphatic: ⌈Do not touch!⌉ This is typed:

\fbox{Do not touch!}

## 3-7. Lines, paragraphs, and pages

**3-7.1. Lines.** $\mathcal{A}_{\mathcal{M}}\mathcal{S}$-LaTeX typesets the article a paragraph at a time; see Section C-2. It tries to split the paragraph into lines; if it fails to do that successfully, and a line is too wide, you get the dreaded overfull \hbox message. Here is a typical example:

```
Overfull \hbox (16.8332pt too wide) in paragraph at lines 452--454
[]\cmr/m/n/10 Example: if you do not want ''{\tt database}''
hy-phen-ated, type it as []\cmtt/m/n/10 \text{database}
\cmr/m/n/10 .
```

```
\hbox(6.94444+1.94444)x348.0, glue set - 1.0
.\hbox(0.0+0.0)x12.0
.\cmr/m/n/10 E
.\cmr/m/n/10 x
.\cmr/m/n/10 a
.\cmr/m/n/10 m
.etc.
```

The log file records which lines are too wide. To see a warning in the typeset version as well, add the command

```
\overfullrule=5pt
```

Then $\mathcal{AMS}$-LaTeX displays a black box (affectionately known as the "slug") on the margin of every line that is too wide. For the final printing, comment this line out, or change it to

```
\overfullrule=0pt
```

The slug is also displayed if the draft document style option is used:

```
\documentstyle[amscd,amssymb,verbatim,draft]{amsart}
```

The first line of defense for an overfull \hbox, is to see whether optional hyphens would help; see Section 3-4.8. Reading the message carefully, you may be able to pick out how $\mathcal{AMS}$-LaTeX means to hyphenate the words. Maybe a simple rephrasing of the paragraph will do the trick.

72 points make an inch. So if the message indicates a 0.55812pt overflow, you may safely ignore it.

**Tip**. If you do not want the 0.55812pt overflow reported whenever the source file is typeset, enclose the offending paragraph with the lines

```
{ \hfuzz=2pt
```

and

```
}% end of \hfuzz=2pt
```

Choose the number (2pt) to exceed slightly the error reported. This does not affect the typesetting, but the error report is suppressed.

You can force a linebreak in a paragraph with \linebreak; this breaks the line at the point of insertion and stretches out the line; if $\mathcal{AMS}$-LaTeX thinks that there was too little left on the line you get an

```
Underfull \hbox (badness 4328) in paragraph at lines 8--12
```

error message.

You can qualify \linebreak with an optional argument: 0 to 4; the higher the argument, the more it forces. \linebreak[4] is the same as \linebreak; \linebreak[0] allows the linebreak but does not force it.

\newline breaks the line but does not stretch it. The text after \newline starts at the beginning of the next line, not indented. The command \\ is the same as \newline.

The commands \nolinebreak and \nolinebreak[0] to \nolinebreak[4] play the opposite role. \nolinebreak[0] is the same as \linebreak[0]; and similarly, \nolinebreak[4] is the same as \nolinebreak.

The nolinebreak commands are seldom used: ~ and \text accomplish the same most of the time; see Sections 3-4.3 and 3-4.8.

As you recall (see Rule 2 of Section 3-2), the end-of-line character is treated by $\mathcal{AMS}$-LATEX as a space. You may want to redefine this: a line should mean a line. This is achieved with the \obeylines command, as illustrated by the following example:

```
{\obeylines
You    do not have to      worry
 about the number of    spaces
separating words,
as long as there is    one space or end-of-line separating
any two words.   }% end \obeylines
```

prints:

> You do not have to worry
> about the number of spaces
> separating words,
> as long as there is one space or end-of-line separating
> any two words.

This did not come out quite right, all the lines are indented. So we get rid of the indentation for each line (\parindent contains the distance by which a paragraph is indented; $\mathcal{AMS}$-LATEX sets it to 20pt):

```
{\obeylines \setlength{\parindent}{0pt}
You    do not have to      worry
 about the number of    spaces
separating words,
as long as there is    one space or end-of-line separating
any two words.   }% end \obeylines
```

and then it prints fine:

You do not have to worry
about the number of spaces
separating words,
as long as there is one space or end-of-line separating
any two words.

You can combine \obeylines with \obeyspaces of Section 3-2; it prints everything as expected, except that the spaces at the beginning of lines will disappear.

**Double spacing.** It is very convenient to proofread articles double spaced. Some journals **demand** that articles be submitted double spaced.

To print the article double spaced, include the command

\renewcommand{\baselinestretch}{2}

in the Command section of the Preamble. Similarly, "line and a half" spacing is provided by

\renewcommand{\baselinestretch}{1.5}

**3-7.2. Paragraphs.** Paragraphs are separated by a blank line or by the command \par. Error messages show new paragraphs always as \par. The \par form is very useful for defining commands and environments, see the together environment in Section 11-3.

Lines are automatically indented in the first line of a paragraph (in our document style). Indentation may be eliminated with \noindent or may be forced with \indent.

You can also override the document style's choice of interline space at the end of a paragraph. Break the line with \\[length], where length is the interline length you wish, for instance, 12pt, .5in, 1.2cm. Note how the units are abbreviated. Example:

Note how the units are abbreviated.\\[15pt]  Example.

Prints:

Note how the units are abbreviated.

Example.

**Tip.** \\ is the same as \newline in text but not in environments or arguments of commands.

Sometimes—for instance, in a schedule, a glossary, or an index—you may want the first line of a paragraph not indented, and all the others indented by a specified amount. This is called a *hanging indent*, and it is done with the command \hangindent, specifying the amount of indentation.

The following example from a TEX glossary illustrates the use of these commands (see Section 6-4.2 for another example):

**sentence** is a groups of words terminated by the period, the exclamation mark, or the question mark.
**paragraph** is a group of sentences terminated by a blank line or by the command \par.

typed as

```
\hangindent=30pt
\noindent
{\bf sentence} is a groups of words terminated by
 the period, the exclamation
mark, or the question mark.
```

```
\hangindent=30pt
\noindent
{\bf paragraph} is a group of sentences terminated by a
blank line or by the
command $\backslash$ {\tt par}.
```

Notice that the two commands are repeated for each paragraph. Sometimes, we may also use the command \hangafter, specifying the number of lines not to be indented.

```
\hangafter = 1
```

is the default.

**3-7.3. Pages.** There are pagebreaking commands which are analogous to the line breaking commands:

```
\newpage;
\pagebreak;
\pagebreak[0] to \pagebreak[4].
\nopagebreak;
\nopagebreak[0] to \nopagebreak[4].
\nopagebreak[0] is the same as \pagebreak[0].
\nopagebreak[4] is the same as \nopagebreak.
```

There are special commands for allowing or forbidding pagebreaks in multiline math displays; see Section 8-6. Sometimes we may want two adjacent paragraphs to be on the same page. In word processing, the instruction for a paragraph to stay on the same page as the next: "keep with next paragraph".

$\mathcal{AMS}$-LaTeX handles these situation with ease. Place the brace and the commands:

```
{\samepage
```

at the start of the paragraph(s) you want to keep together, and place } at the end. Example:

```
{\samepage
```

```
And this is the total of these expenses:
```

```
\$12,341,189.15
```

```
}%end of samepage
```

Make sure that the scope of \samepage contains the blank lines marking the paragraph(s). See also Section 10-2.

### 3-8. Spaces

**3-8.1. Horizontal spaces.** In typing text, there are three commands that are most often used to create (horizontal) white space (the white space created by these commands is shown between the |-s):

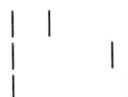

| \␣ | \| \| | (interword space) |
| \quad | \|  \| | |
| \qquad | \|    \| | |

A quad is 1 em, and a qquad is 2 em; see Section 3-8.3.

There are other commands creating smaller units of spaces; all the commands of Section 4-4.1 can also be used in text; see Section B-6.

More appropriate for text are the commands: \hspace and \phantom.

\hspace works with a distance:

\hspace{12pt}, \hspace{.5in},\hspace{1.5cm}.

Example (recall, $|$ prints |):

```
$|$\hspace{12pt}$|$ \\
$|$\hspace{.5in}$|$ \\
$|$\hspace{1.5cm}$|$
```

prints:

```
|  |
|      |
|          |
```

\phantom{argument} produces the same space as the space occupied by the argument.

Illustration:

```
$|$need space$|$\\
$|$\phantom{need space}$|$
```

prints:

```
|need space|
|          |
```

**Horizontal space variant.** At the beginning and end of each line (except at the beginning and end of a paragraph) $\mathcal{AMS}$-LaTeX removes all spaces. This includes the removal of space produced by \hspace. The variant \hspace* creates a space that is not removed by $\mathcal{AMS}$-LaTeX.

Example:

```
And text\\
\hspace{20pt}And text\\
\hspace*{20pt}And text
```

prints:

And text
And text
    And text

Use \hspace*, for instance, for customized indentation. To indent a paragraph 24 pt, give the command:

```
\noindent \hspace*{24pt}And text
```

It prints:

    And text

**3-8.2. Vertical spaces.** Vertical spaces are normally required to make room for a picture or to add some interline space for emphasis. The latter, as we have seen in Section 3-7.1, can be accomplished with the command \\[dist]. Both goals can be easily accomplished with the \vspace command which works just like \hspace (see Section 3-8.1), except that it creates vertical space. Examples: \vspace{12pt}, \vspace{.5in}, \vspace{1.5cm}.

Standard amounts of vertical space are provided by the three commands:

```
\smallskip,    \medskip,    \bigskip
```

These spaces depend on the style and the font size, however, in the style and font we are using, they represent a horizontal space of 3pt, 6pt, and 12pt, respectively (12pt is the distance from line to line in typeset $\mathcal{A}_{\mathcal{M}}S$-LATEX articles).

**Rule 1**. All vertical space commands must start in a new paragraph.

To print

end of text.

New paragraph after vertical space

type

```
end of text.
```

```
\vspace{12pt}
New paragraph after vertical space
```

The following is incorrect:

```
end of text.
\vspace{12pt}
Text after vertical space
```

It prints

end of text. Text after vertical space

**Vertical space variant.** $\mathcal{A}_{\mathcal{M}}S$-LaTeX removes vertical spaces at the beginning and end of each page. This includes the removal of space produced by \vspace. The variant \vspace* creates space that is not removed by $\mathcal{A}_{\mathcal{M}}S$-LaTeX.

**3-8.3. Relative spaces.** The length of a space was given in *absolute units*: 12pt (points), .5cm (centimeter), 1.5in (inches). Sometimes, *relative units* are more appropriate; units that are in size relative to the size of the letters in the currently used font. The units are: 1em is the width of "M"; 1ex is the height of an "x".

Examples: \hspace{12em} and \vspace{12ex}. See also the commands \quad and \qquad in Section 3-8.1.

**3-8.4. Expanding spaces.** The commands

\hfill, \dotfill, and \hrulefill

fill all available space in the line with spaces, dots, or a horizontal line. If there are two of these in the same line pushing against each other, the space is equally divided. These commands can be used to center text, to fill lines with dots in a Table of Contents, and so on. To obtain

2. Boxes . . . . . . . . . . . . . . . . . . . . . . . . . . . . . . . . . . . . . . . . . . . . . . . . . . . . . . . . 34

type

2. Boxes\dotfill 34

To print

a                                   and                                          a

type

a\hfill and\hfill a

To get

a_____and_____a

type

a\hrulefill and\hrulefill a

For instance, in a centered environment—such as the \title (Section 5-4.1) or the center environment (Section 9-1)—you may use \hfill to flush a line right, as in:

This is the title

First Draft

Author

To achieve this, type

```
\begin{center}
This is the title\\
\hfill First Draft\\
Author
\end{center}
```

### 3-9. Boxes

Sometimes it is useful to typeset text in an imaginary "box", and use this box as a single "large" character. A one-line box is made with the \text command; a box with a given length is created with the \parbox command.

**3-9.1. Line box.** The command \text defines a "line box"; it typesets the argument in a single line. The resulting box is handled by $\mathcal{A}_{\mathcal{M}}\mathcal{S}$-LaTeX as a "long" character. For instance, \text{database} typesets "database" and handles the eight characters as if they were one.

This has a number of uses: it prevents $\mathcal{A}_{\mathcal{M}}\mathcal{S}$-LaTeX from hyphenating the word (see Section 3-4.8), and it allows the word to be used in math mode; see Section 4-3.

**Line box—refinement.** The command \text is a short form of the command \makebox. The full form of this command is

\makebox[length][alignment]{argument}

where

> **length:** the length of the box, optional; the default, as long as necessary;
> **alignment:** l or r, optional; l flushes the argument left, r right; the text is centered as a default;
> **argument:** the text in the box.

Length can be specified in inches (in), centimeters (cm), points (pt), or in the relative measurement ex; see Section 3-8.3.

Examples:

```
\makebox{Short title.}End\\
\makebox[2in][l]{Short title.}End\\
\makebox[2in]{Short title.}End\\
\makebox[2in][r]{Short title.}End
```

prints:

Short title.End
Short title.                    End
            Short title.        End
                        Short title.End

The command \framebox works the same way, and draws a frame around the imaginary box:

\framebox[2in][l]{Short title.}

prints:

| Short title. |

**3-9.2. Paragraph box.** The command \parbox typesets its second argument in a paragraph with a line length supplied as the first argument; the resulting box is handled by $\mathcal{A}_{\mathcal{M}}\mathcal{S}$-L⁣ATEX as a "large" character. To print a column three inches wide:

The command parbox typesets its second argument in a paragraph with a line length supplied as the first argument.

type

```
\parbox{3in}{The command parbox typesets its second
argument in a paragraph with a line length supplied
as the first argument.}
```

This is especially useful in the tabular environment; see "Refinements" in Section 9-4 for multiline entries.

The length of the parbox can be specified in inches (in), centimeters (cm), points (pt), in the relative measurement ex (see Section 3-8.3), to mention a few.

**Tip**. The \parbox command requires two arguments. Dropping the first argument may give the error message

```
! Missing number, treated as zero.
<to be read again>
                 T
...
1.175
```

Dropping the second argument gives no error message.

**Paragraph box refinement.** The "character" created by \parbox is placed on the line so that its horizontal center is aligned with the center of the line. An optional first argument b or t forces the bottom or the top to be so aligned. For an example, see Section 9-4.

**3-9.3. Marginal comment.** A paragraph box is used to make marginal comments. The command is \marginpar. For example:

```
\parbox{Careful, tricky computation!}
```

Do not use more than one or two marginal comments a page; $\mathcal{A}_{\mathcal{M}}\mathcal{S}$-L⁣ATEX may get confused, and misplace the marginal comments. It may even cause $\mathcal{A}_{\mathcal{M}}\mathcal{S}$-L⁣ATEX to run out of memory.

**3-9.4. Solid box.** A solid rectangular filled box is made with the \rule command; the first argument is the width, the second is the height. For instances, to print

end of proof symbol: ■

type

```
end of proof symbol: \rule{1.6ex}{1.6ex}
```

In fact, you may notice that this symbol is usually slightly lowered:

End of proof symbol: ■

This is done with an optional first argument:

End of proof symbol: \rule[-.23ex]{1.6ex}{1.6ex}

**Tip**. If a command expects two arguments and none or only one is supplied, $\mathcal{AMS}$-L#T#X gives an error message. For instance, \rule{1.6ex} will give the message:

! Paragraph ended before \@rule was complete.
<to be read again>
                    \par
1.124

\@rule suggests that the problem is with the \rule command. So check the rules for the \rule command, and you will find that an argument is missing.

Solid boxes of width 0 are called *struts*. Struts are invisible, but they force $\mathcal{AMS}$-L#T#X to make room for them, changing the vertical alignment of lines. Struts are especially useful in fine-tuning formulas; see Section 4-12 and the end of Section 9-4 for examples.

**Tip**. 0pt, 0in, 0cm, 0em all stand for length 0; 0 by itself will not be accepted. \rule{0}{1.6ex} gives the error message:

! Illegal unit of measure (pt inserted).
<to be read again>
                    h
...
1.251 \rule{0}{1.6ex}

**3-9.5. Fine-tuning boxes.** The command \raisebox raises (and with a negative value, lowers) boxes. This allows us to play games:

fine-\raisebox{.5ex}{tun}\raisebox{-.5ex}{ing}

prints: fine-^tun_ing. More importantly, \raisebox has two optional arguments:

\raisebox{0ex}[1.5ex][.75ex]{Fine}

which forces $\mathcal{AMS}$-L#T#X to typeset "Fine" as if it extended 1.5ex above and .75ex below the line, resulting in a change in the interline space before and after the line. A simple version of this command: \smash is discussed in Section 4-12.

### 3-10. Footnotes

Footnotes are placed as the arguments of the \footnote command. Footnotes are not encouraged in articles with the exception of the first page footnotes, the \thanks command in the Topmatter; see Section 5-4.2. To show the use of footnotes, we place one here[1], typed as

---

[1]Footnotes are easy to place.

```
\footnote{Footnotes are easy to place.}
```

**3-10.1. Fragile commands.** As a rule, $\mathcal{A}_{\mathcal{M}}\mathcal{S}$-LaTeX reads a paragraph of the source file, typesets it, then goes on to the next paragraph; see Section C-2. Some part of the source file, however, is typeset, and then stored for later use. Examples include the (short) title of an article, which is reused as a running head (Section 5-4.1), titles of parts, sections, subsections, subsubsections, which are stored to be used in the Table of Contents (Sections 6-2 and 6-4), footnotes, titles (captions) of tables and figures (Section 6-5), and index entries (Section 6-4). These are *movable arguments*, and the some commands in them must be protected from damage when being moved. The $\mathcal{A}_{\mathcal{M}}\mathcal{S}$-LaTeX commands that need such protection are called *fragile*. The math mode commands: \( and \) are fragile; oddly enough, $ is not.

In a movable argument fragile commands have to be protected with the command: \protect. So

```
The function \( f(x^{2}) \)
```

is not an appropriate section title, but

```
The function \protect \( f(x^{2}) \protect \)
```

is. Of course, so is

```
The function $f(x^{2})$
```

To be on the safe side, protect every command in a movable argument.

### 3-11. Splitting up the file

Sometimes, it is convenient to write the article in several pieces. There are two commands that combine separate files into one document.

**3-11.1. Input.** Typically, every $\mathcal{A}_{\mathcal{M}}\mathcal{S}$-LaTeX user develops a set of user-defined commands; see Section 11-2. These are used for every article, so they are usually kept in a separate document which is \input-ed in the source file; see the line

```
\input{macros02}
```

in the sample article article2.tex (on the DISK and in Section 11-3).

**Rule 1**. An \endinput command must terminate every file that is \input-ed.

You could also use \input for the parts of the Preamble and Topmatter that are shared by all the articles, although, this is not commonly done.

**3-11.2. Include.** You can also put together a long article with the \include command. For instance,

```
\include{sec1}
\include{sec2}
\include{sec3}
\include{sec4}
\include{sec5}
\include{append}
```

where sec1.tex, ..., sec5.tex are the five sections, and append.tex is the appendix.

**Rule 2.** Every file \include-d must be terminated with \endinput.

\include has some advantages over \input. The most important advantage is the \includeonly command. If you work on Section 4, put the command

\includeonly{sec4}

in the Preamble, and only Section 4 will be typeset; the page numbers, section numbers, and cross-references will be correct. (Almost. They are derived from the last typesetting; see Section C-2.4.) You could also have

\includeonly{sec4,sec5}

All included files start on a new page. If this does not suit you, with cut and paste merge the source files for final printing; as an alternative, change all \include commands to \input.

**Tip.** In the Command section, place the line

%\renewcommand{\include}{\input}

When you want to change all \include commands to \input, just uncomment the line (remove the %).

**Tip.** The command \includeonly does not like blanks.

\includeonly{sec4 ,sec5}

includes only sec5, and

\includeonly{sec4, sec5}

includes only sec4.

# CHAPTER 4

# Typing Math

The math in the source file is typeset *inline*: $a \equiv b \ (\theta)$ and $\int_0^\pi \sin x \, dx = 2$ or *displayed*:

$$a \equiv b \quad (\theta)$$

and

$$\int_0^\pi \sin x \, dx = 2.$$

Notice that the spacing in the first formula changed, as did the size of the integral sign in the second.

How to inform $\mathcal{AMS}$-LATEX that the math should be typeset as an inline formula? You probably expect a \math command whose argument is to be typeset as math. $\mathcal{AMS}$-LATEX implements this differently.

### 4-1. Math environments

Inline and displayed math formulas are implemented with math environments. For inline formulas:

```
\begin{math}
\end{math}
```

and for displayed formulas:

```
\begin{displaymath}
\end{displaymath}
```

**Rule 1.** No blank line is permitted in the displaymath environment.

Inline formulas occur too often for this system to be convenient. Consider this sentence:

Let $a$ be a real number, and let $f$ be a function.

This may be typed:

```
Let
\begin{math}
   a
\end{math}
be a real number, and let
\begin{math}
   f
\end{math}
be a function.
```

This is too verbose. So $\mathcal{A}_{\mathcal{M}}S$-LaTeX allows the use of the special braces \( and \) for the math environment, and \[ and \] for the displaymath environment. In fact, $ and $ is an even shorter, and more distinctive, version for the braces of the math environment. Using these, the sentence may be typed as follows:

```
Let \( a \) be a real number, and let \( f \) be a function.
```

or

```
Let $ a $ be a real number, and let $ f $ be a function.
```

$ as a delimiter for the math environment is a bit of an anomaly: it is both the opening and closing brace. This can easily cause trouble. Leave one out and $\mathcal{A}_{\mathcal{M}}S$-LaTeX does not know whether an opening or a closing brace is missing. For instance,

```
Let $ a be a real number, and let $ f $ be a function.
```

would be interpreted by $\mathcal{A}_{\mathcal{M}}S$-LaTeX as follows: "Let" is text. Then

```
$ a be a real number, and let $
```

indicates the math environment. Then "f" is text, and

```
$ be a function.
```

is again a math environment (opened by $). A math environment is closed by the next $ in the paragraph. When we run out of $-s, we get the error message:

```
! Missing $ inserted.
```

and the line number shows the end of the paragraph. If the paragraph is long, and you cannot find the missing $, place a $ at the end of the paragraph, and typeset it. For instance, our example will print:

Let $abearealnumber, and let fbea function.$

because the math environment ignores the spaces. It is now obvious that the $ is missing after the first math letter $a$.

Now if we make the same mistake, but use \( and \):

```
Let \( a  be a real number, and let  \( f \) be a function
```

then we get the error message:

```
! Bad math environm
\@latexerr ....}\er:
```

```
...
1.3 ...a real number
```

with the correct line numbe
environment, so the second

Multiline math displays
discussed in Chapter 8. D
User-defined environments a

**4-2.**

**4-2.1. Equations.** The equ
same except that the formula i

(1)

typed as

```
\begin{equation} \label{E:
    \int_{0}^{\pi} \sin x \
\end{equation}
```

It is optional to include the command \label in the equation. If \label is included, then the number assigned to the equation can be referenced with the command \ref. In our example,

```
see (\ref{E:int})
```

prints: see (1). The parentheses are automatically placed with \eqref:

```
see \eqref{E:int}
```

prints: see (1). See also Section 6-3.

$\mathcal{AMS}$-LaTeX numbers the equations consecutively throughout the article; if you wish the equations numbered in each section: (1.1), (1.2), ... in Section 1, (2.1), (2.2), ... in Section 2, etc., then in the Command section of the Preamble (see Section 5-3), include the command:

```
\numberwithin{equation}{section}
```

"Manual control" of numbering is discussed in Section 11-4.1.

You attach a * to an equation to kill the numbering; so

```
\begin{equation*}
    \int_{0}^{\pi} \sin x \, dx = 2.
\end{equation*}
```

prints the same as

(rotated margin text:)
\[ \int_{0}^{\pi} \sin x \, dx

\]

There is however one differe
see Section 4-2.2.

**Rule 1.** No blank l

If you type:

\begin{eq

\in

= 2.

...ce; in the equation* environment you can still tag;

...ne is permitted in the equation or equation* environment.

...ation}
...`_{0}^{\pi} \sin x \, dx = 2.\tag{Int}`

`\end{equation}`

you get the error message:

```
Runaway argument?
\Invalid@ \\ \int _{0}^{\pi } \sin x \, dx = 2.\tag {\ETC.
! Paragraph ended before \equation was complete.
<to be read again>
                    \par
1.29
```

**4-2.2. Tagging.** In the equation and the equation* environments,

`\tag{name}`

will attach the "tag" (name) to the formula; for the equation environment, the tag replaces the number.

The numbering of an equation is *relative*; the number assigned is relative to the position of the equation to others in the article. The tagging of an equation is *absolute*; the tag remains the same after rearrangement. A numbered equation needs a `\label{E:xxx}` so `\ref{E:xxx}` can reference the number generated by $\mathcal{AMS}$-LaTeX.

Note that if there is a tag, the equation and the equation* environments are equivalent. Example:

(Int) $$\int_{0}^{\pi} \sin x\, dx = 2.$$

may also be typed as

```
\begin{equation*}
   \int_{0}^{\pi} \sin x \, dx = 2.\tag{Int}
\end{equation*}
```

`\tag*` is the same as `\tag` except that it does not automatically use parentheses. So to get

A–B $$\int_{0}^{\pi} \sin x\, dx = 2.$$

one should type

```
\begin{equation}
   \int_{0}^{\pi} \sin x \, dx = 2.\tag*{A--B}
\end{equation}
```

### 4-3. Text in math

In math environments, type text in the argument of the `\text` command. For instance,

$$A = \{x \in X \mid x \in X_i \text{ for some } i \in I\}$$

is typed as

```
\[
   A = \{ x \in X \mid x \in X_{i} \text{ for some } i \in I \}
\]
```

Note that we have to leave space before "`for`" and after "`some`" inside the argument of `\text`. The argument of `\text` is typeset in one line. Sometimes it is convenient to go into math mode in `\text`:

$$A = \{x \in X \mid \text{for } x \text{ large}\}$$

may be typed as:

```
\[
   A = \{ x \in X \mid \text{ for \( x \) large} \}
\]
```

When typeset, the argument of `\text` changes size as necessary; for instance, in subscript and superscript.

### 4-4. Spacing

We deal with spacing in a line in this section. For vertical spacing; see Section 4-12.

**4-4.1. The spacing rules.** In text, the most important spacing rule is that one space equals any number of spaces. The math environments are even nicer:

**Rule 1.** Spacing in math does not matter for $\mathcal{AMS}$-LATEX.

In other words, all spacing is done by $\mathcal{AMS}$-LATEX. Witness:

```
\(a+b=c\)
```

and

```
\( a  +  b  =  c \)
```

are both typeset as $a + b = c$. However, do not forget to terminate a command with a space. Also keep also in mind:

**Rule 2.** Space in math so that the source file is easy to read.

It is a good practice

- To leave a space after \( and before \).
- To place \[ and \] on a line by itself.
- To leave spaces before and after binary operations and binary relations (including =).
- To indent environments so they stand out (we indent each line by three spaces).
- Not to break formulas at the end of the line (in math, the end-of-line character is ignored by $\mathcal{AMS}$-LaTeX, but this may break up the formula visually in the source file).

Develop your own distinctive style of writing math, and stick with it.

**Tip.** Type $a$, $b \in B$ as follows:

\( a \), \(b \in B \)

If you type

\( a , b \in B \)

you get the math spacing between "$a$," and "$b$" which you may find too narrow: $a, b \in B$.

**4-4.2. Adjustments.** $\mathcal{AMS}$-LaTeX provide a large variety of math symbols: Greek characters ($\alpha$), binary operations ($\circ$), binary relations ($\leq$), negated binary relations ($\nleq$), arrows ($\nearrow$), delimiters ($\{$), etc. All the math symbols are listed in the tables of Appendix A.

Consider the formula:

$$A = \{x \in X \mid x\beta \geq xy > (x + 1)^2 - \alpha\}$$

typed as

\[
    A = \{ x \in X \mid x \beta \geq  x y > (x + 1)^{2} - \alpha \}
\]

In this formula, a number of symbols occur:

$$A \quad = \quad \{ \quad x \quad \in \quad X \quad | \quad \beta \quad \geq \quad y \quad > \quad ( \quad + \quad 1 \quad ) \quad 2 \quad - \quad \alpha \quad \}$$

The spacing of the symbols in the formula varies. In $x\beta$, the two symbols are very close. In $x \in X$, there is some space around $\in$. In $x + 1$, there is somewhat less space around $+$. There is a little space after $\{$ and before $\}$.

$\mathcal{AMS}$-LaTeX bases the spacing of these symbols on the classification of the symbols into several categories: binary relations ($=$, $\geq$, $>$), binary operations ($+$, $-$), delimiters ($\{$, $($), and so on. In the above formula, $=$, $\in$, $|$, $\geq$, and $>$ are binary relations; $+$ and $-$ are binary operations, and $\{$, $\}$, $($, and $)$ are delimiters.

As a rule, you do not have to be concerned whether or not $+$ is a binary operation. $\mathcal{AMS}$-LaTeX knows it, and will typeset the formula correctly. However, in some situations, $\mathcal{AMS}$-LaTeX does not know how to typeset the formula, and you will have to give it a helping hand by adding spacing commands. Luckily, $\mathcal{A}_{\mathcal{M}}\mathcal{S}$-LaTeX provides a large variety of spacing commands:

| Short form: | Full form: | Short form: | Full form: |
|---|---|---|---|
| \, | \thinspace | \! | \negthinspace |
| \: | \medspace | | \negmedspace |
| \; | \thickspace | | \negthickspace |
| @, | | @! | |
| | \quad | | |
| | \qquad | | |

Spacing commands

\quad and \qquad are normally used to adjust aligned formulas (see Chapter 8) or to add space before text in a math formula. The space between the two |-s is a quad: |     |, and this is a qquad: |        |.

\, and \! are most useful for fine-tuning math formulas. @, and @! are one-tenth in size of these.

Here are some examples of fine-tuning; many more are given in this chapter; see also Section 2-4. At the beginning of Section 4-2.1, we typed the equation

(1)
$$\int_0^{\pi} \sin x \, dx = 2.$$

as

```
\begin{equation}  \label{E:int}
   \int_{0}^{\pi} \sin x \, dx = 2.
\end{equation}
```

Those of you with sharper eyes may have noticed that we put "\," between f(x) and dx. Indeed, without it, $\mathcal{A}_{\mathcal{M}}\mathcal{S}$-LaTeX would crowd $f(x)$ and $dx$.

```
\begin{equation}  \label{E:int}
   \int_{0}^{\pi} \sin x dx = 2.
\end{equation}
```

prints:

(1)
$$\int_0^{\pi} \sin x dx = 2.$$

Another example: $|-f(x)|$ (typed as \( | -f(x) | \)) is spaced incorrectly; $\mathcal{A}_{\mathcal{M}}\mathcal{S}$-LaTeX assumes that | and f are regular symbols, and $-$ is a binary operation. To get the correct spacing, type \( \left| -f(x) \right| \) which prints $|-f(x)|$; this form tells $\mathcal{A}_{\mathcal{M}}\mathcal{S}$-LaTeX that the first | is a left delimiter (see Section 4-6), therefore $-$ is the minus sign, and not the binary operation, minus.

Here are two examples of the use of \!:

| Type: | Print: |
|---|---|
| `\( \sqrt{5} \, \text{side} \)` | $\sqrt{5}$ side |
| `\( \sin x / \! \log n \)` | $\sin x/\log n$ |

Some symbols are represented by different commands depending on the role they play (the spacing they demand). For instance, the symbol | in a math formula could be

- an ordinary math symbol, typed as |;
- a binary relation, typed as `\mid`;
- a left delimiter, typed as `\left|`;
- a right delimiter, typed as `\right|`;

Observe the spacing in $a|b$ and $a \mid b$ typed as `\( a | b \)` and `\( a \mid b \)`, respectively.

See Section 4-11.2 on how to declare the type of a symbol.

One more symbol with special spacing, invoked with the command `\colon`, should be mentioned here. `\colon` is a colon (:) for formulas of the type

$$f \colon A \to B$$

typed as

```
\[
    f \colon A \to B
\]
```

### 4-5. Basic constructs

**4-5.1. Arithmetic.** The arithmetic operations are typed as expected. To get: $a+b$, $a - b$, $-a$, $a/b$, $ab$, type

`\( a + b \)`, `\( a - b\)`, `\( -a \)`, `\( a / b \)`, `\( a b \)`

If you wish the · for multiplication, use the math symbol `\cdot`; $a \cdot b$ is typed as `\(a \cdot b\)`; see Section A-4.

In displayed formulas, fractions are not typed with / but with the command `\frac`. To get

$$\frac{1 + 2x}{x + y + xy}$$

type

```
\[
    \frac{1 + 2x}{x + y + xy}
\]
```

Subscripts are typed with _ and superscripts with ˆ. Remember to enclose in braces the subscript and the superscript:

\[
    a_{1}, a_{i_{1}}, a^{2}, a^{b^{c}}, a^{i_{1}}, a_{i} + 1,
    a_{i + 1}
\]

prints:

$$a_1, a_{i_1}, a^2, a^{b^c}, a^{i_1}, a_i + 1, a_{i+1}$$

For $a^{b^c}$, type \( a^{b^{c}} \); not \( a^b^c \). If you type the latter, you get the error message:

! Double superscript.
1.224 $a^b^
          c$

Similarly, $a_{b_c}$ is typed as \( a_{b_{c}} \); not as \( a_b_c \).

In many instances, the braces for the subscripts and superscripts can be omitted; see Section C-2.2. It is a good practice always to type them.

There is one symbol that incorporates the ^, the apostrophe '. $f'(x)$ is typed: \( f'(x) \).

Sometimes, you may want a symbol to appear superscripted (subscripted) by itself as in

we use the symbol † to indicate the dualspace

typed as

we use the symbol \( {}^\dagger \) to indicate the dualspace

{} is the *empty group*. It can be used to separate symbols, or as the base for subscripting and superscripting.

**4-5.2. Fraction refinements.** You can use math display style fractions inline with \dfrac and math inline style fractions displayed with \tfrac. Examples: $\dfrac{1}{2}$ is typed as

\( \dfrac{1}{2} \)

and

$$\tfrac{1}{2}$$

typed as

\[
    \tfrac{1}{2}
\]

The thickness of the fraction line can be set with an optional argument. For example:

\[
    \frac{a}{b + c} \frac[0.5pt]{a}{b + c} \frac[1pt]{a}{b + c}
    \frac[1.5pt]{a}{b + c} \frac[2pt]{a}{b + c}
\]

prints:

$$\frac{a}{b+c}\frac{a}{b+c}\frac{a}{b+c}\frac{a}{b+c}\frac{a}{b+c}$$

Finally, there is \fracwithdelims; for instance, $\left(\frac{a}{b+c}\right]$ is typed as

$$\text{\fracwithdelims()[1pt]\{a\}\{b + c\}.}$$

Delimiters are listed in Section 4-6.

**4-5.3. Roots.** \sqrt produces square root; e.g.,

```
\( \sqrt{5} \)              prints:  √5
\( \sqrt{a + 2b + c^{2}} \)  prints:  √(a + 2b + c²)
```

Roots other than the square root are done with an optional argument; to print $\sqrt[3]{5}$ type \( \sqrt[3]{5} \).

**Root refinement.** The placement of the optional parameter is not always very pleasing, witness $\sqrt[g]{5}$. So there are two additional commands: \leftroot and \uproot to move the root *left* (with a negative argument, *right*) and *up* (with a negative argument, *down*). You may find the following variants an improvement:

$\sqrt[g]{5}$  typed as  \( \sqrt[ \leftroot{2} \uproot{2} g ]{5} \)
$\sqrt[g]{5}$  typed as  \( \sqrt[ \uproot{2} g ]{5} \)

Experiment with the numbers in the arguments of \leftroot and \uproot.

**4-5.4. Binomials.** The command for binomials is \binom.
Examples inline: $\binom{a}{b+c}$ and $\binom{\frac{n^2-1}{2}}{n+1}$, and displayed:

$$\binom{a}{b+c} \text{ and } \binom{\frac{n^2-1}{2}}{n+1}$$

typed as:

```
\[
   \binom{a}{b + c} \text{ and }
   \binom{\frac{n^{2} - 1}{2}}{n + 1}
\]
```

You can use display style binomial inline with \dbinom, and inline style binomial displayed with \tbinom; example: $\binom{a}{b}$ is typed as \( \dbinom{a}{b} \).

**4-5.5. Integrals.** We have already seen both the inline and displayed versions of the formula $\int_0^\pi \sin x\, dx = 2$ . The lower limit is a subscript and the upper limit is a superscript. You can change this with the command \limits; to print $\int\limits_0^\pi \sin x\, dx$ type

\( \int \limits_{0}^{\pi} \sin x \, dx \)

Other variants: \oint ($\oint$), \iint ($\iint$), \iiint ($\iiint$), \iiiint ($\iiiint$), and \idotsint ($\int \cdots \int$).

For complicated bounds, use the subscript and superscript environments; see Section 4-9.1.

**4-5.6. Ellipses.** As in text mode, \dots produces the ellipsis:

$$F(x_1, x_2, \ldots, x_n)$$

typed as

```
\[
    F(x_{1}, x_{2}, \dots , x_{n})
\]
```

In math, we either use low dots as in the last example, or centered dots as in $x_1 + x_2 + \cdots + x_n$ typed as

```
\( x_{1} + x_{2} +  \dots  + x_{n} \)
```

$\mathcal{AMS}$-L^AT_EX picks out the symbol following \dots, and decides whether to use low or centered dots. If the decision reached by $\mathcal{AMS}$-L^AT_EX is not appropriate, you can force low dots with \ldots and centered dots with \cdots. For instance, $\mathcal{AMS}$-L^AT_EX typesets

```
\[
    \alpha( x_{1}+ x_{2} + \dots)
\]
```

as

$$\alpha(x_1 + x_2 + \ldots)$$

To get the desired typesetting:

$$\alpha(x_1 + x_2 + \cdots)$$

type

```
\[
    \alpha( x_{1}+ x_{2} + \cdots)
\]
```

You can exercise even more control with \dotsc for dots with a comma, \dotsb for dots with a binary operations or relation, \dotsm for dots with multiplication, and \dotsi for dots with integrals. These not only force the dots low or center them, but also adjust the spacing.

In math mode, you can print vertical dots $\vdots$ with \vdots and diagonal dots $\ddots$ with \ddots.

## 4-6. Delimiters

Delimiters are parentheses-like symbols that bracket a formula, for example: $(a)$ and $\left(\dfrac{1}{2}\right)$. Delimiters in $\mathcal{A}\mathcal{M}\mathcal{S}$-LaTeX come in two varieties: fixed sized and variable sized that stretch to enclose the formula.

| Name: | Type: | Print: | Name: | Type: | Print: |
|---|---|---|---|---|---|
| Left paren. | ( | ( | Right paren. | ) | ) |
| Left bracket | [ | [ | Right bracket | ] | ] |
| Left brace | \{ | { | Right brace | \} | } |
| Reverse slash | \backslash | \ | Forward slash | / | / |
| Left angle br. | \langle | ⟨ | Right angle br. | \rangle | ⟩ |
| Vertical line | | | | | Double vert. line | \| | ‖ |
| Left floor br. | \lfloor | ⌊ | Right floor br. | \rfloor | ⌋ |
| Left ceiling br. | \lceil | ⌈ | Right ceiling br. | \rceil | ⌉ |

Standard delimiters

| Name: | Type: | Print: |
|---|---|---|
| Upward arrow | \uparrow | ↑ |
| Double upward arrow | \Uparrow | ⇑ |
| Downward arrow | \downarrow | ↓ |
| Double downward arrow | \Downarrow | ⇓ |
| Up-and-down arrow | \updownarrow | ↕ |
| Double up-and-down arrow | \Updownarrow | ⇕ |

More delimiters

**4-6.1. Fixed sized delimiters.** The delimiters are listed in the two tables above. Two synonyms are not shown: \vert is the same as |; the command \Vert is the same as the command \| (printing ‖).

$\mathcal{A}\mathcal{M}\mathcal{S}$-LaTeX knows that these symbols are delimiters, and spaces them accordingly. Notice the difference between $\|a\|$ and $\|a\|$; the first was typed incorrectly: \( || a || \) since || is not a delimiter—as a result the two vertical bars in $\|a\|$ are too far apart. The second was typed correctly: \( \| a \| \), since \| is a delimiter; $\|a\|$ is properly spaced.

Delimiters are normally used in pairs but they can also be used singly, for instance, \( F(x) |^{b}_{a} \) prints $F(x)|^b_a$.

$\mathcal{A}\mathcal{M}\mathcal{S}$-LaTeX provides \bigl and \bigr to produce slightly bigger delimiters, and \biggl and \biggr to produce two-line tall delimiters:

\( (\bigl( \biggl( \)

prints: $\Big(\!\bigg(\!\Bigg(.$

For instance,

```
\[
   \left( \int \limits_{a}^{b} f(x) \, dx \right)
   \biggl( \int \limits_{a}^{b} f(x) \, dx \biggr)
\]
```

prints:

$$\left( \int_{a}^{b} f(x)\, dx \right) \left( \int_{a}^{b} f(x)\, dx \right)$$

Which pair of delimiters looks better?

For integral evaluation, you can choose one of the following:

$$F(x)|_{a}^{b} \quad F(x)\Big|_{a}^{b} \quad F(x)\Bigg|_{a}^{b}$$

typed as

```
\[
   F(x)  |^{b}_{a} \quad  F(x) \bigr|^{b}_{a} \quad
   F(x) \biggr|^{b}_{a}
\]
```

**4-6.2. Delimiters that stretch.** To request that $\mathcal{A}\mathcal{M}\mathcal{S}$-LaTeX enclose a formula with delimiters of the appropriate size, type

$$\( \left\ delim1\ formula\ \right\ delim2\ \)$$

where *delim1* and *delim2* are chosen from the delimiter tables. $\mathcal{A}\mathcal{M}\mathcal{S}$-LaTeX will read the formula and decide on the size of the delimiters. Such delimiters *must be paired* in order for $\mathcal{A}\mathcal{M}\mathcal{S}$-LaTeX to know the extent of the material to be measured; however, the matching delimiters need not be the same.

Since these delimiters must be paired, we need a *blank delimiter* to pair with any other delimiter; the blank delimiter is designated by . as in \left. or \right.

Examples of delimiters:

$$\left| \frac{a+b}{2} \right|, \quad \|A^2\|, \quad \left( \frac{a}{2}, b \right], \quad F(x)|_{a}^{b}$$

typed as:

```
\[
   \left| \frac{a + b}{2} \right|, \quad \left\| A^{2} \right\|,
   \quad \left( \frac{a}{2}, b \right], \quad
   \left. F(x) \right|_{a}^{b}
\]
```

\left\langle can be abbreviated as \left<, and \right\rangle can be abbreviated as \right>.

The delimiters | and ‖ are special: the same symbol (typed in math mode as | or \vert, and \| or \Vert) represents the left delimiter and the right delimiter. If this causes problems, use \left| and \right| to tell $\mathcal{A}_{\mathcal{M}}S$-LaTeX whether | is a left or right delimiter; similarly, for \Vert.

**4-6.3. Delimiters as symbols and binary relations.** The symbol | is used as a delimiter as well as a binary relation. To use it as a delimiter, type |. As a binary relation it is invoked by \mid: $\{x \mid x^2 \leq 2\}$ is typed as

\( \{ x \mid x^{2} \leq 2 \} \)

\big and \bigg produce larger delimiters, spaced as symbols; \bigm and \biggm produce larger delimiters, spaced as binary relations. Examples:

$$\binom{4}{2} \bigg/ \binom{2}{1} \quad \left\{ x \;\middle|\; \int_0^x t^2\, dt \leq 5 \right\}$$

typed as

\[
    \binom{4}{2} \bigg/ \binom{2}{1}
    \left\{ x \, \biggm| \, \int_{0}^x t^{2} \, dt \leq 5 \right\}
\]

For fine tuning, there is also \Big and \Bigg. Example:

\( a\big| \ a\Big|\ a\Bigg| \)

prints $a\big| \; a\Big| \; a\Bigg|$.

## 4-7. Operators

You cannot just type "sin x" for the sine function in math mode;

\( sin x \)

prints $sinx$ instead of $\sin x$. You get this right by typing:

\( \sin x \)

The command \sin prints "sin" in the proper style, and takes care of the spacing. $\mathcal{A}_{\mathcal{M}}S$-LaTeX calls \sin an *operator*.

There are a number of operators such as \sin. They come in two varieties: the simple ones like \sin and those which can take a "limit" in displayed mode, exemplified by \lim:

$$\lim_{x \to 0} f(x) = 0$$

which is typed as

\[
    \lim_{x \to 0} f(x) = 0
\]

The operators are listed in the following two tables (and also in Section A-10):

| \arccos | \arcsin | \arctan | \arg |
|---------|---------|---------|------|
| \cos | \cosh | \cot | \coth |
| \csc | \dim | \exp | \hom |
| \ker | \lg | \ln | \log |
| \sec | \sin | \sinh | \tan |
| \tanh | | | |
| \varliminf | \varlimsup | \varinjlim | \varprojlim |

Operators

| \det | \gcd | \inf | \injlim |
|------|------|------|---------|
| \lim | \liminf | \limsup | \max |
| \min | \projlim | \Pr | \sup |

Operators with limits

Let us illustrate the last four entries in the first table:

$$\varliminf_{x\to 0} \quad \varlimsup_{x\to 0} \quad \varinjlim_{x\to 0} \quad \varprojlim_{x\to 0}$$

typed as:

```
\[
   \varliminf_{x \to 0} \quad \varlimsup_{x \to 0}
   \quad \varinjlim_{x \to 0} \quad \varprojlim_{x \to 0}
\]
```

And we illustrate some entries from the second table:

$$\injlim_{x\to 0} \quad \liminf_{x\to 0} \quad \limsup_{x\to 0} \quad \projlim_{x\to 0}$$

typed as:

```
\[
   \injlim_{x \to 0} \quad \liminf_{x \to 0} \quad
   \limsup_{x \to 0} \quad \projlim_{x \to 0}
\]
```

You can force the limits in a displayed formula into the subscript position with the \textsyle command. Example:

$$\injlim_{x\to 0} \quad \liminf_{x\to 0} \quad \limsup_{x\to 0} \quad \projlim_{x\to 0}$$

typed as:

```
\[
   \textstyle
   \injlim_{x \to 0} \quad \liminf_{x \to 0} \quad
   \limsup_{x \to 0} \quad \projlim_{x \to 0}
\]
```

**4-7.1. Congruences.** Congruences are typeset in one of four flavors with \mod, \bmod, \pmod, and \pod:

| Type: | Print: |
|---|---|
| \( a \equiv v \mod{\theta} \) | $a \equiv v \mod \theta$ |
| \( a \equiv v \bmod{\theta} \) | $a \equiv v \bmod \theta$ |
| \( a \equiv v \pmod{\theta} \) | $a \equiv v \pmod{\theta}$ |
| \( a \equiv v \pod{\theta} \) | $a \equiv v \ (\theta)$ |

See Section 11-1.4 for a macro for congruences.

## 4-8. Math accents

The accents used in text (see Section 3-4.6) cannot be used in math. We collected all math accents in one table (see also Section A-11):

| | | | | | | | |
|---|---|---|---|---|---|---|---|
| \hat{a} | $\hat{a}$ | \Hat{a} | $\hat{a}$ | \widehat{a} | $\widehat{a}$ | a\sphat | $a^{\frown}$ |
| \tilde{a} | $\tilde{a}$ | \Tilde{a} | $\tilde{a}$ | \widetilde{a} | $\widetilde{a}$ | a\sptilde | $a^{\sim}$ |
| \acute{a} | $\acute{a}$ | \Acute{a} | $\acute{a}$ | | | | |
| \bar{a} | $\bar{a}$ | \Bar{a} | $\bar{a}$ | | | | |
| \breve{a} | $\breve{a}$ | \Breve{a} | $\breve{a}$ | | | a\spbreve | $a^{\breve{}}$ |
| \check{a} | $\check{a}$ | \Check{a} | $\check{a}$ | | | a\spcheck | $a^{\vee}$ |
| \dot{a} | $\dot{a}$ | \Dot{a} | $\dot{a}$ | | | a\spdot | $a^{\cdot}$ |
| \ddot{a} | $\ddot{a}$ | \Ddot{a} | $\ddot{a}$ | | | a\spddot | $a^{\cdot\cdot}$ |
| \dddot{a} | $\dddot{a}$ | | | | | a\spdddot | $a^{\cdot\cdot\cdot}$ |
| \ddddot{a} | $\ddddot{a}$ | | | | | | |
| \grave{a} | $\grave{a}$ | \Grave{a} | $\grave{a}$ | | | | |
| \vec{a} | $\vec{a}$ | \Vec{a} | $\vec{a}$ | | | | |

Math accents

Use the capitalized commands for double accents: \( \Hat{\Hat{A}} \) prints $\hat{\hat{A}}$; do not type \( \hat{\hat{A}} \) which prints $\hat{\hat{A}}$.

The two "wide" varieties, \widehat and \widetilde, open up: $\widehat{A}$, $\widehat{ab}$, $\widehat{iii}$, $\widehat{aiai}$, $\widehat{iiiii}$, and $\widetilde{A}$, $\widetilde{ab}$, $\widetilde{iii}$, $\widetilde{aiai}$, $\widetilde{iiiii}$ (the last one typed as \( \widetilde{iiiii} \)). If the "base" is too wide, the accent will be centered: $\widehat{ABCDE}$.

The "sp" varieties, the last column in the table, are used for superscripts, as illustrated in the table. If you use a lot of accented characters, you will appreciate the macro shortcut suggested in Section 10-1.

Notice the difference between $\bar{a}$ and $\overline{a}$ typed as

\( \bar{a}   \overline{a} \)

For more on the command \overline, see Section 4-10.

## 4-9. Sums and products

The sum $\sum_{i=1}^{n} x_i^2$ behaves a little differently from the integral. In displayed form:

$$\sum_{i=1}^{n} x_i^2$$

the sum symbol is larger, and the subscript and superscript become *limits*. Such operators are called *large operators*. The next table shows the complete list of large operators shown inline, and also in displayed mode.

| Type: | Print: | Type: | Print: |
|---|---|---|---|
| \prod_{i=1}^{n} | $\prod_{i=1}^{n}$ | \coprod_{i=1}^{n} | $\coprod_{i=1}^{n}$ |
| \bigcap_{i=1}^{n} | $\bigcap_{i=1}^{n}$ | \bigcup_{i=1}^{n} | $\bigcup_{i=1}^{n}$ |
| \bigvee_{i=1}^{n} | $\bigvee_{i=1}^{n}$ | \bigwedge_{i=1}^{n} | $\bigwedge_{i=1}^{n}$ |
| \bigsqcup_{i=1}^{n} | $\bigsqcup_{i=1}^{n}$ | \biguplus_{i=1}^{n} | $\biguplus_{i=1}^{n}$ |
| \bigotimes_{i=1}^{n} | $\bigotimes_{i=1}^{n}$ | \bigoplus_{i=1}^{n} | $\bigoplus_{i=1}^{n}$ |
| \bigodot_{i=1}^{n} | $\bigodot_{i=1}^{n}$ | \sum_{i=1}^{n} | $\sum_{i=1}^{n}$ |

Large operators

$$\prod_{i=1}^{n} \quad \coprod_{i=1}^{n} \quad \bigcap_{i=1}^{n} \quad \bigcup_{i=1}^{n} \quad \bigvee_{i=1}^{n} \quad \bigwedge_{i=1}^{n} \quad \bigsqcup_{i=1}^{n} \quad \biguplus_{i=1}^{n} \quad \bigotimes_{i=1}^{n} \quad \bigoplus_{i=1}^{n} \quad \bigodot_{i=1}^{n} \quad \sum_{i=1}^{n}$$

Large operators displayed

Use the \textstyle command if you wish to show limits of large operators as subscripts and superscripts in a displayed environment. Example:

$$\bigvee_{\mathfrak{m}} X = a$$

typed as

```
\[
    \textstyle
    \bigvee_{ \frak m } X = a
\]
```

**4-9.1. Subscript and superscript environments.** For large operators, we sometimes need multi-line subscripts and superscripts; these should be typed with the Sb and Sp subsidiary math environments.

For instance,

$$\sum_{\substack{1 \leq i \leq n \\ n \text{ is odd}}} x_i^2$$

is typed:

```
\[
  \sum
  \begin{Sb}
    1 \leq i \leq n\\
    n\text{ is odd}
  \end{Sb}
  {x_{i}^{2}}
\]
```

There is only one rule to remember: use the line separator \\. You can use the Sb and Sp environments wherever subscripts and superscripts can be used.

**4-10. Lines that stretch**

**4-10.1. Arrows.** There are a large number of fixed size arrows, see the table in Section A-6.

Very long arrows to accommodate labels on top of, or under, the arrow can be produced with @>>> and @<<<. The label on top should be typed between the first and second > (<) symbols, while the label underneath should be typed between the second and third > (<) symbols.
Examples:

$$A \xrightarrow{abc} B, \quad A \xrightarrow[abcd]{} B, \quad A \xleftarrow{abcde} B, \quad A \xleftarrow[abcdef]{} B$$

typed as

```
\[
  A @>{abc}>> B, \quad A @>>{abcd}> B, \quad
  A @<{abcde}<< B, \quad A @<<{abcdef}< B
\]
```

See Section 8-5 for commutative diagrams utilizing such arrows.

**4-10.2. Horizontal braces.** \overbrace places a brace of variable size over the argument, as in

$$\overbrace{a + b + \cdots + z}$$

typed as

```
\[
  \overbrace{a + b + \dots + z}
\]
```

A superscript adds a label to the brace, as in

$$\overbrace{a + a + \cdots + a}^{n}$$

typed as

```
\[
    \overbrace{a + a + \dots + a}^{n}
\]
```

**\underbrace** works similarly, placing a brace under the argument; a subscript adds a label to the brace, as in

$$\underbrace{a + a + \cdots + a}_{n}$$

typed as

```
\[
    \underbrace{a + a + \dots + a}_{n}
\]
```

The following example combines these two commands:

$$\underbrace{\overbrace{a + \cdots + a}^{(m-n)/2} + \underbrace{b + \cdots + b}_{n} + \overbrace{a + \cdots + a}^{(m-n)/2}}_{m}$$

typed as

```
\[
    \underbrace{
        \overbrace{a + \dots + a}^{(m - n)/2}
        + \underbrace{b + \dots + b}_{n}   +
        \overbrace{a + \dots + a}^{(m - n)/2}
    }_{m}
\]
```

**4-10.3. Over- and underlining.** Similarly, we can overline and underline in a formula with the commands \overline and \underline. Example:

$$\overline{\overline{X} \cup \overline{\overline{X}}} = \overline{\overline{X}}$$

typed as

```
\[
    \overline{ \overline{X} \cup \overline{ \overline{X} } } =
    \overline{ \overline{X} }
\]
```

## 4-11. Building symbols

$\mathcal{AMS}$-L^AT_EX provides you with a large variety of math symbols. But no matter how many symbols there are, we seem to want more. $\mathcal{AMS}$-L^AT_EX gives us excellent tools to build new symbols from the existing ones.

**4-11.1. Stacking symbols.** In addition to placing an accent on a symbol (Section 4-8), underlining and overlining a symbol, and putting a bar on top of a symbol (Section 4-10.3), you can place *any symbol* on top, or under, the given one. The commands are \overset and \underset, with two arguments; the first argument is over (or under) set in a smaller size, the second argument is the symbol modified. Examples:

$$\overset{\alpha}{a} \qquad X \qquad \overset{\alpha}{a_i} \qquad \overset{\alpha}{a_i} \qquad \overset{\alpha}{a}_i$$

typed as

```
\[
    \overset{\alpha}{a} \qquad \underset{\boldsymbol \cdot}{X}
    \qquad \overset{\alpha}{ a_{i} } \qquad
    \overset{\!\!\alpha}{ a_{i} } \qquad  \overset{\alpha}{a}_{i}
\]
```

Note that in the third example: $\overset{\alpha}{a_i}$, the $\alpha$ seems to be sitting too far to the right; the fourth and fifth examples correct that in two different ways.

You can use these commands also for binary relations, as in

$$f(x) \overset{\text{def}}{=} x^2 - 1$$

typed as

```
\[
    f(x) \overset{ \text{def} }{=} x^{2} - 1
\]
```

Note that $\overset{\text{def}}{=}$ remains a binary relation, as witnessed by the spacing on either side. Here is another example:

$$\frac{a}{b} \overset{u}{\sim} \frac{c}{d} \overset{l}{\sim} \frac{e}{f}$$

typed as

```
\[
    \frac{a}{b} \overset{u}{\sim} \frac{c}{d}
    \overset{l}{\sim} \frac{e}{f}
\]
```

Finally, $\mathcal{AMS}$-LATEX gives the command \sideset which has the strange form

```
\sideset{ _{ll}^{ul} }{ _{lr}^{ur} }{symbol}
```

where "ll" stands for the symbol to be placed at the lower left, "ul" for upper left, "lr" for lower right, and "ur" for upper right; "symbol" is the symbol to which these are attached. Examples: $X_*^*$   $^*X$ typed as

```
\( \sideset{}{ _{*}^{*} }{X} \quad \sideset{ ^{*} }{}{X} \)
```

**4-11.2. Declaring the type.** We have seen that some symbols are binary relations and some are binary operations. In fact, we can declare any symbol to be either.

\mathop declares its argument to be a binary operation, for instance,

\mathop{\alpha}

makes \alpha behave like a binary operation, as in $a \alpha b$ typed as

\( a \mathop{\alpha} b \)

Use \mathrel to declare a binary relation, as in

\mathrel{ \text{fine} }

Then in the formula $a$ fine $b$ , typed as

\( a \mathrel{ \text{fine} } b \)

"fine" is spaced as a binary relation.

Anything can be declared an operator or an operator with limits. For instance, to use **Trunc** as an operator, type

\( \operatorname{ \bold{Trunc} } f(x) \)

which will print: $\mathbf{Trunc}\, f(x)$.

To use **Trunc** as an operator with limits, type

\[
    \operatornamewithlimits{ \bold{Trunc} }_{x \in X} A_{x}
\]

which prints:

$$\mathbf{Trunc}_{x \in X}\, A_x$$

And as an inline formula: $\mathbf{Trunc}_{x \in X}\, A_x$.

Of course, you would introduce a user-defined command for **Trunc** for brevity; see Section 10-1.

## 4-12. Vertical spacing

The formula $\sqrt{a} + \sqrt{b}$ does not look right; the square roots are not uniform in size. You can help this with \mathstrut which inserts an invisible vertical space:

\( \sqrt{\mathstrut a} + \sqrt{\mathstrut b} \)

This prints: $\sqrt{\mathstrut a} + \sqrt{\mathstrut b}$. See also Section 3-9.4.

The command \smash directs $\mathcal{AMS}$-$\LaTeX$ to pretend that the argument of the command does not reach above or below the line. There is also \smash[t] just for the top, and \smash[b] just for the bottom.

For instance, the two lines of the admonition:

It is **very important** that you memorize the integral $\int \frac{1}{\sqrt{x}}\, dx = 2\sqrt{x} + C$ which will appear on the next test.

are too far apart; $\mathcal{AMS}$-LaTeX had to make room for the fraction $\frac{1}{\sqrt{x}}$. However, in this instance, this is not necessary because the second line is very short. So we redo the two lines:

```
It is {\bf very important} that you memorize the integral
\( \int \smash[b]{ \frac{1}{ \sqrt{x} } } \, dx =
2\sqrt{x} + C \) which will appear on the next test.
```

which prints:

It is **very important** that you memorize the integral $\int \frac{1}{\sqrt{x}} \, dx = 2\sqrt{x} + C$ which will appear on the next test.

### 4-13. Special styles

**4-13.1. Font changes.** \cal, \frak, and \Bbb select special fonts, used only in math modes.

\cal produces the *Calligraphic* font, upper case letters only: $\mathcal{A}, \mathcal{B}, \mathcal{C}, \mathcal{D}, \mathcal{E}, \mathcal{F}, \mathcal{G}, \mathcal{H}, \mathcal{I}, \mathcal{J}, \mathcal{K}, \mathcal{L}, \mathcal{M}, \mathcal{N}, \mathcal{O}, \mathcal{P}, \mathcal{Q}, \mathcal{R}, \mathcal{S}, \mathcal{T}, \mathcal{U}, \mathcal{V}, \mathcal{W}, \mathcal{X}, \mathcal{Y}, \mathcal{Z}$. Type \cal{A} in math mode to get $\mathcal{A}$. In text mode, a font change command is in effect within its scope (that is, within the braces it appears) or until it is changed; in math mode, a change font command **affects only one letter**. In the rare occasions when you need two calligraphic letters, say, $\mathcal{AB}$, type \( \cal{AB} \).

*Fraktur* (or Gothic) font is invoked with \frak: $\mathfrak{a}, \mathfrak{b}, \mathfrak{c}, \mathfrak{d}, \mathfrak{e}, \mathfrak{f}, \mathfrak{g}, \mathfrak{h}, \mathfrak{i}, \mathfrak{j}, \mathfrak{k}, \mathfrak{l}, \mathfrak{m}, \mathfrak{n}, \mathfrak{o}, \mathfrak{p}, \mathfrak{q}, \mathfrak{r}, \mathfrak{s}, \mathfrak{t}, \mathfrak{u}, \mathfrak{v}, \mathfrak{w}, \mathfrak{x}, \mathfrak{y}, \mathfrak{z}, \mathfrak{A}, \mathfrak{B}, \mathfrak{C}, \mathfrak{D}, \mathfrak{E}, \mathfrak{F}, \mathfrak{G}, \mathfrak{H}, \mathfrak{I}, \mathfrak{J}, \mathfrak{K}, \mathfrak{L}, \mathfrak{M}, \mathfrak{N}, \mathfrak{O}, \mathfrak{P}, \mathfrak{Q}, \mathfrak{R}, \mathfrak{S}, \mathfrak{T}, \mathfrak{U}, \mathfrak{V}, \mathfrak{W}, \mathfrak{X}, \mathfrak{Y}, \mathfrak{Z}$. For instance, $\mathfrak{a}$ is typed as \( \frak{a} \).

*Blackboard bold* is provided by \Bbb, uppercase letters only: $\mathbb{A}, \mathbb{B}, \mathbb{C}, \mathbb{D}, \mathbb{E}, \mathbb{F}, \mathbb{G}, \mathbb{H}, \mathbb{I}, \mathbb{J}, \mathbb{K}, \mathbb{L}, \mathbb{M}, \mathbb{N}, \mathbb{O}, \mathbb{P}, \mathbb{Q}, \mathbb{R}, \mathbb{S}, \mathbb{T}, \mathbb{U}, \mathbb{V}, \mathbb{W}, \mathbb{X}, \mathbb{Y}, \mathbb{Z}$. For instance, $\mathbb{A}$ is typed as \( \Bbb{A} \) .

Finally, the new *Euler script* is a real improvement aesthetically over the old calligraphic style: $\mathscr{A}, \mathscr{B}, \mathscr{C}, \mathscr{D}, \mathscr{E}, \mathscr{F}, \mathscr{G}, \mathscr{H}, \mathscr{I}, \mathscr{J}, \mathscr{K}, \mathscr{L}, \mathscr{M}, \mathscr{N}, \mathscr{O}, \mathscr{P}, \mathscr{Q}, \mathscr{R}, \mathscr{S}, \mathscr{T}, \mathscr{U}, \mathscr{V}, \mathscr{W}, \mathscr{X}, \mathscr{Y}, \mathscr{Z}$. See Section 11-2 on how to introduce a command that will make Euler script available.

**4-13.2. Style changes.** In math, most of the style selections are made by $\mathcal{AMS}$-LaTeX. The exception is boldface.

To make a *letter* bold, use the \bold command. For instance, in

let the vector **v** be chosen ...

the bold "v" is produced by

\( \bold{v} \)

**Tip.** It is easy to make the mistake of typing \bf for \bold. $\mathcal{AMS}$-LaTeX ignores \bf in math mode. There is no error message.

To obtain *bold numbers*, *bold Greek letters*, and *bold math symbols*, use the command \boldsymbol; for instance, $\boldsymbol{5}, \boldsymbol{\alpha}, \boldsymbol{\Lambda}, \boldsymbol{a \equiv b \pmod{\theta}}, \boldsymbol{\rightarrow}$ typed as

```
\( \boldsymbol{5}, \boldsymbol{\alpha}, \boldsymbol{\Lambda},
 a \boldsymbol{\equiv} b \pmod{\theta}, \boldsymbol{\to} \)
```

If you do not have AMSFonts Version 2.1 (or later) installed, many bold symbols in this book will not be available.

To make a whole formula bold, use \boldmath as in

```
{\boldmath \( a \equiv c \pmod \theta \)}
```

which prints: $a \equiv c \pmod{\theta}$. Within the scope of \boldmath, you can have \unboldmath that undoes the effect of \boldmath. Note that the \boldmath command is given before the formula, not in math mode; it has an effect within its scope.

So to get $\mathcal{AMS}$ type

```
\( \boldsymbol{ \cal{A} } \boldsymbol{ \cal{M} }
  \boldsymbol{ \cal{S} } \)
```

or

```
{\boldmath \( cal{A} \cal{M} \cal{S} \)}
```

Not all symbols have bold variants, type

```
\( \sum \quad \boldsymbol{\sum} \)
```

it prints: $\sum \quad \sum$ (there is no change). To obtain a bold version, use the *poor man's bold* invoked with the command \pmb. This prints the symbol three times very close to each other. For some symbols the result is satisfactory. However, \pmb destroys the "type" of the symbol: \pmb{\sum} is no longer a large operator. To make it into a large operator, declare it as in Section 4-11.2:

```
\mathop{\pmb{\sum}}
```

Compare the following three variants of sum:

$$\sum_{i=1}^{n} i^2 \quad \textstyle\sum_{i=1}^{n} i^2 \quad \sum_{i=1}^{n} i^2$$

The first sum is typed (in displayed math mode) as

```
\sum_{i = 1}^{n} i^{2}
```

The second uses poor man's bold, but does not declare the result a large operator:

```
\pmb{\sum}_{i = 1}^{n} i^{2}
```

The third uses poor man's bold, and it does declare the result a large operator:

```
\mathop{\pmb{\sum}}_{i = 1}^{n} i^{2}
```

**4-13.3. Size changes.** There are four math sizes, invoked by the commands:

- \textstyle
  the normal size for inline formulas. See Sections 2-4 (Example 8) and 4-9 for examples of its use.
- \displaystyle
  the normal size for displayed formulas;

- \scriptstyle
  the normal size for subscripted/superscripted symbols;
- \scriptscriptstyle
  the normal size for doubly subscripted/superscripted symbols.

For instance, if, for some reason, you want $x_i$ (instead of the usual $x_i$), type

\( x_{ \textstyle{i} } \)

**Continued fractions.** Fractions where all the numbers remain display style could be typed with \frac, \dfrac (Section 4-5.2), and \displaystyle. $\mathcal{AMS}$-LaTeX makes it easier with \cfrac:

$$\cfrac{1}{2 + \cfrac{1}{3 + \cdots}}$$

typed as

\[
    \cfrac{1}{2 + \cfrac{1}{3 + \cdots}}
\]

Use \lfrac (\rfrac) to place the numerator on the left (right).

**4-13.4. Boxed formulas.** The command \boxed puts the formula in the argument in a box, as in

$$\boxed{\int_{0}^{\pi} \sin x \, dx = 2}$$

typed as

\[
    \boxed{ \int_{0}^{\pi} \sin x \, dx = 2 }
\]

This command can also be used with a text argument.

# CHAPTER 5

# The Preamble
# and the Topmatter

We divide the source file of an article into the following parts:

(1) The *Preamble* is the part of the source file before the

\begin{document}

line; it contains definitions and instructions for the whole article, in the Style, the Declaration, and the Command sections.

(2) The *Topmatter* is between the lines

\begin{document}

and

\maketitle

It contains the information on the title, author, and so on, from which the "titlepage" is put together. The command

\maketitle

instructs $\mathcal{AMS}$-LaTeX to create the "titlepage". If there is no Topmatter, there is no need for this command.

(3) The article proper in the source file is called the *Body*; it is between the line

\maketitle

and the line

\end{document}

it starts, optionally, with the abstract environment, and ends, optionally, with the Bibliography.

So the document environment consists of the Topmatter and the Body.

In this chapter, we deal with the Preamble and the Topmatter. If you are satisfied with the article template set up in Section 2-7, then this chapter is not presently needed. However, if you have to modify the template, or require a brand new one, this chapter presents the rules to follow.

The organization of the Body is taken up in Chapter 6. Usually, the Body concludes with the *Bibliography* which is in the `thebibliography` environment just before the line

`\end{document}`

The Bibliography is discussed in detail in Chapter 7.

## 5-1. Preamble: Style section

In $\mathcal{A}_{\mathcal{M}}\mathcal{S}$-LaTeX, the Style section of the Preamble consists of a single line (see page xxii of the sample article article.tex):

`\documentstyle[amscd,amssymb,verbatim]{amsart}`

amsart.sty is the name of the document style: $\mathcal{A}_{\mathcal{M}}\mathcal{S}$ article.
amscd.sty, amssymb.sty, and verbatim.sty
are options (see optional argument, Section 3-3). We include these options, so that all the features they provide be available.

Alternatively, you may use:

`\documentstyle[amscd,amssymb,verbatim,12pt]{amsart}`

This prints the characters 20% larger.

There **must be** a Style section. $\mathcal{A}_{\mathcal{M}}\mathcal{S}$-LaTeX cannot typeset even the simplest note without it.

**Tip**. $\mathcal{A}_{\mathcal{M}}\mathcal{S}$-LaTeX is extremely fussy how the Preamble is typed, and not particularly helpful to make corrections. A single space

`\documentstyle[amscd,amssymb,verbatim␣]{amsart}`

will result in the query:

```
I can't read ''verbatim'' (not found)
Shall I try another file?
```

If you get this question, check whether you spelled "`verbatim`" correctly, and that it is not followed by a space!

If you enclose the optional argument in braces:

`\documentstyle{amscd,amssymb,verbatim}{amsart}`

$\mathcal{A}_{\mathcal{M}}\mathcal{S}$-LaTeX asks

```
I can't read ''amscd,amssymb,verbatim'' (not found)
Shall I try another file?
```

If you drop the last brace:

`\documentstyle[amscd,amssymb,verbatim]{amsart`

you get the error message:

```
Runaway argument?
{amsart
! Paragraph ended before \@documentstyle was complete.
<to be read again>
                    \par
1.6
```

The Style section for the articles in this book is very seldom changed.

### 5-2. Preamble: Declaration section

A *declaration* is a theorem, definition, corollary, note, and so on. The Declaration section of the Preamble of an article defines which of these are available, in which style they are printed, and how they are numbered. The actual declarations are in the Body of the article; see Section 5-2.3.

A simple note may have no Declaration section.

The sample article illustrates the three declaration styles (see pages xviii–xx); let us start by introducing them. When the article is printed in a journal, these styles may look different.

**5-2.1. The three styles.** Declarations come in three flavors.

**The plain style.** The most distinctive style is called *plain*. The lemmas and the theorems in the sample article article.tex are in this style (see pages xix and xx). Here is an example of a theorem in plain style:

**Theorem 1.** *There exists an infinite complete distributive lattice $K$ with only the two trivial complete congruence relations.*

Note that the name is bold, the text is emphasized, and the theorem is separated from the text by some additional interline spaces.

**The definition style.** This is less emphatic. The definitions in the sample article article.tex are in this style (see pages xviii and xix). Here is an example of a declaration in definition style:

**Definition 1.** A complete lattice $V$ is called *complete-simple* if $\omega$ and $\iota$ are the only two complete congruences of $V$.

In this style, the name is bold, the text is not emphasized.

**The remark style.** This is the least emphatic style; the Notation in the sample article article.tex is in this style—and is unnumbered; see page xix. Here is an example of an unnumbered declaration in definition style:

*Notation.* The two trivial congruence relations are denoted by $\omega$ and $\iota$, respectively.

In this style, the name is emphasized, the text is not emphasized, and there is little interline space separating the declaration from the following text.

**5-2.2. Setting up a declaration.** A declaration is set up in the Declaration section with two commands, \theoremstyle and \newtheorem. For instance:

\theoremstyle{plain}
\newtheorem{Thm}{Theorem}

This sets up the Thm environment which will produce a theorem in plain style.

\newtheorem is preceded by the style setting command \theoremstyle. If it is not, the default is the plain style. The \theoremstyle command stays in effect until another one is given.

\theoremstyle has an argument: plain, definition, or remark.

The full form of \newtheorem is:

\newtheorem{envname}[counter]{Name}[section]

where

envname: The name of the environment created by this command. This also gives the name for the counter used by $\mathcal{AMS}$-LaTeX to number the invocations of this declaration. For instance, we use Thm for the envname of a theorem; so a theorem is typed in the Thm environment. Of course, envname is just a label; you are free to choose any environment name, theorem, or th, or t, or george.

counter: $\mathcal{AMS}$-LaTeX sets up a counter for the environment; this counter is used to number the invocations of this environment. As a rule, if Thm is the envname for the environment being set up, then the name of the counter is theThm. The counter is an *optional argument*; it equates the counter for the new environment being defined with the counter of a previously defined declaration; counter must be the envname of a previously defined declaration. As a result, the two declarations will be jointly numbered. (See Examples (2) and (3) below.)

Name: When invoking the declarations, this is the name typeset. So if Theorem is the Name, then in the article we shall get **Theorem 1**, **Theorem 2**, and so on.

section: This optional argument will cause the Name declaration to be numbered within sections; so if Theorem is the Name, then in Section 1 it will be **Theorem 1.1**, **Theorem 1.2**, and so on; in Section 2, **Theorem 2.1**, **Theorem 2.2**, and so on. If this optional argument is missing, then the Thm declaration will be consecutively numbered in the whole article as **Theorem 1**, **Theorem 2**, **Theorem 3**, and so on.

**No numbering.** If the declaration Name should not be numbered, we add a third command:

\renewcommand{\theName}{}

For instance, if we do not want the theorems numbered, and the theorems were defined by the Thm environment, then the command is

\renewcommand{\theThm}{}

See Section 11-4.1 for an explanation of this command, and Example (4) below for an illustration.

**Tip.** Normally, the definition of a command or environment may be placed anywhere in the article, and will take effect where it is placed; see Section 10-1. Declarations, however, are special. They **must be placed** in the Preamble. If you violate this rule, you get the error message:

```
LaTeX error.  See LaTeX manual for explanation.
            Type  H <return>  for immediate help.
! Can be used only in Preamble.
\@latexerr ....}\errmessage {#1}
```

```
l.61 \theoremstyle
                {plain}
```

$\mathcal{AMS}$-LaTeX is very fussy about how declarations are typed. For instance, in the sample article article.tex in the paragraph (see page xxii):

```
%Declaration section
\theoremstyle{plain}
\newtheorem{Thm}{Theorem
\newtheorem{Cor}{Corollary}
\newtheorem{Main}{Main Theorem}
\renewcommand{\theMain}{}
\newtheorem{Lem}{Lemma}
\newtheorem{Prop}{Proposition}
```

drop the closing brace from the end of the third line as shown. You get the error message:

```
Runaway argument?
{Theorem \newtheorem {Cor}{Corollary} \newtheorem {Mai\ETC.
! Paragraph ended before \@nthm was complete.
<to be read again>
                \par
l.16
```

The line number is the end of the paragraph. So check all the \newtheorems, and see which is incorrect.

Next, drop an argument. Change the third line of the same paragraph to:

```
\newtheorem{Theorem}
```

You get the error message:

```
LaTeX error.  See LaTeX manual for explanation.
            Type  H <return>  for immediate help.
! Missing \begin{document}.
\@latexerr ....}\errmessage {#1}
```

```
<to be read again>
                      C
1.11 \newtheorem{C
              or}{Corollary}
```

The line

```
! Missing \begin{document}.
```

usually means that $\mathcal{A}_{\mathcal{M}}S$-LaTeX got confused; it is trying to typeset "C" as text. Somehow it convinced itself that there is some text typed in the Preamble, and therefore this text should be moved past the line

```
\begin{document}
```

The mistake could be anywhere in the Preamble. If you encounter such a problem, try to isolate the trouble by commenting out parts of the Preamble; see Section 3-5.

**Examples of declarations.**

(1) `\theoremstyle{plain}`
`\newtheorem{Thm}{Theorem}`

Sets up the Thm environment to be named and numbered as **Theorem 1, Theorem 2, Theorem 3,** and so on. (The counter is `\theThm`.)

(2) `\theoremstyle{plain}`
`\newtheorem{Lem}{Lemma}`
`\newtheorem{Prop}[Lem]{Proposition}`

Sets up the Lem and Prop environments to be named and jointly numbered as **Lemma 1, Proposition 2, Proposition 3,** and so on. (The counter for both is `\theLem`.)

(3) `\theoremstyle{plain}`
`\newtheorem{Lem}{Lemma}[section]`
`\newtheorem{Prop}[Lem]{Proposition}`

Sets up the Lem and Prop environments to be named and jointly numbered as **Lemma 1.1, Proposition 1.2,** ... , **Proposition 2.1,** and so on.

(4) `\theoremstyle{remark}`
`\newtheorem{Note}{Note}`
`\renewcommand{\theName}{}`

Sets up the Note environment in the remark style to be named **Note** and not numbered. The counter `\theNote` is empty; {} is the empty group, see Section 4-5.1.

Full examples of the Declaration section of an article can be found in Section 2-7; see also the file article.tpl on the DISK.

**5-2.3. Invoking declarations.** The declarations we have defined are environments, and are invoked as such. For instance, if we use Option 5 in the Declaration section of article.tpl (see Section 2-7), then we have defined the Thm, Cor, Main, Lem, Prop, Def, and Notation environments. To type a lemma:

```
\begin{Lem} \label{L:xxx}
Text of the lemma.
\end{Lem}
```

These environments have an *optional argument*: a name for the decla
placed in parenthesis. For instance,

**Theorem 5 (The Conversion Formula).** *Text of the theorem.*

is typed

```
\begin{Thm}[The Conversion Formula] \label{T:ConvForm}
Text of the theorem.
\end{Thm}
```

`\ref{T:ConvForm}` will reference the theorem

## 5-3. Preamble: Command section

A simple note may omit the Command section.

To make sure that the error messages you will see are similar to the ones in this book, $\mathcal{AMS}$-LaTeX be told:

```
\errorcontextlines=0
```

The Command section of article.tex (page xxii) has one more command, to introduce `\rm` as discussed in Section 3-6.2. In the sample article article2.tex (see the DISK or Section 11-3), the Command section is continued with

```
\input{macros02}
```

where macros02.tex is the file containing the standard commands used by the author of the sample article (available on the DISK and in Section 11-2).

This is normally followed by a list of user-defined commands and environments that are special to the article. You will learn in Sections 10-1 and 10-2 about user-defined commands and environments.

**Tip**. Almost any typing error in the Command section of the Preamble will result in a

```
Runaway argument?
```

or

```
! Missing \begin{document}.
```

error message. $\mathcal{AMS}$-LaTeX is even easier to confuse with new commands than with declarations, since it does not know what commands or environments you wish to define. Checklist:

(1) The command to be defined must be in braces.
(2) \ precedes the name of the command.
(3) The optional argument must be in brackets, not braces.
(4) The braces must balance for every command (Section 3-3.1).

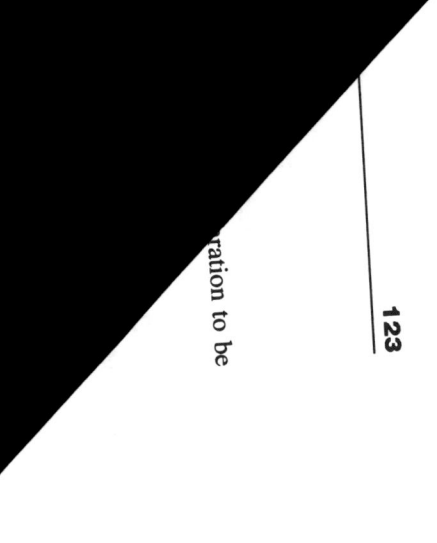

ɔu want the equations numbered in each section,
line:

n}

**Topmatter**

ion on the title, author, and so on, from which
ɔrmation provided in the Topmatter is placed
We group the items in the Topmatter roughly
ɔument style: article information, information
ɪuired by the $\mathcal{AMS}$.
ɔr.
ɔd as arguments of commands. Most of this
ɛe sure that all commands are \protect-ed;

### 5-4.1. Article info.

**Title.**

**Rule 1.** *Title.*

- Command: \title.
- Separate lines with \\.
- Optional argument: short title for running head.
- Do not put a period at the end of the title.

Most titles are too long to be typeset in one line in the large type used by $\mathcal{AMS}$-LaTeX for titles. It is suggested that you indicate to $\mathcal{AMS}$-LaTeX where the line should be broken.

The *running head* (the top line of the page, the "header") is the title on odd numbered pages, set in capital letters. If the title is more than a few words long, use the optional argument to specify a short title for the running head; do not use \\ in the short title.

Examples. A title:

```
\title{A construction of  distributive lattices}
```

A title with a short title (running head):

```
\title[Complete-simple distributive lattices]{A construction
   of complete-simple \\ distributive lattices}
```

**Translator.**

**Rule 2.** *Translator.*

- Command: \translator.
- Do not punctuate.

Example:

```
\translator{Harry M. Goldstein}
```

**Dedication.**

**Rule 3.** *Dedication.*

- Command: \dedicatory.
- Separate lines with \\.

It is suggested that you indicate to $\mathcal{A}\mathcal{M}\mathcal{S}$-L∧TEX where the line should be broken. Example:

```
\dedicatory{To the memory of my esteemed
   friend and teacher, \\ Harry M. Goldstein}
```

**Date.**

**Rule 4.** *Date.*

- Command: \date.

Examples:

```
\date{January 22, 1991}
```

You can use the \today command to get today's date.

```
\date{\today}
```

**5-4.2. Author info.**

**Author.**

**Rule 5.** *Author.*

- Command: \author.
- Optional argument: short form of name for running head.

Examples. An author:

```
\author{George A. Menuhin}
```

An author with a short form of the name for the running head:

```
\author[G. A. Menuhin]{George A.  Menuhin}
```

**Address.**

**Rule 6.** *Address.*

- Command: \address.
- Separate lines with \\.
- Optional argument: name of author.

Example:

DEPARTMENT OF APPLIED MATHEMATICS, UNIVERSITY OF WINEBAGO, WINEBAGO MIN-
NESOTA 23714

typed as

```
\address{Department of Applied Mathematics \\
  University of Winebago \\
  Winebago Minnesota 23714}
```

Observe that $\mathcal{AMS}$-LaTeX replaces the \\ line separators with commas.

If there are several authors, it may not be clear how to associate the addresses with the authors. In such cases use the optional argument of \address (the authors' name) to avoid ambiguity. See Example (4) in Section 5-4.5 for a complete example.

### Current address.

**Rule 7.** *Current address.*

- Command: \curraddress.
- Separate lines with \\.
- Optional argument: name of author.

If there are several authors, it may not be clear how to associate the current addresses with the authors. In such cases use the optional argument (the authors' name) of \address to avoid ambiguity.

Example: same as for \address in Section 5-4.5.

### Electronic mail address.

**Rule 8.** *Email.*

- Command: \email.
- Type @@ to get @.
- Optional argument: name of author.

Some European email addresses also contain %; recall (Section 3-4.4) that you have to type \% to get %.

Examples:

```
\email{gmen@@ccw.uwinebago.edu}
\email{h1175moy\%ella@@relay.eu.net}
```

"Generic" email addresses contain _; recall (Section 3-4.4) that you have to type \_ to get _. Example:

```
\email{George\_Gratzer@@umanitoba.ca}
```

### Research support.

**Rule 9.** *Research support.*

- Command: \thanks.

- Do not indicate linebreak.

Example:

```
Research  was supported in part by NSF grant~ PAL-90-23466.
```

**5-4.3.** $\mathcal{AMS}$ **info.** The following are collected at the bottom of the first page as unmarked footnotes.

### $\mathcal{AMS}$ subject classification.

**Rule 10.** *$\mathcal{AMS}$ subject classification.*

- Command: \subjclass.
- $\mathcal{AMS}$-LaTeX adds a period at the end.

The argument should be "Primary:" and a five digit code, semicolon, followed by "Secondary:", five digit code, no period, or just a single five digit code.

Examples:

```
\subjclass{06B10}
\subjclass{Primary: 06B10; Secondary: 06D05}
```

The current subject classification scheme is in a document on the $\mathcal{AMS}$-computer, see Appendix D on how to access it.

### Keywords.

**Rule 11.** *Keywords.*

- Command: \keywords.
- Do not indicate line break.
- $\mathcal{AMS}$-LaTeX supplies "*Key words and phrases.* and a period at the end.

Example:

```
\keywords{Complete lattice, distributive lattice, complete
   congruence, congruence lattice}
```

**Further footnotes.** An additional \thanks becomes an additional footnote.

Examples:

```
\thanks{This is a preliminary version of this article,
   prepared for the Second Annual Meeting of the
   Statistical Association of Winebago.}
\thanks{This article is in final form, and no version of it
   will be submitted elsewhere.}
```

The second example may be used in conference proceedings to indicate that the article should be reviewed.

**5-4.4. Multiple authors.** If the article has several authors, the author information should be repeated for each one. Take care that the email follows the address.

In case two authors have the same address, omit the \address for the second author (who can still have \email). In this case, the additional footnote should be a \thanks following the \thanks of the *last author*. Since the footnotes are not marked, the argument of the \thanks for research support should contain a reference to the author:

```
\thanks{The research  of the first author was supported in part by
    NSF grant~ PAL-90-23466.}
\thanks{The research of the second author was supported in part by
    the  Hungarian National Foundation for Scientific Research,
    under Grant No.~9901.}
```

Finally, if an article has so many authors that even the short form of the authors' name is too long for the running head, use only one \author command as in the following example:

```
\author[G.  A. Menuhin, E. T. Moynahan, \em{et al.}]
    {G.~ A.~ Menuhin, E.~T.~Moynahan, R. ~S. ~Treblinski,
    P. ~G. ~Viznobranski, and B. ~R. ~Wojdicko}
```

Now write the author info as usual, and use no more \author command. So for the second, third, and so on author you only type \address, \email, and \thanks.

If there are multiple authors, sometimes it may not be clear whose address, current address, or email address is being given. In such cases give the name of the author as an optional argument. Example:

*Email address*, E. T. Moynahan: emoy@ccw.uwinebago.edu.

typed as

```
\email[E. T. Moynahan]{emoy@@ccw.uwinebago.edu}
```

See also Example (4) in Section 5-4.5.

**5-4.5. Examples.** Here are some examples of Topmatter, available on the DISK in the file topmat.tpl.

(1) One author:

```
%Article info
\title[Complete-simple distributive lattices]
    {A construction of complete-simple \\
    distributive lattices}
\date{\today}
%Author info
\author{G.  A.  Menuhin}
\address{Computer Science Department \\
    University of Winebago \\
    Winebago,  Minnesota 23714}
```

```
\email{gmen@@ccw.uwinebago.edu}
\thanks{This research was supported by
    the NSF under grant number~ 23466.}
%AMS info
\keywords{Complete lattice, distributive lattice,
    complete congruence, congruence lattice}
\subjclass{Primary: 06B10; Secondary: 06D05}
```

This is a fairly typical Topmatter. In \title, the optional argument (the running head) is the rule, not the exception. You may prefer

```
\title[Complete-simple distributive
    lattices]{A construction of \\
    complete-simple distributive lattices}
```

All the items are necessary, except \email.

(2) Two authors. We only show the author info section; the others are unchanged:

```
%Author info
\author{G.  A.  Menuhin}
\address{Computer Science Department \\
    University of Winebago \\
    Winebago,  Minnesota 23714}
\email{gmen@@ccw.uwinebago.edu}
\thanks{The research of the first author was
    supported by the NSF under grant number~ 23466.}
\author{E. T. Moynahan}
\address{Mathematical Research Institute
    of the Hungarian  Academy of Sciences \\
    Budapest,  P.O.B.  127, H-1364 \\
    Hungary}
\email{h1175moy\%ella@@relay.eu.net}
\thanks{The research of the second author
    was supported in part by the  Hungarian
    National Foundation for Scientific Research,
    under Grant No.~9901.}
```

(3) Two authors, same department. We only show the author info section; the others are unchanged:

```
%Author info
\author{G.  A.  Menuhin}
\address{Computer Science Department \\
    University of Winebago \\
    Winebago,  Minnesota 23714}
\email[G.  A.  Menuhin]{gmen@@ccw.uwinebago.edu}
\thanks{The research of the first author was
    supported by the NSF under grant number~ 23466.}
```

```
\author{E. T. Moynahan}
\email[E. T. Moynahan]{emoy@@ccw.uwinebago.edu}
\thanks{The research of the second author
    was supported in part by the  Hungarian National
    Foundation for Scientific Research,
    under Grant No.~9901.}
```

(4) Three authors, the first two from the same department, the second and third with email addresses and research support. We only show the author info section; the others are unchanged. There are various ways of doing this, here is one possibility:

```
%Author info
\author{G.  A.  Menuhin}
\address[G.  A.  Menuhin and E. T. Moynahan]%
    {Computer Science Department \\
        University of Winebago \\
        Winebago, Minnesota 23714}
\author{E. T. Moynahan}
\email[E. T. Moynahan]{emoy@@ccw.uwinebago.edu}
\thanks{The research of the second author was
    supported in part by the Hungarian National
    Foundation for Scientific Research,
    under Grant No.~9901.}
\author{F. R. Richardson}
\address[F. R. Richardson]%
    {Department of Mathematics \\
        California United Colleges \\
        Frasco,  CA 23714}
\email{frich@@ccu.frasco.edu}
\thanks{The research of the third author was
    supported by the NSF under grant number~ 23466.}
```

**Tip.** The most typical mistake in Topmatter is the misspelling of a command name, for instance, \adress. This is no problem because the error message:

```
! Undefined control sequence.
l.37 \adress
            {Computer Science Department \\
```

is very helpful. Similarly, if you drop a closing brace, for instance:

```
\email{menuhin@@ccw.uwinebago.edu
```

you are told what went wrong:

```
Runaway argument?
{menuhin@@ccw.uwinebago.edu \thanks {The research of th\ETC.
! Paragraph ended before \email was complete.
```

```
<to be read again>
                    \par
1.52
```

If you drop an opening brace:

```
\author  G. A. Menuhin}
```

you get the error message:

```
! Too many }'s.
1.43 \author  G. A. Menuhin}
```

If you enclose an optional argument by braces, for instance:

```
\title{Complete-simple distributive lattices}%\
        {A construction of complete-simple \\
        distributive lattices}
```

$\mathcal{A}_{\mathcal{M}}S$-LaTeX makes the short title into the title, and the title is printed before the short title. There is no error message.

# CHAPTER 6

# The Body
# of the Article

In this chapter, we deal with the organization of the article itself, the Body (see the introductory comments in Chapter 5), which lies in the source file between the line

`\maketitle`

and the line

`\end{document}`

We start with the abstract, and continue with the division of the article into sections. Then we take up cross-referencing, a major strength of $\mathcal{A}_{\mathcal{M}}$S-LaTeX.

The next section deals with Table of Contents and Index. These are not very important for the typical article, but they may be useful for longer ones.

Finally, there is a brief discussion of tables and figures.

The Body, optionally, ends with the Bibliography, discussed in Chapter 7.

### 6-1. Abstract

The abstract is typed in an environment:

`\begin{abstract}`

`\end{abstract}`

$\mathcal{A}_{\mathcal{M}}$S-LaTeX types ABSTRACT. and typesets the text in a smaller type with wider margins.

**Tip**. Do not type the `abstract` environment, and delay writing the abstract until later. The `abstract` environment cannot stay empty. If it is, you get the error message

```
! Something's wrong--perhaps a missing \item.
\@latexerr ....}\errmessage {#1}
```

```
...
1.62 \end{abstract}
```

Either comment out the `abstract` environment, or insert something temporary, such as "Yet to do!"

## 6-2. Sectioning

**6-2.1. Section.** The Body of a typical article is divided into *sections*. $\mathcal{A}_{\mathcal{M}}S$-LaTeX centers the titles of sections and sets them in small capitals.

$\mathcal{A}_{\mathcal{M}}S$-LaTeX is instructed to start a section with the `\section` command. This command has an argument: the title of the section. $\mathcal{A}_{\mathcal{M}}S$-LaTeX will typeset the number (automatically produced) and the title. Of course, `\section` should be followed by `\label` so we can refer to the number generated by $\mathcal{A}_{\mathcal{M}}S$-LaTeX.

Example:

1. INTRODUCTION

is typed

```
\section{Introduction} \label{S:intro}
```

The command `\ref{S:intro}` will refer to the number of the section.

The `\section*` command works the same way, except that the section will not be numbered. A `\section*` cannot have a label.

**6-2.2. Other sectioning commands.** A section may be subdivided into *subsections*, and there are even *subsubsections*. Subsection titles are typeset flush left in bold; subsections are numbered within the section (in Section 1, they are numbered 1.1, 1.2, and so on).

Subsubsections are typeset flush left emphasized; they are numbered within the subsection (in Subsection 3 of Section 2, they are numbered 2.3.1, 2.3.2, and so on).

It is important to understand that the three levels of sectioning are not just three different styles of typesetting (such as the three different styles of declarations; see Section 5-2.1); there is no subsection without a section, and there is no subsubsection without a subsection.

In the section, 1. INTRODUCTION, to get a subsection

**1.1. Birkhoff's contributions.** To start out, let us

type

```
\subsection{Birkhoff's contributions}\label{SS:contrib}
To start out, let us
```

Notice that $\mathcal{A}_{\mathcal{M}}S$-LaTeX placed a period at the end of the title.

Finally, in this subsection, we may want a subsubsection:

*1.1.1. The years 1935–1945.* Already, in his formative

typed as

```
\subsubsection{The years 1935--1945}\label{SSS:1935}
Already, in his formative
```

Notice again the period.

And this is all about sectioning. There is one more marker, the *part*, but it has no effect on other sectioning commands. The command is \part; for instance,

**Part I. Theory**

is typed as

\part{Theory} \label{Theory}

The text following the part is set in a new paragraph with a generous interline space.

There are also the commands \subsection*, \subsubsection*, and \part* for the nonnumbered variants.

To learn how to change the formatting of the section numbers, see Section 11-4.2. See also Section 11-4.1 on how to influence which sectioning levels be numbered.

**6-2.3. Appendix.** The \appendix command marks the start of the appendices. Each subsequent section becomes an appendix. For example

APPENDIX A. A GEOMETRIC PROOF OF THE MAIN THEOREM

is typed

\appendix
\section{A geometric proof of the Main Theorem}\label{S:geom}

Subsections are numbered A.1, A.2, and so on, and sububsections in A.1 are numbered A.1.1, A.1.2, and so on.

If you want an unnumbered appendix, such as:

APPENDIX. A GEOMETRIC PROOF OF THE MAIN THEOREM

type:

\appendix
\renewcommand{\thesection}{}
\section{A geometric proof of the Main Theorem}

**6-2.4. Equations.** Equations (see Section 4-2.1) are numbered sequentially in the article. The command:

\numberwithin{equation}{section}

in the Command section of the Preamble will cause the equations to be numbered within sections; so in Section 1, the equations will be numbered (1.1), (1.2) and so on.

## 6-3. Cross-referencing

There are three types of cross-referencing in $\mathcal{AMS}$-LaTeX:

- Symbolic referencing with \ref.
- Page referencing with \pageref.
- Bibliographic referencing with \cite.

In this section, we discuss the first two; the third is discussed in Chapter 7, in particular, in Sections 7-1 and 7-3.1.

Wherever $\mathcal{AMS}$-LaTeX generates a number, you can place a \label command:

\label{symbol}

Then at any place in the text you can use the command \ref:

\ref{symbol}

to reproduce the number.

You can use labels for sections, subsections, subsubsections, parts, equations, figures, tables, items in an enumerated environment (see Section 9-3.1), and most importantly, for theorems and other declarations.

If the equation, labeled E:int, is the fifth in the article, then the label E:int will store the number 5; \ref{E:int} will produce the number 5. If the equation is numbered within sections (see Section 6-2.4), say, this equation is the third in Section 2, then the label E:int will store the number 2.3; \ref{E:int} will produce the number 2.3.

**Example 1.** The title of the present section of this book is typed

\section{Cross-referencing} \label{S:cref}

So \ref{S:cref} will produce the number 6.3. (See Section 11-4.2 for an explanation of why in this book we get this number in the style 6-3.)

**Example 2.**

\begin{equation}\label{E:int}
\int_{0}^{\pi} \sin x \, dx = 2.
\end{equation}

\ref{E:int} produces a number such as 1 (or 3.1, if the equations are numbered within sections); it does not give the parentheses. If you want a reference: (1), you must type:

(\ref{E:int})

or use the command \eqref which supplies the parentheses.

In fact, \eqref does somewhat more: even if the text is emphasized (as in theorems), the parentheses and the number will not be slanted.

**Tip.** Do not use \label in tagged equations.

**Example 3.**

```
\begin{Thm} \label{T:fund}
Statement of theorem.
\end{Thm}
```

`\ref{T:fund}` produces the number of the theorem.

It is hard to overemphasize how much help cross-referencing gives in the writing of an article. There are three simple tools to make cross-referencing easier.

- User-defined commands (see Section 10-1) may cut the typing necessary for referencing.
- Systematize the labels. We start the label for a section with "`S:`", subsection with "`SS:`", subsubsection "`SSS:`", theorem "`T:`", lemma "`L:`", definition "`D:`", and so on.
- While working on an article, typeset it with the labels shown on the margin; see Section 11-1.5.

Closely related to labels are citations; see Section 7-1.

**Tip.** Remember that you have to **typeset twice** to see a change in a cross-reference.

**6-3.1. Page-referencing.** The command

`\pageref`

produces the page number of the page where the corresponding `\label` appears.

Example:

```
There may be three types of problems with the
construction of such lattices.\label{problem}
```

And somewhere else:

```
Because of the problems associated with
the construction (see page ~\pageref{problem})
```

## 6-4. Table of Contents and Index

$\mathcal{AMS}$-LaTeX can generate a Table of Contents and an Index.

**6-4.1. Table of Contents.** $\mathcal{AMS}$-LaTeX creates a toc file when so instructed by the command `\tableofcontents`. If the source file is article.tex, the toc file is article.toc. This file lists all the parts, sections, subsections, subsubsections, their titles and page numbers; and also the References.

If you already have a toc file, the command `\tableofcontents` instructs $\mathcal{AMS}$-LaTeX to create a new toc file, and creates a Table of Contents from the last toc file. The Table of Contents is inserted at the point where the `\tableofcontents` command appears.

You can add a line to the Table of Contents formatted like a section title with the command:

```
\addcontentsline{toc}{section}{The line to be added}
```

There are three arguments. The first argument informs $\mathcal{A}_{\mathcal{M}}\mathcal{S}$-LATEX that the third argument is to be added to the Table of Contents. The second argument specifies how the line is to be formatted in the Table of Contents. In the example, the second argument is `section`, so the line will be formatted as a section title is formatted in the Table of Contents. The second argument must be `part`, `section`, `subsection`, or `subsubsection`.

You can add a line (not formatted) to the Table of Contents with the command:

`\addtocontents{toc}{The line to be added}`

**Tip**. The toc file is easy to read; the lines are self-explanatory. These are typical lines:

```
\contentsline {section}{\numberline {5-4.}Topmatter}{119}
\contentsline {subsection}{\numberline {5-4.1.}Article info}{119}
\contentsline {subsection}{\numberline {5-4.2.}Author info}{121}
```

before the final printing you should

- Edit the toc file; for instance, add `\samepage` commands to keep a section together with at least one subsection; see Section 3-7.3. You can add `\dotfill` commands (see Section 3-8.4) to connect with dots the titles with the page numbers:

  `\contentsline{section}{\numberline{5-4.}Topmatter\dotfill}{119}`

- Then add the `\nofiles` command to the Preamble of the document. This will prevent $\mathcal{A}_{\mathcal{M}}\mathcal{S}$-LATEX from generating a new toc file, so that the pretty toc file you have created will not be overwritten.

We can influence which levels of sectioning should go into the Table of Contents; see Section 11-4.1.

**6-4.2. Index.** Using the commands `\label` and `\pageref` (see Section 6-3), it is quite simple to produce an Index:

INDEX

At every point in the text which you want to reference in the Index, place a \label command. This will be referenced in the Index with a \pageref.

Start the Index as follows:

```
\renewcommand{\e}{\par \setlength{\hangindent}{12pt} \noindent}
  %entry
\renewcommand{\se}{\par \setlength{\hangindent}{24pt} \noindent
  \hspace*{12pt} }%subentry
\renewcommand{\sse}{\par \setlength{\hangindent}{36pt} \noindent
  \hspace*{24pt}} %subsubentry
```

```
\section*{Index}
```

The commands \e, \se, \sse introduce an entry, subentry, and subsubentry, respectively. If you require vertical spacing when the first letter changes (say, between the "h" entries and the "i" entries), use the command \newalph. Change the numbers in these commands to suit your taste. Now edit in the Style section the \documentstyle command in the article to read:

```
\documentstyle[amscd,amssymb,verbatim,multicol]{amsart}
```

and copy the file multicol.sty from the DISK to the TeX input directory/folder.

The index entries are typed in the multicols environment. Here are some examples (the labels used in these examples are the labels we used when compiling the Index for this book; the symbols used have no intrinsic meaning):

```
\begin{multicols}{2}
\e article info, \pageref{x26}
  \se date, \pageref{x31}
  \se dedication, \pageref{x30}
  \se translator, \pageref{x29}
  \se title, \pageref{x27}
\e {\tt article.tex}, \pageref{r27}, \pageref{s56}
\e {\tt article.tpl}, \pageref{r34}, \pageref{x19}, \pageref{y4},
    \pageref{y8}
\e  {\tt article1.bbl}, \pageref{bbl}
\e  {\tt article1.bib}, \pageref{y32}, \pageref{y35}
\e  {\tt article1.blg}, \pageref{blg}

\newalph
\e bibliographic entry, \pageref{y12}
  \se field of, \pageref{y13}
      \sse required, \pageref{y16}
  \se type, \pageref{y14}
      \sse ARTICLE, \pageref{y15}, \pageref{y18}
      \sse BOOK, \pageref{y15}, \pageref{y19}
```

```
\newalph
\e \disk/, \pageref{di1}, \pageref{di2}, \pageref{r5},
    \pageref{r27}, \pageref{x19}, \pageref{x23}, \pageref{x47},
    \pageref{di3}, \pageref{x73}, \pageref{y4}, \pageref{y9},
    \pageref{y17}, \pageref{C:Multidisp}, \pageref{C:Tenv},
    \pageref{z44}, \pageref{z45}, \pageref{z48}, \pageref{z56},
    \pageref{di4}
\e displayed math, \pageref{q39}, \pageref{t47}, \pageref{t50}
\e {\tt displaymath} environment, \pageref{t50}, \pageref{y44}
\e Doob, Michael, \pageref{p6}, \pageref{z55}, \pageref{w26}
\end{multicols}
```

$\mathcal{AMS}$-LaTeX also provides the \index command which has a limited ability to help you compile an Index. The entries are placed in the text as arguments of \index, for instance,

```
\index{page-referencing}
```

If you place the command \makeindex in the Preamble, $\mathcal{AMS}$-LaTeX will create a file with the extension idx containing all the entries along with the page numbers on which they appear.

Most LaTeX installations have the MakeIndex program written by P. Chen and L. Lamport. If you follow the instructions of this program on how to code the index entries, MakeIndex will convert the idx file into an Index. You have to use the amsbook document style to utilize MakeIndex for $\mathcal{AMS}$-LaTeX. Both for the **PC** and the **Mac**, the MakeIndex program is available from the TUG; see Section D-5.

**Editing macros.** It is hard to overemphasize the importance of a good editor for typing an $\mathcal{AMS}$-LaTeX source file. A good editor should have "macro" capability, meaning that a single keystroke should be able to produce a sequence of keystrokes (and mouse clicks, file selections, and so on).

For instance, if you use the command \index, you may want to define a macro, invoked with ˆI (pressing the control key and I at the same time) which does the following: it types \index{, then does a "paste", then types }. So to enter an index entry in the source file, select the text, "copy" it, then type ˆI.

See also the user-defined command \ie in Section 10-1.1.

### 6-5. Tables and figures

The table environment is set up as follows:

```
\begin{table}
```

Place the table here

```
    \caption{name of table}
\end{table}
```

The \caption is optional. A table can have more than one caption.

The `table` environment is used mostly for tables made with the `tabular` environment; see Section 9-4. The auxiliary file for the list of tables is named lot.

There are two examples of tables in Chapter 9.

For `\begin{table}` you can specify an optional argument b for bottom of page, h for here, t for top of page, and p for separate page. In fact, you can list your priorities, for instance,

`\begin{table}[bht]`

The default is tbp. Remember, this option *requests* $\mathcal{A}_{\mathcal{M}}S$-L\TeX to place the table as indicated. $\mathcal{A}_{\mathcal{M}}S$-L\TeX may or may not be able to comply.

The information for the List of Tables is placed by $\mathcal{A}_{\mathcal{M}}S$-L\TeX in the lot file if so instructed by the

`\listoftables`

command. The List of Tables is inserted into the Body where this command appears.

The analogs of the Table of Contents commands:

`\addcontentsline{lot}{section}{The line to be added}`

`\addtocontents{lot}{The line to be added}`

add a line to the List of Tables.

Since $\mathcal{A}_{\mathcal{M}}S$-L\TeX is not very good in handling many tables (it may run out of memory, and refuse to typeset the article), merging them (making two tables into one) may be the only way to have more than one table on a page.

The `figure` environments handle figures that cannot be broken across pages. It provides a caption for the figure. The captions are numbered by $\mathcal{A}_{\mathcal{M}}S$-L\TeX; if labels are used, these numbers can be cross-referenced. A List of Figures can be compiled just as the Table of Contents is done.

Many implementations of \TeX allow you to include a picture, not just to paste one in.

The List of Figures is compiled with the command

`\listoffigures`

which creates the auxiliary file lof.

We also have

`\addcontentsline{lof}{section}{The line to be added}`

`\addtocontents{lof}{The line to be added}`

which add a line to the List of Figures.

# CHAPTER 7

# The Bibliography

$\mathcal{A}_{\mathcal{M}}\mathcal{S}$-LaTeX provides two ways to create the Bibliography of an article:

- Bibliography in the article.
- Bibliographic database document processed by BibTeX.

In the sample article (see page xxix) and in the discussion in Section 2-8.3, we used the simpler method: Bibliography in the article. In Section 7-1, we discuss this method in more detail. The advantage of this method is its simplicity. The disadvantage is that there is no "document style" for the bibliographic items, so the journal in which you publish the article probably will have to edit the Bibliography.

The second method requires to create first a bibliographic database document, as described in Section 7-2. Then use the program BibTeX and a bibliographic style (see Section 7-3), to produce the bibliographic listing. This procedure has two major advantages:

- To change the style of the bibliography, the journal only has to change the bibliographic style.
- The bibliographic database document is reusable, so in the long run, you save a lot of typing.

And the disadvantages are the following:

- This process is more complicated, and it requires the use of the program BibTeX which is not part of $\mathcal{A}_{\mathcal{M}}\mathcal{S}$-LaTeX.
- BibTeX sometimes does not put the references in the proper order, so the journal will have to do a little more than just change the name of the bibliographic style.

In the article, the Bibliography is titled "References".

## 7-1. Bibliography in the article

The simplest way to handle the Bibliography is to put it right in the article. For a short example, see the sample article article.tex (page xxix). Here is a more complete example:

### REFERENCES

1. H. H. Albert, *Free torsoids*, Current Trends in Lattice Theory, D. Van Nostrand, 1970.
2. H. H. Albert, *Free torsoids*, Current Trends in Lattice Theory (G. H. Birnbaum, ed.), vol. 7, D. Van Nostrand, Princeton-Toronto-London-Melbourne, January 1970, no translation available, pp. 173–215. (Hungarian)
3. S.-K. Foo, *Lattice constructions*, Ph.D. thesis, University of Winebago, 1990.
4. S.-K. Foo, *Lattice constructions*, Ph.D. thesis, University of Winebago, Winebago MN, December 1990, final revision not yet available. (Chinese)
5. G. H. Foster, *Computational complexity in lattice theory*, Tech. report, Carnegie Mellon University, 1986.
6. G. H. Foster, *Computational complexity in lattice theory*, Research Note 128A, Carnegie Mellon University, Pittsburgh PA, December 1986, research paper in preparation. (English)
7. P. Konig, *Composition of functions*, Proceedings of the Conference on Universal Algebra (Kingston, 1969).
8. P. Konig, *Composition of functions*, Proceedings of the Conference on Universal Algebra, 1969 (G. H. Birnbaum, ed.), vol. 7, Canadian Mathematical Society, Queen's Univ., available from the Montreal office, pp. 1–106. (English)
9. W. A. Landau, *Representations of complete lattices*, Abstract: Notices Amer. Math. Soc., 18, 937.
10. W. A. Landau, *Representations of complete lattices*, Abstract: Notices Amer. Math. Soc. 18, 937, December 1975. (English)
11. G. A. Menuhin, *Universal algebra*, D. van Nostrand, Princeton-Toronto-London-Melbourne,1968.
12. G. A. Menuhin, *Universal algebra*, University Series in Higher Mathematics, vol. 58, D. van Nostrand, Princeton-Toronto-London-Melbourne, second ed., March 1968, no Russian translation. (English)
13. E. T. Moynahan, *On a problem of M. H. Stone*, Acta Math. Acad. Sci. Hungar. 8 (1957), 455–460.
14. E. T. Moynahan, *On a problem of M. H. Stone*, Acta Math. Acad. Sci. Hungar. 8 (1957), 455–460, Russian translation available. (English)

These sample bibliographic items contain two each (one short and one long) of the seven most often used forms.

Type the Bibliography in the `thebibliography` environment, as shown in this example (you can find these entries in inbibl.tpl on the DISK; also the templates for these entries are reproduced in `article.tpl` following the line `\end{document}`):

```
\begin{thebibliography}{99}
\bibitem{hA70}
   H. H. Albert, {\em Free torsoids}, Current Trends in Lattice
   Theory, D. ~Van~ Nostrand, 1970.
\bibitem{hA70a}
H. H. Albert, {\em Free torsoids}, Current Trends in Lattice
   Theory (G.~H. Birnbaum, ed.), vol.~7, D. ~Van~ Nostrand,
   Princeton-Toronto-London-Melbourne,   January 1970,
   no translation available,   pp.~173--215. (Hungarian)
\bibitem{sF90}
   S.-K. Foo, {\em Lattice constructions}, Ph.D. thesis,
   University of Winebago,  1990.
\bibitem{sF90a}
   S.-K. Foo, {\em Lattice constructions}, Ph.D. thesis,
   University of Winebago,  Winebago MN, December 1990,
   final revision not yet available. (Chinese)
\bibitem{gF86}
   G. H. Foster, {\em Computational complexity in lattice
   theory}, Tech. report,  Carnegie Mellon University, 1986.
\bibitem{gF86a}
   G. H. Foster, {\em Computational complexity in lattice
   theory}, Research Note 128A,  Carnegie Mellon University,
   Pittsburgh PA,  December 1986,
   research article in  preparation.  (English)
\bibitem{pK69}
   P. Konig, {\em Composition of functions}, Proceedings of
   the Conference on  Universal Algebra (Kingston, 1969).
\bibitem{pK69a}
   P. Konig, {\em Composition of functions}, Proceedings of
   the Conference on  Universal Algebra, 1969
   (G.~H. Birnbaum, ed.),  vol.~7, Canadian Mathematical
   Society, Queen's Univ., available from the Montreal office,
   pp.~1--106. (English)
\bibitem{wL75}
W. A. Landau, {\em Representations of complete lattices},
   Abstract: Notices Amer. Math. Soc., {\bf 18}, 937.
\bibitem{wL75a}
   W. A. Landau, {\em Representations of complete lattices},
```

```
   Abstract: Notices Amer.  Math. Soc. {\bf 18}, 937, December
   1975. (English)
\bibitem{gM68}
   G. A. Menuhin, {\em Universal algebra}, D.~ van ~Nostrand,
   Princeton-Toronto-London-Melbourne, 1968.
\bibitem{gM68a}
   G. A. Menuhin, {\em Universal algebra}, University Series
   in Higher Mathematics,  vol.~58, D.~ van ~Nostrand,
   Princeton-Toronto-London-Melbourne, second ed.,
   March 1968, no Russian translation. (English)
\bibitem{eM57}
   E. T. Moynahan, {\em On a problem of M. H. Stone},
   Acta Math. Acad. Sci.  Hungar. {\bf 8} (1957), 455--460.
\bibitem{eM57a}
   E. T. Moynahan, {\em On a problem of M. H. Stone},
   Acta Math. Acad. Sci. Hungar.  {\bf 8} (1957), 455--460,
   Russian translation available. (English)
\end{thebibliography}
```

We use the convention that the label for the \bibitem is made up from the initials of the author and the year of publication. The first publication by A. B. Reich in 1987 would have the label: aR87, the second, aR87a. Of course, you can use any label you choose. This convention helps greatly in making the items reusable.

The environment thebibliography has an argument, in the example 99. This tells $\mathcal{A}_{\mathcal{M}}$S-LaTeX that the widest reference number $\mathcal{A}_{\mathcal{M}}$S-LaTeX has to generate is two-characters wide; for the one-character wide case use 9 and for the three-character wide case use 999.

If the argument of \begin{thebibliography} is missing, you get the error message:

```
LaTeX error.  See LaTeX manual for explanation.
             Type  H <return>  for immediate help.
! Something's wrong--perhaps a missing \item.
\@latexerr ....}\errmessage {#1}


...
1.98 \bibitem
            {incoll}
```

Each bibliographic item is introduced with \bibitem, which is just like the \label command. In the text, use \cite which is just like \ref. So if the thirteenth bibliographic item is introduced with

```
\bibitem{eM57}
```

then

```
\cite{eM57}
```

refers to that item: [13].

The Bibliography is numbered by $\mathcal{A}_{\mathcal{M}}\mathcal{S}$-LaTeX.

**Tip**. The command \cite does not ignore spaces; \cite{⊔eM57} will produce [?] for an unknown reference (and so will \cite{eM57⊔}).

You can use \cite in the form:

\cite{hA70,eM57}

(or with more than two labels) which will produce: [1, 13]. (Be careful, and do not type \cite{hA70,⊔eM57}.) There is also an optional argument for \cite:

\cite[pages 2--15]{eM57}

which prints: [13, pages 2–15].

If you wish to use labels, as opposed to numbers, for the listing in the Bibliography and the references in the text, specify this with an optional argument of \bibitem:

[EM57] E. T. Moynahan, *On a problem of M. H. Stone*, Acta Math. Acad. Sci. Hungar. **8** (1957), 455–460.

typed as

\bibitem[EM57]{eM57}
    E.~T. Moynahan, {\em On a problem of M. H. Stone},
    Acta Math. Acad. Sci. Hungar. {\bf 8} (1957), 455--460.

Make sure that the argument of \begin{thebibliography} is wide enough to accommodate all the labels. If this optional argument of \bibitem is used, then the command \cite will produce [EM57].

**Rule 1**. A label cannot start with a space and cannot contain a comma or a space.

The examples illustrate the $\mathcal{A}_{\mathcal{M}}\mathcal{S}$ article styles. Seven major types of references are shown, each with two examples, a typical one and a rather long one. Most of the references will be articles, such as [13], or books, such as [11]. You can find the templates for these entries in the file article.tpl on the DISK, following \end{document}.

Only the titles are emphasized, and only the volume number of the journals are set in boldface. Otherwise, just watch the order in which the items are given, the punctuation, and the capitalization.

If an author appears repeatedly as the author of a bibliographic item, use the \bysame command. Example:

\bibitem{gF86}
    G. H. Foster, {\em Computational complexity in lattice
    theory}, Tech. report,  Carnegie Mellon University, 1986.
\bibitem{gF86a}
    \bysame, {\em Computational complexity in lattice
    theory}, Research Note 128A,  Carnegie Mellon University,
    Pittsburgh PA, December 1986, research article in
preparation.  (English)

See article.tex (page xxix) for another example.

**Tip**. If you want a different title for the Bibliography, say, "My title", place the command

```
\renewcommand{\bibname}{My title}
```

before the Bibliography.

**Tip**. You may have more than one thebibliography environments in an article. In each the entries will be numbered from 1.

### 7-2. The database document

To use BiBTEX for bibliographies, we first have to learn how to create the database documents from which BiBTEX will create the Bibliography. This will be done in the present section.

A bibliographic database document, the bib file, contains the bibliographic entries. We shall discuss in Section 7-3.1 how the database documents are utilized.

**7-2.1. Entry types.** A bibliographic entry is given in "pieces" called *fields*; the bibliographic style (see Section 7-3.1) will specify how the fields are handled. Here is a typical example of an entry:

```
@BOOK(gM68,
   AUTHOR = {G.  A.  Menuhin},
   TITLE = {Universal Algebra},
   PUBLISHER = {D.~ van ~Nostrand},
   ADDRESS = {Princeton-Toronto-London-Melbourne},
   YEAR = {1968}
   )
```

The entry *type* is "BOOK" marked by @. There are five *fields*: AUTHOR, TITLE, PUBLISHER, ADDRESS, and YEAR. The field name is followed by "=" and the content of the field in braces; there is a comma separating the fields (there is no comma after the last field).

There are many types of entries:

**ARTICLE:** An article from a journal or magazine.
**BOOK:** A book with a publisher.
**BOOKLET:** Printed work without a publisher.
**INBOOK:** A part of a book, such as a chapter.
**INCOLLECTION:** A part of a book with its own title.
**INPROCEEDINGS:** An article in a conference proceedings.
**MANUAL:** Technical documentation.
**MASTERSTHESIS:** A Master thesis.
**MISC:** Whatever does not fit in any other category.
**PHDTHESIS:** A Ph.D. thesis.
**PROCEEDINGS:** The proceedings of a conference.

**TECHREPORT:** An article published by a school or institution.

**UNPUBLISHED:** An unpublished article.

Each entry has a number of fields chosen from the following list:
ADDRESS, AUTHOR, BOOKTITLE, CHAPTER, EDITION, EDITOR,
HOWPUBLISHED, INSTITUTION, JOURNAL, LANGUAGE, MONTH,
NOTE, NUMBER, ORGANIZATION, PAGES, PUBLISHER, SCHOOL,
SERIES, TITLE, TYPE, VOLUME, YEAR.

For each entry type there are some *required fields* and some *optional fields*. In the examples of this section, the first example of an entry type is a typical example, while the second is a maximal example, showing all possible fields.

All the examples of this section can be found in the file template.bib on the DISK. Some rules about fields:

**Rule 1.** $\mathcal{AMS}$-LaTeX converts the TITLE to lower case, except for the first letter. If you need a letter in upper case, put it in braces. The same rule applies to the field EDITION.

Example: title is "Distributive lattices of type Stone, II." You need both "S" (in "Stone") and "II" (for part II) in upper case. So the title is typed:

```
TITLE = {Distributive lattices of type {S}tone, {II}}
```

**Rule 2.** Remember to use -- for the page range in the field PAGES.

**Rule 3.** Do not put a punctuation mark at the end of a field; BibTeX will supply it.

Example:

```
PAGES = {23--45}
```

**Tip.** Make sure you type the field name correctly; if there is an error in the field name, $\mathcal{AMS}$-LaTeX will ignore the field. There is no warning or error message.

**7-2.2. Article.**

**ARTICLE:**

**Required:** AUTHOR, TITLE, JOURNAL, YEAR

**Optional:** VOLUME, NUMBER, PAGES, MONTH, NOTE, LANGUAGE

Examples (one short, one long):

13. E. T. Moynahan, *On a problem of M. H. Stone*, Acta Math. Acad. Sci. Hungar. **8** (1957), 455–460.
14. E. T. Moynahan, *On a problem of M. H. Stone*, Acta Math. Acad. Sci. Hungar. **8** (1957), 455–460, Russian translation available. (English)

typed as

```
@ARTICLE(eM57,
    AUTHOR =  {E. T. Moynahan},
    TITLE = {On a problem of {M. H. Stone}},
    JOURNAL = {Acta Math. Acad. Sci. Hun\-gar.},
    PAGES = {455--460},
    VOLUME = {8},
    YEAR = {1957}
    )
@ARTICLE(eM57a,
    AUTHOR = {E. T. Moynahan},
    TITLE = {On a problem of {M. H. Stone}},
    JOURNAL = {Acta Math. Acad. Sci. Hun\-gar.},
    PAGES = {455--460},
    VOLUME = {8},
    YEAR = {1957},
    MONTH = feb,
    NOTE = {Russian translation available},
    LANGUAGE = {English}
    )
```

Observe that the field MONTH is ignored because both VOLUME and YEAR are given.

### 7-2.3. Book.

**BOOK:**
**Required:** AUTHOR (or EDITOR), TITLE, PUBLISHER, YEAR
**Optional:** VOLUME, SERIES, ADDRESS, EDITION, MONTH,
NOTE, LANGUAGE
Examples:

11. G. A. Menuhin, *Universal algebra*, D. van Nostrand, Princeton-Toronto-London-Melbourne, 1968.
12. G. A. Menuhin, *Universal algebra*, University Series in Higher Mathematics, vol. 58, D. van Nostrand, Princeton-Toronto-London-Melbourne, Second ed., March 1968, no Russian translation. (English)

typed as

```
@BOOK(gM68,
    AUTHOR = {G.  A.  Menuhin},
    TITLE = {Universal {A}lgebra},
    PUBLISHER = {D. ~van~ Nostrand},
    ADDRESS = {Princeton-Toronto-London-Melbourne},
    YEAR = {1968}
    )
@BOOK(gM68,
    AUTHOR = {G.  A.  Menuhin},
```

```
    TITLE = {Universal {A}lgebra},
    PUBLISHER = {D. ~van~ Nostrand},
    ADDRESS = {Princeton-Toronto-London-Melbourne},
    YEAR = {1968},
    SERIES = {University Series in Higher Mathematics},
    VOLUME = {58},
    EDITION = {{S}econd},
    MONTH = {March},
    NOTE = {no Russian translation},
    LANGUAGE ={English}
    )
```

Second variant, with editor:

15. R. S. Prescott, ed., *Universal Algebra*, D. van Nostrand, Princeton-Toron to-London-Melbourne, 1968.

typed as

```
@BOOK(gM68,
    EDITOR = {R.  S.  Prescott},
    TITLE = {Universal {A}lgebra},
    PUBLISHER = {D. ~van~ Nostrand},
    ADDRESS = {Princeton-Toronto-London-Melbourne},
    YEAR = {1968}
    )
```

BIBTEX sends the error message:

```
"abcxyz" is a string literal, 'author' is a missing field
---they aren't the same literal types for entry one
while executing---line 1118 of file amsplain.bst
'author' is a missing field, not a string, for entry one
while executing---line 1118 of file amsplain.bst
(There were 2 error messages)
```

but it does the job.

### 7-2.4. Conference proceedings and collections.

**INPROCEEDINGS:**
**Required:** AUTHOR, TITLE, BOOKTITLE, YEAR
**Optional:** EDITOR, PAGES, ORGANIZATION, PUBLISHER,
ADDRESS, MONTH, NOTE, LANGUAGE
Examples:

7. P. Konig, *Composition of functions*, Proceedings of the Conference on Universal Algebra,1969.
8. P. Konig, *Composition of functions*, Proceedings of the Conference on Universal Algebra, 1969 (G. H. Birnbaum, ed.), vol. 7, Canadian Mathematical

Society, Queen's Univ., available from the Montreal office, pp. 1–106. (English)

typed

```
@INPROCEEDINGS(inproc,
   AUTHOR = {P. Konig},
   TITLE = {Composition of functions},
   BOOKTITLE = {Proceedings of the Conference on
   Universal Algebra, 1969},
   YEAR = {1970}
   )
@INPROCEEDINGS(inprocfull,
   AUTHOR = {P. Konig},
   TITLE = {Composition of functions},
   BOOKTITLE = {Proceedings of the Conference on
      Universal Algebra, 1969},
   PUBLISHER = {Queen's Univ., Kingston ON},
   ORGANIZATION = {Canadian Mathematical Society},
   EDITOR = {G. H. Birnbaum},
   PAGES = {1--106},
   VOLUME = {7},
   YEAR = {1970},
   MONTH = dec,
   NOTE = {available from the Montreal office},
   LANGUAGE ={English}
   )
```

**INCOLLECTION:**
**Required:** AUTHOR, TITLE, BOOKTITLE, PUBLISHER, YEAR
**Optional:** EDITOR, CHAPTER, PAGES, ADDRESS, MONTH, NOTE
Examples:

1. H. H. Albert, *Free torsoids*, Current Trends in Lattice Theory, D. Van Nostrand, 1970.
2. H. H. Albert, *Free torsoids*, Current Trends in Lattice Theory (G. H. Birnbaum, ed.), vol. 7, D. Van Nostrand, Princeton-Toronto-London-Melbourne, January 1970, first volume of the series "Current Trends", pp. 173–215. (German)

typed

```
@INCOLLECTION(incoll,
   AUTHOR = {H. H. Albert},
   TITLE = {Free torsoids},
   BOOKTITLE = {Current Trends in Lattice Theory},
   PUBLISHER = { D. Van Nostrand},
```

```
        YEAR = {1970}
        )
@INCOLLECTION(incollfull,
        AUTHOR = {H.  H.  Albert},
        EDITOR = {G. H. Birnbaum},
        CHAPTER = {Third},
        TITLE = {Free torsoids},
        BOOKTITLE = {Current Trends in Lattice Theory},
        PUBLISHER = {D. Van Nostrand,
         Princeton-Toronto-London-Melbourne},
        LANGUAGE = {German},
        PAGES = {173--215},
        VOLUME = {7},
        YEAR = {1970},
        MONTH = jan,
        NOTE = {first volume of the series ''Current Trends''}
        )
```

The ADDRESS field should contain the location of the meeting (if appropriate); the address of the publisher should be typed in the PUBLISHER field, as shown.

### 7-2.5. Thesis.

**MASTERSTHESIS or PHDTHESIS:**
**Required:** AUTHOR, TITLE, SCHOOL, YEAR
**Optional:** ADDRESS, MONTH, NOTE, LANGUAGE
    Examples:

3. S.-K. Foo, *Lattice constructions*, Ph.D. thesis, University of Winebago, 1990.
4. S.-K. Foo, *Lattice constructions*, Ph.D. thesis, University of Winebago, Winebago MN, December 1990, final revision not yet available. (Chinese)

typed

```
@PHDTHESIS(sF90,
        AUTHOR = {S.-K. Foo},
        TITLE = {Lattice constructions},
        SCHOOL = {University of Winebago},
        YEAR = {1990}
        )
@PHDTHESIS(sFa90,
        AUTHOR = {S.-K. Foo},
        TITLE = {Lattice constructions},
        SCHOOL = {University of Winebago},
        ADDRESS = {Winebago MN},
        YEAR = {1990},
        MONTH = dec,
```

```
NOTE = {final revision not yet available},
LANGUAGE ={Chinese}
)
```

### 7-2.6.  Technical report.

**TECHREPORT:**
**Required:** AUTHOR, TITLE, INSTITUTION, YEAR
**Optional:** TYPE, NUMBER, ADDRESS, MONTH, NOTE, LANGUAGE
Examples:

5. G. H. Foster, *Computational complexity in lattice theory*, Tech. report, Carnegie Mellon University, 1986.
6. G. H. Foster, *Computational complexity in lattice theory*, Research Note 128A, Carnegie Mellon University, Pittsburgh PA, December 1986, research article in preparation. (English)

typed

```
@TECHREPORT(tech,
    AUTHOR = {G. H. Foster},
    TITLE = {Computational complexity in lattice theory},
    INSTITUTION = {Carnegie Mellon University},
    YEAR = {1986}
    )
@TECHREPORT(techfull,
    AUTHOR = {G. H. Foster},
    TITLE = {Computational complexity in lattice theory},
    INSTITUTION = {Carnegie Mellon University},
    YEAR = {1986},
    TYPE = {Research Note},
    ADDRESS = {Pittsburgh PA},
    NUMBER = {128A},
    MONTH = dec,
    NOTE = {research article in preparation},
    LANGUAGE ={English}
    )
```

### 7-2.7.  Manuscript.

**UNPUBLISHED:**
**Required:** AUTHOR, TITLE, NOTE
**Optional:** MONTH, YEAR, LANGUAGE
Examples:

9. W. A. Landau, *Representations of complete lattices*, Abstract: Notices Amer. Math. Soc. 18, 937.

10. W. A. Landau, *Representations of complete lattices*, Abstract: Notices Amer. Math. Soc. 18, 937, December 1975. (English)

typed

```
@UNPUBLISHED(wL75,
    AUTHOR = {W. A. Landau},
    TITLE = {Representations of complete lattices},
    NOTE = {Abstract:  Notices Amer. Math. Soc. {\bf 18}, 937}
    )
@UNPUBLISHED(wl75a,
    AUTHOR = {W. A. Landau},
    TITLE = {Representations of complete lattices},
    YEAR = {1975},
    NOTE = {Abstract:  Notices Amer. Math. Soc. {\bf 18}, 937},
    MONTH = dec,
    LANGUAGE ={English}
    )
```

**7-2.8. Others.** There are some other types:

**BOOKLET:**
**Required:** TITLE
**Optional:** AUTHOR, HOWPUBLISHED, ADDRESS, MONTH, NOTE

**INBOOK:**
**Required:** AUTHOR or EDITOR, TITLE, CHAPTER and/or PAGES,
PUBLISHER, YEAR
**Optional:** VOLUME, SERIES, ADDRESS, EDITION, MONTH, NOTE

**MANUAL:**
**Required:** TITLE
**Optional:** AUTHOR, ORGANIZATION, ADDRESS, EDITION,
MONTH, YEAR, NOTE

**MISC:**
**Required:**
**Optional:** AUTHOR, TITLE, HOWPUBLISHED, MONTH, YEAR, NOTE

**PROCEEDINGS:**
**Required:** TITLE, YEAR
**Optional:** EDITOR, PUBLISHER, ORGANIZATION, ADDRESS,
MONTH, NOTE

**7-2.9. Abbreviations.** You may have noticed the field:

```
MONTH = dec,
```

This is an example of an abbreviation. $\mathcal{A}\mathcal{M}\mathcal{S}$-LaTeX comes with the abbreviations for the months: jan, feb, ... , dec. When an abbreviation is used, it is not in braces.

An abbreviation has a *label*, such as "feb;" a label is a string of characters that starts with a letter, does not contain spaces, "=", or comma, nor any of the special keys of Section 3-4.4.

An abbreviation is defined with the command @STRING. Example:

```
@STRING{au = {Algebra Universalis}}
```

A string definition can be placed anywhere in a bib file, as long as it precedes its first use.

The $\mathcal{A}\mathcal{M}\mathcal{S}$ supplies the file mrabbrev.bib containing abbreviations for many mathematical journals. This is an important file since it contains the correct abbreviated forms. Based on this documents, you can make your own myabbrev.bib file containing all the journals you reference with labels you may find easy to remember.

If you use this scheme, the command specifying the bib files will always start with

```
\bibliography{myabbrev, }
```

### 7-3. Using BibTeX

In Section 7-2, we learned how to create bibliographic database files (the sample bib files are template.bib and article1.bib, see the DISK). In this section, we learn how to use BibTeX to process these files.

You obtain article1.tex from the sample article article.tex by deleting the bibliography, and adding the two lines

```
\bibliographystyle{amsplain}
\bibliography{article1}
```

just before

```
\end{document}
```

You can also find article1.tex on the DISK.

article1.bib is the bibliographic file for article1.tex:

```
@BOOK(gM68,
    AUTHOR = {G.~ A.~ Menuhin},
    TITLE = {Universal {A}lgebra},
    PUBLISHER = {D. van Nostrand},
    ADDRESS = {Princeton-Toronto-London-Melbourne},
    YEAR = {1968}
)


@BOOK(fR82,
    AUTHOR = {F.~R. Richardson},
    TITLE = {General {L}attice {T}heory},
    EDITION = {Expanded and Revised},
    LANGUAGE = {Russian},
```

```
    PUBLISHER = {MIR},
    ADDRESS = {Moscow},
    YEAR = {1982}
)


@ARTICLE(eM57,
    AUTHOR = {E.~T.~Moynahan},
    TITLE = {On a problem of {M. H. Stone}},
    JOURNAL = {Acta Math. Acad. Sci. Hungar.},
    PAGES = {455--460},
    VOL = {8},
    YEAR = {1957}
)


@ARTICLE(eM57a,
    AUTHOR = {E.~T.~Moynahan},
    TITLE = {Ideals and congruence relations in lattices. {II}},
    JOURNAL = {Magyar Tud. Akad. Mat. Fiz. Oszt. K\"ozl.},
    LANGUAGE = {Hungarian},
    PAGES = {417--434},
    VOL = {7},
    YEAR = {1957}
)


@PHDTHESIS(sF90,
    AUTHOR = {S.-K. Foo},
    TITLE = {Lattice constructions},
    SCHOOL = {University of  Winebago},
    ADDRESS = {Winebago MN},
    MONTH = dec,
    YEAR = {1990}
)
```

Type in article1.bib, or copy it from the DISK.

Before you start BIBTEX, make sure that everything is set up properly.

**7-3.1. The setup.** You will specify which references go into the Bibliography with the \cite commands in the article. If you choose to include a reference that is not mentioned in the text, pull it in the article with a \nocite command. Example:

\cite{pK57}

and

\nocite{pK57}

One of the bib files specified in the argument of the \bibliography command must contain an entry with the label "pK57".

The article must contain the instructions naming the bib files to be used and specifying the style for the Bibliography. For instance, the sample article article1.tex contains the lines:

```
\bibliographystyle{amsplain}
\bibliography{article1}
```

The instruction

```
\bibliographystyle{amsplain}
```

names amsplain.bst as the "bibliographic style".

The \bibliography command names the bib file: article1.bib; it may name several bib files:

```
\bibliography{myabbrev,gg,lattice,article1}
```

where myabbrev.bib contains my standard abbreviations, gg.bib contains my articles, and lattice.bib contains lattice theoretical articles by other authors, and article1.bib contains the additional references needed for article1.

**Tip.** If you used LATEX, it is easy to make the mistake of typing

```
\bibliographystyle{plain}
```

plain.bst is a bibliographic style in LATEX but it will not be accepted by $\mathcal{A}_{\mathcal{M}}S$-LATEX.

It is important to make sure that the BiBTEX program, the bibliographic style amsplain.bst, the bib file(s), and the article are in subdirectories/folders in which BiBTEX can reach them all. One way to make sure is to copy all of them in one subdirectory/folder.

**7-3.2. The steps.** To use BiBTEX, use the following steps:

**Step 1.** Check that BiBTEX, the article, the bib files are placed in the appropriate subdirectories/folders (see the comment at the end of Section 7-3.1).

**Step 2.** Typeset the article to get a fresh aux file.

**Step 3.** Run BiBTEX, and name/select the new aux file. If BiBTEX finds a fatal error, it will abort. The reason why it aborted will be written in a blg (bibliography log) file named after the article. Correct the errors, and run BiBTEX again. A successful run creates a bbl (bibliography) file, and also a blg file.

**Step 4.** Typeset the article **twice**.

**7-3.3. The files of BiBTEX.** To illustrate the contents of the various files in the process, let us go through the steps with the sample article, article1.tex.

**Step 1.** Let us start fresh; delete the aux, blg, and bbl files, if they are present.

**Step 2.** Now typeset the article article1.tex to get the aux file. The log file contains warnings about the missing references. The aux file has a number of lines we are not currently interested in. The lines containing the bibliographic information are:

```
\citation{fR82}
\citation{gM68}
\citation{eM57}
```

```
\citation{sF90}
\citation{eM57a}
\bibdata{article1}
\bibstyle{amsplain}
```

Each \citation in this file corresponds to a \cite (or \nocite) in the article, and the lines

```
\bibliographystyle{amsplain}
\bibliography{article1}
```

of the article are translated as

```
\bibstyle{amsplain}
\bibdata{article1}
```

**Step 3.** Now run BIBTEX and choose the file article1.aux. BIBTEX generates two new files, article1.blg and article1.bbl. Let us look at article1.blg:

```
This is BibTeX, C Version 0.99c
The top-level auxiliary file: article1.aux
The style file: amsplain.bst
Database file #1: article1.bib
```

At present, this file does not contain important information; however, if there are any errors, this is the file to read.

You will find the other file, article1.bbl, more interesting; in this file, we created the thebibliography environment just as it was described in Section 7-1:

```
\ifx\undefined\bysame
\newcommand{\bysame}{\leavevmode\hbox to3em{\hrulefill}\,}
\fi
\begin{thebibliography}{1}

\bibitem{sF90}
S.-K. Foo, {\em Lattice constructions}, Ph.D. thesis, University
  of Winebago,  Winebago MN, December 1990.

\bibitem{gM68}
G.~A. Menuhin, {\em Universal {A}lgebra}, D. van Nostrand,
  Princeton-Toronto-London-Melbourne, 1968.

\bibitem{eM57a}
E.~T. Moynahan, {\em Ideals and congruence relations
  in lattices. {II}}, Magyar Tud. Akad. Mat. Fiz. Oszt. K\"ozl.
  (1957), 417--434 (Hungarian).

\bibitem{eM57}
\bysame, {\em On a problem of {M. H. Stone}}, Acta Math.
```

Acad. Sci. Hungar. (1957), 455--460.

```
\bibitem{fR82}
F.~R. Richardson, {\em General {L}attice {T}heory}, expanded
  and revised ed., MIR, Moscow, 1982 (Russian).
```

```
\end{thebibliography}
```

**Step 4.** Now typeset the article. In the typeset form, the References section appears (it was built from the bbl file); however, in the new log file, you still get all the warnings about the missing bibliographic references. The new aux file contains five lines of interesting new information:

```
\bibcite{sF90}{1}
\bibcite{gM68}{2}
\bibcite{eM57a}{3}
\bibcite{eM57}{4}
\bibcite{fR82}{5}
```

which identifies the bibliographic reference label "sF90" (see line 1 above—the label "sF90" is the label for Foo's thesis in article1.bib) with "1", and so on. Now typeset article1.tex again, and all the references are correctly given in the typeset form.

Observe:

(1) The crucial step is Step 3: the running of the program BibTeX; this gives you different error messages and obeys different rules (as compared with $\mathcal{A}_{\mathcal{M}}\mathcal{S}$-LaTeX—see Section 7-3.4).

(2) The file article1.bbl was created running BibTeX. It will not be changed by running $\mathcal{A}_{\mathcal{M}}\mathcal{S}$-LaTeX. So you can edit this file, and use the edited form; running $\mathcal{A}_{\mathcal{M}}\mathcal{S}$-LaTeX will not undo the changes you make.

**Tip.** If the tex file consists of \nocite-s only, the references will not be typeset.

### 7-3.4. BibTeX rules and messages.

**Rule 1.** You cannot comment out lines with %. For example, the following item

```
@ARTICLE(eM57,
    AUTHOR = {E. T. Moynahan},
    TITLE = {On a problem of {M. H. Stone}},
    JOURNAL = {Acta Math. Acad. Sci. Hungar.},
    % PAGES = {455--460},
    VOLUME = {8},
    YEAR = {1957}
    )
```

will cause BibTeX to give the error message:

```
You're missing a field name---line 5 of file onebib.bib
    :
```

```
:   % PAGES = {455--460},
```
(Error may have been on previous line)
I'm skipping whatever remains of this entry
Warning--year missing in eM57
Warning--empty pages in eM57
(There was 1 error message)

**Rule 2.** Do not abbreviate field names. For instance, if you abbreviate VOLUME to VOL:

```
@ARTICLE(eM57,
    AUTHOR =  {E. T. Moynahan},
    TITLE = {On a problem of {M. H. Stone}},
    JOURNAL = {Acta Math. Acad. Sci. Hun\-gar.},
    PAGES = {455--460},
    VOL = {8},
    YEAR = {1957}
    )
```

The volume is simply ignored; this item will print:

12. E. T. Moynahan, *On a problem of M. H. Stone*, Acta Math. Acad. Sci. Hungar. (1957), 455–460.

**Tip.** BIBTEX has a lot of messages you may not be able to recognize. For instance, if an item is:

```
@BOOK(gM68,
    EDITOR = {R.   S.   Prescott},
    TITLE = {Universal Algebra},
    SERIES = {University Series in Higher Mathematics},
    PUBLISHER = {D. ~van~ Nostrand},
    ADDRESS = {Princeton-Toronto-London-Melbourne},
    YEAR = {1968}
    )
```

BIBTEX sends the error message:

```
"abcxyz" is a string literal, 'author' is a missing field
---they aren't the same literal types for entry gM68
while executing---line 1118 of file amsplain.bst
'author' is a missing field, not a string, for entry gM68
while executing---line 1118 of file amsplain.bst
ptr=1, stack=
{\em Universal algebra}
---the literal stack isn't empty for entry gM68
while executing---line 1136 of file amsplain.bst
(There were 3 error messages)
```

Would you guess what the error is? If you have a field SERIES, there must also be VOLUME or NUMBER.

**Tip**. Make sure that every line, except the last, is terminated with a comma; if not, you may get the error message:

```
I was expecting a ',' or a ')'---line 5 of file onebib.bib
 :
 :    PUBLISHER = {D. ~van~ Nostrand},
(Error may have been on previous line)
I'm skipping whatever remains of this entry
"abcxyz" is a string literal, 'author' is a missing field
---they aren't the same literal types for entry gM68
while executing---line 1118 of file amsplain.bst
'author' is a missing field, not a string, for entry gM68
while executing---line 1118 of file amsplain.bst
Warning--empty publisher in gM68
Warning--empty year in gM68
ptr=1, stack=
{\em Universal algebra}
---the literal stack isn't empty for entry gM68
while executing---line 1136 of file amsplain.bst
(There were 4 error messages)
```

All this because the comma on the line preceding PUBLISHER was missing. Dropping the closing brace from the same line gives the message:

```
Illegal end of database file---line 9 of file onebib.bib
 :
 :
(Error may have been on previous line)
I'm skipping whatever remains of this entry
"abcxyz" is a string literal, 'author' is a missing field
---they aren't the same literal types for entry gM68
while executing---line 1118 of file amsplain.bst
'author' is a missing field, not a string, for entry gM68
while executing---line 1118 of file amsplain.bst
Warning--empty publisher in gM68
Warning--empty year in gM68
(There were 3 error messages)
```

Line 9 is one line past the last line in the test file.

Finally, drop the opening brace in the SERIES line:

```
SERIES = University Series in Higher Mathematics},
```

You get the error message:

```
Warning--string name "university" is undefined
--line 4 of file onebib.bib
I was expecting a ',' or a ')'---line 4 of file onebib.bib
 :    series = university
 :                       Series in Higher Mathematics},
I'm skipping whatever remains of this entry
"abcxyz" is a string literal, 'author' is a missing field
---they aren't the same literal types for entry gM68
while executing---line 1118 of file amsplain.bst
'author' is a missing field, not a string, for entry gM68
while executing---line 1118 of file amsplain.bst
Warning--empty publisher in gM68
Warning--empty year in gM68
(There were 3 error messages)
```

$\mathcal{A}_\mathcal{M}S$-LaTeX assumed that "university" is a string, since it was not preceded by a brace.

The obvious conclusion is that one has to be very careful about typing the entries. We recommend that you use the file template.bib that contains templates of the most often used bibliographic entries. Copy the form you need and fill in the blanks; this will avoid typing errors that lead to confusing messages.

**7-3.5. Editing the bib file.** The bib file contains the Bibliography in the form described in Section 7-1. You may not like the result. For instance, Part I of an article may be after Part II since the order only reflects the names of the authors and the year of publication. In such a case, you may want to rearrange the order. You understand now from Section 7-3.3 that the bib file is not going to change until you use BIBTEX again; the bib file is a stable file unlike the aux file or the toc file.

There may be other reasons for editing. For instance, the contents of two fields may be placed side-by-side, parenthesized by the bibliographic style amsplain.bst.

However, any editing of the bib file should be recorded, and transmitted to the journal publishing the article. When the journal changes the name of the bibliographic style for the Bibliography, and runs BIBTEX on the article, the journal may have to carry out on the Bibliography the same editing changes you have recorded.

# CHAPTER 8

# Multiline Math Displays

The `displaymath` environment (Section 4-1) and the `equation` environment (Section 4-2.1) work well with a single formula that can be displayed on one line. In this chapter, we shall discuss how to esthetically display math formulas on more than one line.

The large number of multiline math environments is quite intimidating to the novice user. However, for most math articles, three constructs will do: the *simple align*, the *double align*, and the `cases`. For an introduction to these, see Section 2-5.2. In this chapter, you will find the simple align and the double align in Section 8-1, and the `cases` in Section 8-3.

We start in Section 8-1 with *aligned columns*. One aligned column is the simple align of Section 2-5.2; many aligned columns are done with the `alignat` environment. The double align of Section 8-1.3 is a special case of the latter.

Next we introduce *subsidiary math environments*, which are just like math environments except that they have to be used *within* a math environment.

There are four *centered* one- or *multi-column constructs* discussed in Section 8-3. Instead of being aligned, each column is centered, or flushed left or right. The simplest construct is the `gather` environment (one column, centered). The other three constructs are subsidiary environments: `matrix` (multicolumn, centered), `array` (multicolumn, centered, or flush left or right), and its derivative, `cases` (curly left brace with two columns flush left).

Splitting a long formula is provided by `multline`; see Section 8-4.

Section 8-5 discusses a subsidiary math environment to design simple commutative diagrams.

Finally, Section 8-6 describes how to allow pagebreaks in multiline math environments.

The file multline.tpl on the DISK contains all the multiline formulas of this chapter.

## 8-1. Aligned columns

The lines of many multiline formulas are naturally divided into *columns*. In this sections, we shall consider how to display such formulas with *aligned columns*.

The simplest case is a multiline math formula with a single aligned column. This is implemented with the `align` *environment*. Here is an example:

$$x = y + z, \tag{1}$$

$$u = v + w. \tag{2}$$

where the "=" signs are aligned. The same environment can be used to break a long formula into two:

$$\begin{aligned} h(x) &= \int \left( \frac{f(x) + g(x)}{1 + f^2(x)} + \frac{1 + f(x)g(x)}{\sqrt{1 - \sin x}} \right) dx \\ &= \int \frac{1 + f(x)}{1 + g(x)} \, dx - 2 \tan^{-1}(x - 2) \end{aligned} \tag{3}$$

There is a better way to split a long formula into lines; see the `split` subsidiary math environment in Section 8-2.1.

*Multiple align* allows multiple aligned columns; it is implemented with the `alignat` environment. In the next example, there are two aligned columns:

$$\begin{aligned} f(x) &= x + yz, & g(x) &= x + y + z, \\ h(x) &= xy + xz + yz, & k(x) &= (x + y)(x + z)(y + z). \end{aligned} \tag{4}$$

A special case of this (two columns, the second aligned on the left) is *double align*, which will align the formulas, and align the explanatory text:

$$\begin{aligned} x &= x \wedge (y \vee z) && \text{(by distributivity)} \\ &= (x \wedge y) \vee (x \wedge z) && \text{(by Condition (M))} \\ &= y \vee z \end{aligned} \tag{5}$$

**8-1.1. Simple align.** The rules of the `align` environment:

**Rule 1.** *Simple align.*

    (1) \\ separates the lines; there is no \\ at the end of the last line.
    (2) In each line there is one & marking the alignment point.
    (3) Each line is numbered except those that are \tag-ed and those where numbering is prohibited by \notag.
    (4) No blank line is permitted.

Examples: Formulas (1)–(2) are typed as

```
\begin{align} \label{E:ml1}
    x &= y + z, \\
    u &= v + w. \label{E:ml1a}
\end{align}
```

and formula (3) is

```
\begin{align} \label{E:m12}
   h(x) &= \int \left( \frac{ f(x) + g(x) }{ 1 + f^{2}(x) } +
            \frac{ 1 + f(x)g(x) }{ \sqrt{1 - \sin x} } \right)
            \, dx \\
         &= \int \frac{ 1 + f(x) }{ 1 + g(x) } \, dx
            -2 \tan^{-1}(x - 2) \notag
\end{align}
```

If you place a \\ at the end of the last line, there will be no error message, but a blank (numbered) line is appended to the formula.

If you have two (or more) & symbols in a line, you get the error message:

```
! Extra alignment tab has been changed to \cr.
<template> }\endtemplate
```

```
...
1.57 \end{align}
```

A blank line between \begin{align} and \end{align} gives the error message:

```
Runaway argument?
```

```
! Paragraph ended before \align was complete.
<to be read again>
                    \par
1.57
```

All the multiline math environments use \\ to separate the lines, and & to mark the alignment point. Each line becomes an equation, which is numbered as an equation, unless \notag declares otherwise.

Each multiline math environment has a *-ed version, where each line becomes an equation*, that is, an *unnumbered equation*. \tag works just as it does for equations; see Section 4-2.2. For cross-referencing, use \label the same way as for equations (see Section 6-3). \tag and \label should precede the line separator \\.

**8-1.2. Multiple align.** The formulas (4) are typed:

```
\begin{alignat}{2} \label{E:m13}
   f(x) &= x + yz         & \qquad g(x) &= x +  y + z \\
   h(x) &= xy + xz + yz & \qquad k(x) &= (x + y)(x + z)(y + z)
   \notag
\end{alignat}
```

In this environment, & doubles as a mark for the *alignment point* and as a *column separator*. In the first line of this formula:

```
   f(x) &= x + yz         & \qquad g(x) &= x +  y + z \\
```

the two columns are

```
f(x) &= x + yz
```

and

```
\qquad g(x) &= x +  y + z
```

In each column, you find a single & to mark the alignment point. Of the three & symbols,

- the first & marks the alignment point of the first column;
- the second & marks the end of the first column;
- the third & marks the alignment point of the second column.

As you can see, double align is a special case of this: the second column is flush left.

We use the convention that we put a blank on the left of the alignment point & and no space to the right. We put spaces on both sides of & as a column separator.

In \begin{alignat}, declare the number of columns as an argument:

```
\begin{alignat}{2}
```

You can have two, three, or more columns. For instance, if you declare three:

```
\begin{alignat}{3}
```

there should be five &-s in each line, the two even numbered &-s are column separators, the three odd numbered &-s are alignment marks.

The rules of multiple align:

**Rule 2.** *Multiple align.*

(1) The argument of \begin{alignat} is the number of columns.
(2) \\ separates the lines; there is no \\ at the end of the last line.
(3) If the argument is $n$, in each line put $2n - 1$ symbols &; the even numbered &-s mark the columns, and the odd numbered &-s mark the alignment points.
(4) No blank line is permitted between the lines

```
\begin{alignat}
```

and

```
\end{alignat}
```

If you begin with \begin{alignat}{2} and end with \end{align}, you get the error message:

```
! \begin{alignat} ended by \end{align}.
\@latexerr ....}\errmessage {#1}


...
1.22 \end{alignat}
```

or

```
Runaway argument?

! Paragraph ended before \alignat was complete.
```

```
<to be read again>
                    \par
1.34
```

The argument of `\begin{alignat}` is compulsory. If you forget about it, you get the message:

```
! Missing number, treated as zero.
<to be read again>
                    x

...
1.17 \end{alignat}
```

If there are too few &-s in a line, there is no error message, but the line may be displayed incorrectly. If there are too many &-s on a line, you get the message:

```
AmS-TeX error:
! Extra & on this line.
\err@ ...error:}\errmessage {#1}
                              \fi

...
1.16 \end{alignat}
```

Note the message: "AmS-TeX error", bearing witness to the $\mathcal{A}\mathcal{M}\mathcal{S}$-TEX heritage of the `alignat` environment; see Section C-1.

**8-1.3. Double align.** Double align is implemented with the `alignat` *environment*, with argument 2:

```
\begin{alignat}{2}
\end{alignat}
```

For instance, formula (4) is typed:

```
\begin{alignat}{2} \label{E:ml3}
    x &= x \wedge (y \vee z) & &\quad\text{, by distributivity,} \\
      &= (x \wedge y) \vee (x \wedge z)
                            & &\quad\text{, by Condition (M),}
                                                        \notag \\
      &= y \vee z \notag
\end{alignat}
```

The rules of the double align:

**Rule 3**. *Double align.*

    (1) Use the `alignat` environment with argument 2.

    (2) \\ separates the lines; there is no \\ at the end of the last line.

    (3) In each line place (at most) one & to mark the alignment point in the formula, and place & & to mark the beginning of the text.

(4) Each line is numbered except those that are \tag-ed and those where numbering is prohibited by \notag.

(5) Type the text as the argument of a \text command.

(6) No blank line is permitted.

## 8-2. Enhancing math environments

$\mathcal{AMS}$-LaTeX provides a number of tools to enhance math environments. The most important ones are implemented as *subsidiary math environments*; that is, as math environments that have to appear inside another environment. cases is a subsidiary math environment; it must appear inside a displayed math environment. A subsidiary multiline math environment is like a "large" math symbol you create so that you can use it in a math environment.

The environments align and alignat (see Section 8-1), and the environment gather (see Section 8-3.1) have subsidiary versions: aligned, alignedat, and gathered.

To obtain this display:

$$
\begin{aligned} x &= 3, \\ y &= 4, \\ z &= 5; \end{aligned} \qquad \text{or} \qquad \begin{aligned} x &= 5, \\ y &= 12, \\ z &= 13. \end{aligned}
$$

type:

```
\[
   \begin{aligned}
     x &= 3, \\
     y &= 4, \\
     z &= 5;
   \end{aligned}
   \text{\qquad or \qquad}
   \begin{aligned}
     x &= 5, \\
     y &= 12, \\
     z &= 13.
   \end{aligned}
\]
```

Note how

$$
\begin{aligned} x &= 3, \\ y &= 4, \\ z &= 5; \end{aligned}
$$

and

$$
\begin{aligned} x &= 5, \\ y &= 12, \\ z &= 13. \end{aligned}
$$

are treated as individual "large symbols".

We can use the `aligned` subsidiary math environment to rewrite formula (4) from Section 2-5.2 so that the formula number is centered between the two lines:

(6)
$$\begin{aligned}
h(x) &= \int \left( \frac{f(x) + g(x)}{1 + f^2(x)} + \frac{1 + f(x)g(x)}{\sqrt{1 - \sin x}} \right) dx \\
&= \int \frac{1 + f(x)}{1 + g(x)} dx - 2\tan^{-1}(x - 2)
\end{aligned}$$

This is typed as

```
\begin{equation}
  \begin{aligned} \label{E:longInt2}
     h(x) &= \int \left( \frac{ f(x) + g(x) }{ 1+ f^{2}(x) } +
     \frac{1+ f(x)g(x) }{ \sqrt{1 - \sin x} } \right) \, dx \\
        &= \int \frac{ 1 + f(x) }{ 1 + g(x) } \,
           dx - 2 \tan^{-1} (x-2)
  \end{aligned}
\end{equation}
```

Symbols, as a rule, are "centrally aligned". This is not an issue with normal symbols, but it may be with the large symbols created by subsidiary math environments. These subsidiary math environments can take c, t, and b as an optional argument to force centered, top, or bottom alignment, respectively. The default is c (centered). So to obtain

$$\begin{aligned}
x &= 3, \\
y &= 4, \\
z &= 5;
\end{aligned} \qquad \text{or} \qquad \begin{aligned}
x &= 5, \\
y &= 12, \\
z &= 13.
\end{aligned}$$

type

```
\[
  \begin{aligned}[b]
     x &= 3, \\
     y &= 4, \\
     z &= 5;
  \end{aligned}
  \text{\qquad or \qquad}
  \begin{aligned}[b]
     x &= 5, \\
     y &= 12, \\
     z &= 13.
  \end{aligned}
\]
```

There is no automatic numbering or \tag-ing in subsidiary environments.

**8-2.1. Split.** The split *subsidiary math environment* is used to split up a (very long) formula into aligned parts; it generates only one number for the formula. Example:

$$f = (x_1 x_2 x_3 x_4 x_5 x_6)^2$$

(7)
$$= (x_1 x_2 x_3 x_4 x_5 + x_1 x_3 x_4 x_5 x_6 + x_1 x_2 x_4 x_5 x_6 + x_1 x_2 x_3 x_5 x_6)^2$$

$$= (x_1 x_2 x_3 x_4 + x_1 x_2 x_3 x_5 + x_1 x_2 x_4 x_5 + x_1 x_3 x_4 x_5 + x_2 x_3 x_4 x_5)^2$$

typed as

```
\begin{equation}  \label{E:ml5}
  \begin{split}
    f &= (x_{1} x_{2} x_{3} x_{4} x_{5} x_{6})^{2} \\
      &= (x_{1} x_{2} x_{3} x_{4} x_{5} +
      x_{1} x_{3} x_{4} x_{5} x_{6} +
      x_{1} x_{2} x_{4} x_{5} x_{6} +
      x_{1} x_{2} x_{3} x_{5} x_{6})^{2} \\
      &= (x_{1} x_{2} x_{3} x_{4} + x_{1} x_{2} x_{3} x_{5} +
      x_{1} x_{2} x_{4} x_{5} + x_{1} x_{3} x_{4} x_{5}
      + x_{2} x_{3} x_{4} x_{5})^{2}
  \end{split}
\end{equation}
```

**Rule 1.** split *subsidiary math environment.*

(1) \\ separates the lines; there is no \\ at the end of the last line.
(2) The alignment point is marked by &.
(3) split must be inside another environment: equation, align, or gather.
(4) A split formula has only one tag—automatically generated or declared by \tag, or no tag if so declared by \notag.
(5) \tag and \notag must follow \end{split}.
(6) No blank line is permitted.

If split is used by itself, you get the error message:

```
AmS-TeX error:
! \begin{split} is not allowed here. Try the 'aligned' envir
onment..
\err@ ...error:}\errmessage {#1}
                                        \fi
1.17 \begin{split}
```

Here is an example to illustrate split in align:

$$f = (x_1 x_2 x_3 x_4 x_5 x_6)^2$$
$$(8) \qquad = (x_1 x_2 x_3 x_4 x_5 + x_1 x_3 x_4 x_5 x_6 + x_1 x_2 x_4 x_5 x_6 + x_1 x_2 x_3 x_5 x_6)^2$$
$$= (x_1 x_2 x_3 x_4 + x_1 x_2 x_3 x_5 + x_1 x_2 x_4 x_5 + x_1 x_3 x_4 x_5 + x_2 x_3 x_4 x_5)^2,$$
$$(9) \qquad g = y_1 y_2 y_3.$$

which is typed as follows

```
\begin{align} \label{E:ml6}
  \begin{split}
    f &= (x_{1} x_{2} x_{3} x_{4} x_{5} x_{6})^{2} \\
      &= (x_{1} x_{2} x_{3} x_{4} x_{5} +
         x_{1} x_{3} x_{4} x_{5} x_{6} +
         x_{1} x_{2} x_{4} x_{5} x_{6} +
         x_{1} x_{2} x_{3} x_{5} x_{6})^{2} \\
      &= (x_{1} x_{2} x_{3} x_{4} +
         x_{1} x_{2} x_{3} x_{5} +
         x_{1} x_{2} x_{4} x_{5} +
         x_{1} x_{3} x_{4} x_{5} +
         x_{2} x_{3} x_{4} x_{5})^{2},
  \end{split} \\
    g &= y_{1} y_{2} y_{3}.   \label{E:ml7}
\end{align}
```

Notice the \\ following \end{split} to separate the lines for align. If you omit the \\, you get the error message:

```
AmS-TeX error:
! Extra & on this line.
\err@ ...error:}\errmessage {#1}
                                \fi
...
l.36 \end{align}
```

**8-2.2. Intertext.** A different type of tool to enhance multiline math displays is provided by the command \intertext. It places a line (or more) of text in the middle of an aligned environment (align or alignat). For instance, to obtain the following:

$$(10) \qquad h(x) = \int \left( \frac{f(x) + g(x)}{1 + f^2(x)} + \frac{1 + f(x)g(x)}{\sqrt{1 - \sin x}} \right) dx$$

The reader may find the following form easier to read:

$$= \int \frac{1 + f(x)}{1 + g(x)} \, dx - 2 \tan^{-1}(x - 2)$$

type:

```
\begin{align}  \label{E:ml8}
     h(x) &= \int \left( \frac{ f(x) + g(x) }{1 + f^{2}(x)} +
        \frac{1 + f(x)g(x)}{ \sqrt{1 - \sin x} } \right) \, dx \\
   \intertext{The reader may find the following form easier to
   read:}
        &= \int \frac{1 + f(x)}{1 + g(x)} \, dx  -
        2 \tan^{-1}(x - 2) \notag
\end{align}
```

Another an example with `alignat*`:

$$f(x) = x + yz \qquad\qquad g(x) = x + y + z$$

The reader also may find the following polynomials useful:

$$h(x) = xy + xz + yz \qquad k(x) = (x + y)(x + z)(y + z)$$

typed as

```
\begin{alignat*}{2}
   f(x) &= x + yz & \qquad g(x) &= x + y + z \notag \\
   \intertext{The reader also may find the following
    polynomials useful:}
   h(x) &= xy + xz + yz
                 & \qquad k(x) &= (x + y)(x + z)(y + z)
\end{alignat*}
```

If you place the `\intertext` command before the line separator \\, you get the error message:

```
! Misplaced \noalign.
\intertext #1->\noalign
                      {\vskip \belowdisplayskip \vbox {\no
r...
  ...
1.17 \end{alignat*}
```

The text in `\intertext` can be centered using the center environment; see Section 9-1.

### 8-3. Centered columns

There are four centered one- or multi-column constructs. Instead of being aligned (as in Section 8-1), the columns are *centered*, or *flushed left* or *right*. The simplest construct is provided by the gather environment, which centers a number of formulas, for instance:

$$x_1 x_2 + x_1^2 x_2^2 + x_3,$$
(11)
$$x_1 x_3 + x_1^2 x_3^2 + x_2,$$
$$x_1 x_2 x_3.$$

The other three constructs are subsidiary environments: matrix (multicolumn, centered):

$$
\begin{array}{cccc}
a+b+c & uv & x-y & 27 \\
a+b & u+v & z & 134
\end{array}
$$

array (multicolumn, centered, or flush left or right):

$$
\begin{array}{cccc}
a+b+c & uv & x-y & 27 \\
a+b & u+v & z & 134
\end{array}
$$

(in this example, there are three centered columns and one flush right), and its derivative, cases:

(12)
$$f(x) = \begin{cases} -x^2, & \text{if } x \le 0; \\ 0+x, & \text{if } 0 \le x \le 1; \\ x^2, & \text{otherwise.} \end{cases}$$

**8-3.1. Gather.** Formula (11) is typed:

```
\begin{gather}
  x_{1} x_{2} + x_{1}^{2} x_{2}^{2} + x_{3}, \notag \\
  x_{1} x_{3} + x_{1}^{2} x_{3}^{2} + x_{2}, \label{E:ml9} \\
  x_{1} x_{2} x_{3}. \notag
\end{gather}
```

The rules for the gather environment are very simple:

**Rule 1.** gather *environment.*

(1) \\ separates the lines; there is no \\ at the end of the last line.
(2) Each line is numbered except those that are \tag-ed and those where numbering is prohibited by \notag.
(3) No blank line is permitted between \begin{gather} and \end{gather}.
(4) No & is permitted.

You can put align* and split in gather:

```
\begin{gather} \label{E:ml11}
  \begin{split}
    f &= (x_{1} x_{2} x_{3} x_{4} x_{5} x_{6})^{2} \\
      &= (x_{1} x_{2} x_{3} x_{4} x_{5}
         + x_{1} x_{3} x_{4} x_{5} x_{6} +
```

```
          x_{1} x_{2} x_{4} x_{5} x_{6} +
          x_{1} x_{2} x_{3} x_{5} x_{6})^{2} \\
     &= (x_{1} x_{2} x_{3} x_{4} +
          x_{1} x_{2} x_{3} x_{5} +
          x_{1} x_{2} x_{4} x_{5} +
          x_{1} x_{3} x_{4} x_{5} +
          x_{2} x_{3} x_{4} x_{5})^{2}
   \end{split} \\
   \begin{align*}
     g &= y_{1} y_{2} y_{3} \\
     h &= z_{1}^{2} z_{2}^{2} z_{3}^{2}
   \end{align*}
\end{gather}
```

which prints:

$$f = (x_1 x_2 x_3 x_4 x_5 x_6)^2$$
$$\text{(13)} \quad = (x_1 x_2 x_3 x_4 x_5 + x_1 x_3 x_4 x_5 x_6 + x_1 x_2 x_4 x_5 x_6 + x_1 x_2 x_3 x_5 x_6)^2$$
$$= (x_1 x_2 x_3 x_4 + x_1 x_2 x_3 x_5 + x_1 x_2 x_4 x_5 + x_1 x_3 x_4 x_5 + x_2 x_3 x_4 x_5)^2$$
$$g = y_1 y_2 y_3$$
$$h = z_1^2 z_2^2 z_3^2$$

You cannot put `multline` in `gather`.

**8-3.2. Matrices.** Use the `matrix` *subsidiary math environment* to print matrices. Here is an example:

```
\begin{equation*}
  \begin{matrix}
    a + b + c & uv & x - y & 27 \\
    a  + b & u + v & z & 134
  \end{matrix}
\end{equation*}
```

which prints:

$$
\begin{matrix}
a+b+c & uv & x-y & 27 \\
a+b & u+v & z & 134
\end{matrix}
$$

`matrix` does not stand on its own:

```
\begin{matrix}
  a + b + c & uv & x - y & 27 \\
  a + b & u + v & z & 134
\end{matrix}
```

gives the error message:

```
! Missing $ inserted.
<inserted text>
                    $
...
l.13 \begin{matrix}
```

**Rule 2.** matrix *environment.*

(1) matrix must be included in a math environment.

(2) The columns are separated by &.

(3) \\ separates the rows; there is no \\ at the end of the last row.

(4) No blank line is permitted between the lines

\begin{matrix}

and

\end{matrix}

(5) If you need more than 10 columns, reset the MaxMatrixCols counter, as in the example following.

$\mathcal{AMS}$-L&TEX gives you a matrix of up to 10 *centered* columns. If you need more columns, you have to set the number of columns. In the following example, we set the number of columns to 12:

```
\begin{equation} \label{E:ml12}
    \setcounter{MaxMatrixCols}{12}
    \begin{matrix}
        1 & 2 & 3 & 4 & 5 & 6 & 7 & 8 & 9 & 10 & 11 & 12 \\
        1 & 2 & 3 & \hdotsfor{7} & 11 & 12
    \end{matrix}
\end{equation}
```

which prints:

$$(14) \quad \begin{matrix} 1 & 2 & 3 & 4 & 5 & 6 & 7 & 8 & 9 & 10 & 11 & 12 \\ 1 & 2 & 3 & \hdotsfor{7} & & & & & & & 11 & 12 \end{matrix}$$

More about \setcounter and counters in Section 11-4.1.

You can put dots in a number of columns with the command \hdotsfor; the argument specifies the number of columns as in formula (14). The number in the argument of \hdotsfor indicates how many &-s the command replaces.

**Rule 3.** \hdotsfor must be at the beginning of a row or it must follow a &.

If you violate this rule, you get the error message:

```
! Misplaced \omit.
\multispan #1->\omit
                    \mscount #1 \loop \ifnum \mscount >\@ne
  ...
  ...
```

1.32 \end{equation}

A matrix is a "large" symbol; normally it is centrally aligned with the symbols around it. To align it with its bottom or top, use the optional parameter t or b, as in

\begin{matrix}[b]

**Matrix variants.** Using delimiters (see Section 4-6), we can enclose a matrix as we wish:

$$
\begin{matrix} a+b+c & uv \\ a+b & c+d \end{matrix}
\qquad
\begin{pmatrix} a+b+c & uv \\ a+b & c+d \end{pmatrix}
\qquad
\begin{bmatrix} a+b+c & uv \\ a+b & c+d \end{bmatrix}
$$

$$
\begin{vmatrix} a+b+c & uv \\ a+b & c+d \end{vmatrix}
\qquad
\begin{Vmatrix} a+b+c & uv \\ a+b & c+d \end{Vmatrix}
\qquad
\left. \begin{matrix} a+b+c & uv \\ a+b & c+d \end{matrix} \right]
$$

These matrices are typed as follows:

```
\begin{alignat*}{3}
  &\
  \begin{matrix}
    a   + b + c & uv \\
    a + b & c + d
  \end{matrix}
  \qquad
  &&
  \begin{pmatrix}
    a + b + c & uv \\
    a + b & c + d
  \end{pmatrix}
  \qquad
  &&
  \begin{bmatrix}
    a + b + c & uv \\
    a + b & c + d
  \end{bmatrix}
  \\
  &
  \begin{vmatrix}
    a + b + c & uv \\
    a + b & c + d
  \end{vmatrix}
  \qquad
  &&
  \begin{Vmatrix}
    a + b + c & uv \\
    a + b & c + d
  \end{Vmatrix}
```

```
    \qquad
    &&
    \left(\begin{matrix}
        a + b + c & uv \\
        a + b & c + d
    \end{matrix}
    \right]
\end{alignat*}
```

The first entry is the `matrix` itself. The next four illustrations are matrix variants, with delimiters supplied by $\mathcal{A}\mathcal{M}\mathcal{S}$-LaTeX: `pmatrix`, `bmatrix`, `vmatrix`, and `Vmatrix`. In the last example, we provide our own delimiters. (Note the `alignat*` environment: there are three columns, all flush left; there are five & symbols in a row: two column separators, three alignment points.)

**Small matrix.** If you put a `matrix` in an inline math formula, and you may get a matrix that is too large for your taste, use the environment `smallmatrix`. Compare the regular matrix $\begin{matrix} a+b+c & uv \\ a+b & c+d \end{matrix}$ in this line, typed as follows:

```
\(
    \begin{matrix}
        a + b + c & uv \\
        a + b & c + d
    \end{matrix}
\)
```

with the small matrix in this line $\begin{smallmatrix} a+b+c & uv \\ a+b & c+d \end{smallmatrix}$ typed as

```
\(
    \begin{smallmatrix}
        a + b + c & uv \\
        a + b & c + d
    \end{smallmatrix}
\)
```

The command `\hdotsfor` does not work in a small matrix. There are no variants of `smallmatrix` similar to the variants of `matrix`.

**8-3.3. Arrays.** The `matrix` subsidiary math environment and the `array` *subsidiary math environment* are almost the same. The matrix in the introduction to Section 8-3 is typed as follows as an array:

```
\begin{equation*}
    \begin{array}{cccc}
        a + b + c & uv & x - y & 27 \\
        a + b & u + v & z & 134
    \end{array}
\end{equation*}
```

which prints:

$$a + b + c \quad uv \quad x - y \quad 27$$
$$a + b \quad u + v \quad z \quad 134$$

Here are the rules:

**Rule 4.** array *subsidiary math environment.*

(1) array must be included in a math environment.

(2) The columns are separated by &.

(3) \\ separates the rows; there is no \\ at the end of the last row.

(4) The argument of \begin{array} is compulsory: it is a string made up of the letters l, r, and c; the number of letters is the number of columns; a column is flush left, centered, flush right, if the letter corresponding to it is l, c, and r, respectively.

(5) No blank line is permitted.

So the following is an array that could not have been made with matrix:

$$a + b + c \quad uv \quad x - y \quad 27$$
$$a + b \quad u + v \quad z \quad 134$$

since the last column is flush right. (Of course, this is not quite true; in a matrix, \hfill 27 will flush the entry 27 right; see Section 3-8.4.)

If the argument of \begin{array} is missing:

```
\begin{equation}
   \begin{array}
      a + b + c & uv & x - y & 27 \\
      a + b & u + v  z & 134
   \end{array}
\end{equation}
```

you get the error message:

```
LaTeX error.  See LaTeX manual for explanation.
                Type  H <return>  for immediate help.
! Illegal character in array arg.
\@latexerr ....}\errmessage {#1}


. . .

l.18 \end{equation}
```

If the closing brace of the argument of \begin{array} is missing:

```
\begin{equation}
   \begin{array}{cccc
      a + b + c & uv & x - y & 27 \\
      a + b & u + v & z & 134
   \end{array}
```

\end{equation}

you get the error message:

```
Runaway argument?
\Invalid@ \\ \begin {array}{ a + b + c & uv & x - y & \ETC.
! Paragraph ended before \equation was complete.
<to be read again>
                        \par
l.20
```

**8-3.4. Cases.** The cases *environment* is a *subsidiary multiline math environment*. It must be a part of a displayed math environment, an equation (equation*) environment, or of a line in a multiline math environment.

Formula (12) is typed as:

```
\begin{equation} \label{E:ml10}
   f(x) =
      \begin{cases}
         -x^{2}, &\text{if $x \leq 0$;} \\
         0 + x,  &\text{if $ 0 \leq x \leq 1$;} \\
         x^{2},  &\text{otherwise.}
      \end{cases}
\end{equation}
```

The rules and error messages for cases are the same as for simple align except for rule (3) which does not apply. Since the whole construct has a single tag, you can put \tag and \notag anywhere.

It is easy to code cases as a special case of an array; in formula 18 in Section 2-4, cases is coded with the subsidiary math environment smallmatrix; see Section 8-3.2.

### 8-4. Multiline formulas

The multline *environment* is used to display one very long formula: the first line is flush left, the last is flush right, the middle lines are centered:

$$(15) \quad (x_1x_2x_3x_4x_5x_6)^2 +$$

$$(x_1x_2x_3x_4x_5 + x_1x_3x_4x_5x_6 + x_1x_2x_4x_5x_6 + x_1x_2x_3x_5x_6)^2 +$$

$$(x_1x_2x_3x_4 + x_1x_2x_3x_5 + x_1x_2x_4x_5 + x_1x_3x_4x_5 + x_2x_3x_4x_5)^2$$

This display of a single formula is implemented with the multline environment:

```
\begin{multline}\label{E:ml13}
   (x_{1} x_{2} x_{3} x_{4} x_{5} x_{6})^{2} + \\
   (x_{1} x_{2} x_{3} x_{4} x_{5} + x_{1} x_{3} x_{4} x_{5} x_{6}
   + x_{1} x_{2} x_{4} x_{5} x_{6}
   + x_{1} x_{2} x_{3} x_{5} x_{6})^{2}+  \\
   (x_{1} x_{2} x_{3} x_{4} + x_{1} x_{2} x_{3} x_{5} +
```

```
    x_{1} x_{2} x_{4} x_{5} + x_{1} x_{3} x_{4} x_{5} +
    x_{2} x_{3} x_{4} x_{5})^{2}
\end{multline}
```

The rules for the `multline` environment are very simple:

**Rule 1.** `multline` environment.

(1) \\ separates the lines; there is no \\ at the end of the last line.

(2) Between \begin{multline} and \end{multline}, no blank line is permitted.

(3) No & is permitted.

A typical error is to write "multiline" for "multline", giving the message:

```
! Environment multiline undefined.
\@latexerr ....}\errmessage {#1}
```

```
l.13 \begin{multiline}
```

\tag and \notag should be placed between the lines

\begin{multline}

and

\end{multline}

A \notag placed after \end{multline} is ignored, while a \tag gives the error message:

```
AmS-TeX error:
! \tag not allowed here.
\err@ ...error:}\errmessage {#1}
                                      \fi
```

```
...
l.18 \end{multline}\tag
                    {A}
```

A \label can go between \begin{multline} and \end{multline} or right after \end{multline}.

## 8-5. Commutative diagrams

$\mathcal{A}_{\mathcal{M}}$S-LaTeX provides the subsidiary math environment CD to type some simple commutative diagrams. For instance, to obtain

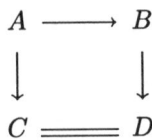

type

```
\[
    \begin{CD}
        A           @>>>        B  \\
        @VVV                    @VVV \\
        C           @=          D
    \end{CD}
\]
```

A commutative diagram is a matrix made up of two kinds of rows: *horizontal rows*; that is, rows with horizontal arrows, and *vertical rows*; that is, rows with vertical arrows. Examples:

```
A           @>>>        B  \\
```

This is a typical horizontal row. It defines two columns, and a connecting horizontal arrow @>>>. The connecting piece can be an extendible arrow (see Section 4-10.1) @>>> or @<<<; or it could be @=, and extendible equal sign. There may be more than two columns, as in:

```
A   @>>>  B   @>>>   C   @=   D   @<<<   E   @<<<   F  \\
```

The arrows may be labeled: @>{label}>> puts label above, and @>>{label}> puts label below the arrow.

```
@VVV                @VVV        @AAA \\
```

is a typical vertical row containing vertical arrows. @VVV is a down arrow and @AAA is an up arrow. @V{label}VV puts label to the left and @VV{label}V puts label to the right. The vertical arrows are placed in the columns from the first on.

Here is a more complicated example, followed by its source:

$$A \xrightarrow{\log} B \underset{\text{bottom}}{\longrightarrow} C \Longequal D \longleftarrow E \longleftarrow F$$

$$1-1\Big\downarrow \qquad \downarrow \qquad \Big\uparrow\text{onto}$$

$$X \Longequal Y \longrightarrow Z$$

$$\beta\Big\uparrow \qquad \Big\uparrow\gamma$$

$$D \xrightarrow{\alpha} E$$

```
\[
    \begin{CD}
        A           @>\log>>        B               @>>\text{bottom}>        C        @=
                    D               @<<<            E               @<<<       F \\
        @V\text{1 -- 1}VV           @VVV                                        @AA\text{onto}A\\
        X           @=              Y               @>>>                        Z \\
        @A{\beta}AA                 @AA{\gamma}A \\
        D           @>\alpha>>      E \\
    \end{CD}
\]
```

More complicated diagrams should be done with a drafting program.

### 8-6. Pagebreak

The math environments of this chapter do not allow *pagebreaks*. For instance, a pagebreak in cases is obviously not desirable, but it may be permissible in simple align or gather

You have to decide whether to allow pagebreaks. To allow pagebreak, use the

`\allowdisplaybreaks`

command. It will allow pagebreaks in a multiline math environment within its scope. For instance,

```
{\allowdisplaybreaks
\begin{align} \label{E:ml14}
    a &= b + c, \\
    d &= e + f, \\
    x &= y + z, \\
    u &= v + w.
\end{align}
}% end of \allowdisplaybreaks
```

allows a pagebreak after any one of the first three lines.

Within the scope of `\allowdisplaybreaks`, use `\\*` to prohibit break at that line.

The line separator `\\` can be modified as in Section 3-7.1 to add some interline space.

Just before the line separator `\\`, you can put `\displaybreak` to force a break, or

`\displaybreak[0]`

to allow one. `\displaybreak[n]`, where n is 1, 2, or 3, are the intermediate steps between allowing and forcing. `\displaybreak[4]` is the same as `\displaybreak`.

# CHAPTER 9

# Displayed Text

We shall discuss the text environments of $\mathcal{A}_{\mathcal{M}}\mathcal{S}$-LaTeX in this chapter. The examples from this chapter are collected in the file textenv.tpl on the DISK.

### 9-1. Style and size environments

The simplest text environments set the printing style and size. They are named the same as the commands: rm (roman), bf (bold), sf (sans serif), sl (slanted), it (italic), sc (small caps), tt (typewriter); tiny, scriptsize, small, normalsize, large. (If \rm is redefined as in Section 3-6.2, the rm environment also works as expected.)

Line placements are controlled by the environments flushleft, flushright, and center. These environments can be used separately or in combinations, as in

The **simplest** text environments set the printing style and size. The commands
and the environments are named the same.

typed as

```
\begin{flushright}
   The
   \begin{bf}
      simplest
   \end{bf}
   text environments set the
   printing style and size.  The commands and the
   environments are named the same.
\end{flushright}
```

There are commands that correspond to the centering and flush environments: \centering (center), \raggedright (flush left), \raggedleft (flush right). The scope of these commands must be whole paragraphs. The effect of one of these commands is almost the same as that of the corresponding environment except that the environment places some vertical space before and after the displayed paragraphs.

### 9-1.1. Some general rules.

**Rule 1**. Blank lines in text environments.

(1) Blank lines are ignored immediately after \begin{name} and immediately before \end{name}.

(2) A blank line after \end{name} forces the following text to start a new paragraph.

(3) As a rule, you should not have a blank line before \begin{name}.

The pagebreaking commands of Section 3-7.3 apply to text environments; as does the \\[dist] linebreaking command of Section 3-7.1.

### 9-2. Proof environment

The pf *text environment* is provided for proofs. Example:

*Proof.* This is the proof.  □

typed as

```
\begin{pf}
   This is the proof.
\end{pf}
```

The interline space separating the proof is larger than normal, and the end of proof is marked with the symbol □

If you do not wish a symbol at the end of a proof, give the command:

```
\renewcommand{\qedsymbol}{}
```

To substitute for "*Proof*" another phrase, like "*Necessity*", as in

*Necessity.* This is the proof.  □

use the pf* environment, and name the phrase as an argument:

```
\begin{pf*}{Necessity}
   This is the proof.
\end{pf*}
```

### 9-3. List environments

**9-3.1. Numbered lists: enumerate.** The most often used list is the *numbered list* created with the enumerate *text environment*. Example:

This space has the following properties:

(1) Grade 2 Cantor.

(2) Half smooth Hausdorff.

(3) Metrizably smooth.

Therefore, we can apply the Main Theorem ...

typed as

```
This space has the following properties:
\begin{enumerate}
   \item Grade 2 Cantor.\label{Cantor}
   \item Half smooth Hausdorff.\label{Hausdorff}
   \item Metrizably smooth.\label{smooth}
\end{enumerate}
Therefore, we can apply the Main Theorem \dots
```

Each item is introduced with `\item`. The numbers generated can be labeled and cross-referenced; see Section 6-3. This construct can be used in theorems and definitions, listing conditions or conclusions.

**9-3.2. Bulleted lists: itemize.** Example:

In this lecture, we set out to accomplish a variety of goals:

- To introduce the concept of smooth functions.
- To show their usefulness in the differentiation of Howard-type functions.
- To point out the efficacy of using smooth functions in Advanced Calculus courses.

We hope that the reader will agree ...

typed as

```
In this lecture, we set out to accomplish a variety of goals:
\begin{itemize}
   \item To introduce the concept of smooth functions.
   \item To show their usefulness in the differentiation
      of Howard-type functions.
   \item To point out the efficacy of using smooth functions
      in Advanced Calculus courses.
\end{itemize}
We hope that the reader will agree \dots
```

**9-3.3. Captioned lists: description.** Example:

In this introduction, we outline the history of this concept. The main contributors were

**J. Perelman:** the first to introduce smooth functions.
**T. Kovács:** who showed their usefulness in the differentiation of Howard type functions.
**A. P. Fein:** the main advocate of using smooth functions in advanced Calculus courses.

We hope that the reader will agree ...

typed as

```
In this introduction, we outline the history of this concept.
The main contributors were
\begin{description}
```

```
\item[J. Perelman] the first to introduce smooth functions.
\item[T. Kov\'acs] who showed their usefulness in the
   differentiation of Howard type functions.
\item[A. P. Fein] the main advocate of using smooth
   functions in advanced Calculus courses.
```
`\end{description}`
```
We hope that the reader will agree \dots
```

### 9-3.4. Rules and combinations.

**Rule 1**. An `\item` must follow `\begin{enumerate}`.

If it does not, you get an error message. For instance,

```
\begin{enumerate}
   This is wrong!
   \item Grade 2 Cantor.
```

gives the error message:

```
LaTeX error.  See LaTeX manual for explanation.
                Type  H <return>  for immediate help.
! Something's wrong--perhaps a missing \item.
\@latexerr ....}\errmessage {#1}


...
1.14 \item G
            rade 2 Cantor.
```

Remember the list environments' only rule, and check for text preceding the first `\item`.

The same rule applies to `\begin{itemize}` and `\begin{description}`.

**Rule 2**. If a declaration starts with a list environment, precede the list by `\hfill`

as in:

```
\begin{Def} \label{D:prime} \hfill
   \begin{enumerate}
      \item \( u \) is {\em meet-irreducible\/} if
         \( u = x \wedge y \) implies that
         \( u = x \) or   \( u = x \).\label{mi1}
      \item \( u \) is {\em meet-irreducible\/} if
         \( u = x \wedge y \) implies that
         \( u = x \) or   \( u = x \).\label{mi2}
      \item \( u \) is {\em completely join-irreducible\/} if
         \( u = \bigvee X \) implies that \( u \in X \).\label{mi3}
   \end{enumerate}
\end{Def}
```

(This assumes that in the Preamble, the declaration

```
\theoremstyle{plain}
\newtheorem{Def}{Definition}
```

was given.)

Up to four list environments can be combined; for instance:

(1) First item Level 1.
 (a) First item Level 2.
  (i) First item Level 3.
   (A) First item Level 4.
   (B) Second item Level 4.
  (ii) Second item Level 3.
 (b) Second item Level 2.
(2) Second item Level 1.

The label: 1(a)iA

typed as

```
\begin{enumerate}
  \item First item Level 1.
  \begin{enumerate}
    \item  First item Level 2.
    \begin{enumerate}
      \item  First item Level 3.
      \begin{enumerate}
        \item  First item Level 4.\label{aa}
        \item  Second item Level 4.
      \end{enumerate}
      \item Second item Level 3.
    \end{enumerate}
    \item Second item Level 2.
  \end{enumerate}
  \item Second item Level 1.
\end{enumerate}
The label: \ref{aa}
```

Note that the label collects together all four counters; see Section 6-3.

In all three types list environments, \item may be followed by an optional argument:

```
\item[label]
```

For instance, here is an itemized list with optional arguments:

In this lecture, we set out to accomplish a variety of goals:

Goal 1. To introduce the concept of smooth functions.
Goal 2. To show their usefulness in the differentiation of Howard-type functions.

Goal 3. To point out the efficacy of using smooth functions in Advanced Calculus courses.

We hope that the reader will agree ...

typed as

```
In this lecture, we set out to accomplish a variety of goals:
\begin{itemize}
    \item[Goal 1.] To introduce the concept of smooth functions.
    \item[Goal 2.] To show their usefulness in the differentiation
    of Howard-type functions.
    \item[Goal 3.] To point out the efficacy of using smooth
    functions in Advanced Calculus courses.
\end{itemize}
We hope that the reader will agree \dots
```

Of course, for the `description` environment the "optional argument" is rather compulsory.

### 9-4. Tabular environment

A `tabular` environment creates a "large symbol", the table. Here is a simple table:

| Name | 1 | 2 | 3 |
|-------|------|-------|------|
| Peter | 2.45 | 34.12 | 1.00 |
| John | 0.00 | 12.89 | 3.71 |
| David | 2.00 | 1.85 | 0.71 |

typed as

```
\begin{tabular}{ | | l | r | r | r | | }
    \hline
    Name     & 1    & 2      & 3      \\ \hline
    Peter    & 2.45 & 34.12 & 1.00 \\ \hline
    John     & 0.00 & 12.89 & 3.71 \\ \hline
    David    & 2.00 & 1.85  & 0.71 \\ \hline
\end{tabular}
```

In this example we have printed the table as a large character in the line.

**Rule 1**. `tabular` *environment*.

- `\begin{tabular}` has an argument consisting of a character l, r, or c (meaning left, right, or center alignment) for each column, and the symbols |; each | indicates a vertical line in the table. Spaces in the argument are ignored (but you should use them for readability).
- Columns are separated by &, and the end of the last column is indicated by \\.
- & absorbs spaces on either side.
- \hline before a row signifies a horizontal line.
- If you use a horizontal line to finish the table, there must be \\ at the end of the last row.

| Name | 1 | 2 | 3 |
|------|------|-------|------|
| Peter | 2.45 | 34.12 | 1.00 |
| John | 0.00 | 12.89 | 3.71 |
| David | 2.00 | 1.85 | 0.71 |

TABLE 9.1. Tabular Table

- \begin{tabular} has an optional argument b or t for bottom or top horizontal alignment. The default is the center alignment.

If you forget to place \\ at the end of the last row before \hline, you get the error message:

```
! Misplaced \noalign.
\hline ->\noalign
                {\ifnum 0='}\fi \hrule \@height \arrayrule
w...
1.14 ...2.00 & 1.85 & 0.71\hline
```

Remember to put the optional argument b or t in brackets, as in

```
\begin{tabular}[b]{ | | l | r | r | r | | }
```

A table, like the previous example, can be centered (with the center environment; see Section 9-1). It can also be placed in a table environment (see Section 6-5), and a caption may be added:

```
\begin{table}
  \begin{center}
    \begin{tabular}{ | | l | r | r | r | | }
      \hline
      Name     & 1     & 2     & 3      \\ \hline
      Peter    &  2.45 & 34.12 & 1.00 \\ \hline
      John     &  0.00 & 12.89 & 3.71 \\ \hline
      David    &  2.00 & 1.85  & 0.71 \\ \hline
    \end{tabular}
  \end{center}
  \caption{Tabular Table} \label{Ta:first}
\end{table}
```

Then the table will be listed in the List of Tables (see Section 6-5), and the table number can be referenced by \ref{Ta:first}.

**Refinements.** \hline can be refined to \cline{a-b} where a and b are column numbers; this draws the horizontal line from column a to column b (inclusive) only; e.g., \cline{1-3}, \cline{4-4}. Another useful command is \multicolumn, which is a single entry for one or more columns, e.g.,
\multicolumn{3}{c}{\em absent}.
The first parameter is the number of columns used by the entry, the second parameter

is alignment (and maybe the vertical line designator | for this row only), the third is the entry. Example:

| Name  | 1    | 2      | 3    |
|-------|------|--------|------|
| Peter | 2.45 | 34.12  | 1.00 |
| John  | *absent* |    |      |
| David | 2.00 | 1.85   | 0.71 |

typed as

```
\begin{tabular}{ | | l | r | r | r | | } \hline
    Name    & 1    & 2      & 3 \\ \hline
    Peter   & 2.45 & 34.12 & 1.00 \\ \hline
    John    & \multicolumn{3}{c | |}{\em absent} \\ \hline
    David   & 2.00 & 1.85   & 0.71 \\ \hline
\end{tabular}
```

The next example makes extensive use of \multicolumn and \cline:

| Name | Month | Week | Amount |
|------|-------|------|--------|
| Peter | Jan. | 1 | 1.00 |
|       |      | 2 | 12.78 |
|       |      | 3 | 0.71 |
|       |      | 4 | 15.00 |
|       | Total: | | 29.49 |
| John | Jan. | 1 | 12.01 |
|      |      | 2 | 3.10 |
|      |      | 3 | 10.10 |
|      |      | 4 | 0.00 |
|      | Total: | | 25.21 |
| Grand Total: | | | 54.70 |

This is typed as follows:

```
\begin{center}
\begin{tabular}{ | | c  c  | c | r | | } \hline
      Name   & Month & Week & Amount \\ \hline
      Peter & Jan.  & 1    & 1.00 \\ \cline{3-4}
            &       & 2    & 12.78 \\ \cline{3-4}
            &       & 3    & 0.71 \\ \cline{3-4}
            &       & 4    & 15.00 \\ \cline{2-4}
            & \multicolumn{2}{| l}{Total: } & 29.49 \\   \hline
      John  & Jan.  & 1    & 12.01 \\ \cline{3-4}
            &       & 2    & 3.10 \\ \cline{3-4}
            &       & 3    & 10.10 \\ \cline{3-4}
            &       & 4    & 0.00 \\ \cline{2-4}
            & \multicolumn{2}{| l}{Total: } & 25.21 \\   \hline
```

```
      \multicolumn{3}{| | l}{Grand Total:} & 54.70 \\ \hline
\end{tabular}
\end{center}
```

\parbox (see Section 3-9.2) can be used for multiline entries; recall that the first argument of \parbox is the width. As an example, let us replace "Grand Total" by "Grand Total for Peter and John":

| Name | Month | Week | Amount |
|------|-------|------|--------|
| Peter | Jan. | 1 | 1.00 |
| | | 2 | 12.78 |
| | | 3 | 0.71 |
| | | 4 | 15.00 |
| | Total: | | 29.49 |
| John | Jan. | 1 | 12.01 |
| | | 2 | 3.10 |
| | | 3 | 10.10 |
| | | 4 | 0.00 |
| | Total: | | 25.21 |
| Grand Total for Peter and John: | | | 54.70 |

typed as

```
\begin{center}
\begin{tabular}{ | | c   c  | c | r | | }
\hline
 Name  & Month & Week & Amount \\ \hline
 Peter & Jan.  & 1    & 1.00 \\ \cline{3-4}
       &       & 2    & 12.78 \\ \cline{3-4}
       &       & 3    & 0.71 \\ \cline{3-4}
       &       & 4    & 15.00 \\ \cline{2-4}
       & \multicolumn{2}{| l}{Total: } & 29.49 \\  \hline
 John  & Jan.  & 1    & 12.01 \\ \cline{3-4}
       &       & 2    & 3.10 \\ \cline{3-4}
       &       & 3    & 10.10 \\ \cline{3-4}
       &       & 4    & 0.00 \\ \cline{2-4}
       & \multicolumn{2}{| l}{Total: }
                      & 25.21 \\  \hline
\multicolumn{3}{| | l}{ \parbox[b]{10em}{Grand Total \\
for Peter and John:}} & 54.70 \\ \hline
\end{tabular}
\end{center}
```

Note that in
```
\parbox[b]{10em}{Grand Total \\ for Peter and John:}
```
we use the bottom alignment option; see Section 3-9.2.

The spacing of "Grand Total" is not quite right. This can be adjusted with a "strut": \rule{0ex}{4.8ex} 4.8 ex in height; see Section 3-9.4.

### 9-5. Tabbing environment

Although of limited use for math, the tabbing *environment* may be useful for typing algorithms, computer programs etc. In a tabular environment (Section 9-4), the width of a column is determined by $\mathcal{A}\mathcal{M}\mathcal{S}$-LaTeX from the widest entry. In the tabbing environment, it is under user control.

End of line is marked by \\; tab stops are set by \=; and \> moves to the next tab position. If there is already a next tab position, \= resets the tab.

A simple example:

```
PrintTime
    Block[{timing},
        timing = Timing[expr];
        Print[ timing[[1]] ];
    ]
End[]
```

typed as

```
\begin{tabbing}
   Prin\= tTime \\
   \>Bloc\=k[\{timing\}, \\
   \>\>timing = Timing[expr]; \\
   \>\>Print[ timing[[1]] ]; \\
   \>] \\
   End[\,] \\
\end{tabbing}
```

An alternative way to proceed is to use a line to set the tab stops, and \kill the line so it does not print. We use the previous example to illustrate this:

```
\begin{tabbing}
   9999\=9999\=    \kill
   PrintTime \\
   \>Block[\{timing\}, \\
   \>\>timing = Timing[expr]; \\
   \>\>Print[ timing[[1]] ]; \\
   \>] \\
   End[\,] \\
\end{tabbing}
```

Observe that there is no \\ in the line containing the \kill command.

There are about a dozen more commands special to this environment; if you need to use this often, please consult Lamport's book [20], especially Section C.9.

### 9-6. Miscellaneous text environments

There are three more displayed text environments, although they are not very often used in articles with mathematical formulas. They are quote, quotation, and verse. A fourth, verbatim, is used by authors who write about TₑX.

The quote environment is used for short (one paragraph) quotations:

> It's not that I'm afraid to die. I just don't want to be there when it happens. *Woody Allen*
> Literature is news that STAYS news. *Ezra Pound*

Typed as:

```
\begin{quote}
   It's not that I'm afraid to die.  I just don't want to be
   there when it happens.
   {\em Woody Allen}

   Literature is news that STAYS news.  {\em Ezra Pound}
\end{quote}
```

The quotes are separated by blank lines. In the quotation environment the blank lines mark new paragraph:

> KATH: Can he be present at the birth of his child?
> ED: It's all any reasonable child can expect if the dad is present at the conception.
>
> *Joe Orton*

typed as

```
\begin{quotation}
   KATH: Can he be present at the birth of his child?

   ED: It's all any reasonable child can expect if the dad
   is present at the conception.
   \begin{flushright}
      {\em Joe Orton}
   \end{flushright}
\end{quotation}
```

Finally, an example of the verse environment:

> I think that I shall never see
> A poem as lovely as a tree.
> Poems are made by fools like me,
> But only God can make a tree.
>
> *Joyce Kilmer*

typed as

```
\begin{verse}
   I think that I shall never see \\
   A poem as lovely as a tree.

   Poems are made by fools like me, \\
   But only God can make a tree.

   \begin{flushright}
      {\em Joyce Kilmer}
   \end{flushright}
\end{verse}
```

Lines are separated by \\, and stanzas by blank lines.

Finally, the verbatim text environment. You may need it if you write *about* TEX (all the displayed source in this book was written in the verbatim environment) or if you need to include TEX source in your writing. For instance, you may write to the $\mathcal{A}\mathcal{M}\mathcal{S}$ about the article you are proofreading:

Formula (2) in Section 3 should be typed as follows:

```
\begin{equation}
   D^{\langle 2 \rangle} = \{ \langle x_0, x_1 \rangle
      \mid x_0, x_1 \in D,\ x_0 = 0 \Rightarrow x_1 =
      0, \text{and } x_1=1\Rightarrow x_0 =1 \}.
\end{equation}
```

Please make the corrections.

The problem is that if you just type

```
\begin{equation}
   D^{\langle 2 \rangle} = \{ \langle x_0, x_1 \rangle
      \mid x_0, x_1 \in D,\ x_0 = 0 \Rightarrow x_1 =
      0, \text{and } x_1=1\Rightarrow x_0 =1 \}.
\end{equation}
```

TEX will typeset this:

$$(1) \quad D^{\langle 2 \rangle} = \{\langle x_0, x_1\rangle \mid x_0, x_1 \in D,\ x_0 = 0 \Rightarrow x_1 = 0, \text{and } x_1 = 1 \Rightarrow x_0 = 1\}.$$

If you want TEX to print the source exactly as typed, place it in the verbatim environment:

```
\begin{verbatim}
\begin{equation}
   D^{\langle 2 \rangle} = \{ \langle x_0, x_1 \rangle
      \mid x_0, x_1 \in D,\ x_0 = 0 \Rightarrow x_1 =
      0, \text{and } x_1=1\Rightarrow x_0 =1 \}.
\end{equation}
\end{verbatim}
```

**Rule 1**. `verbatim` text environment.

- There should be no characters on the line following `\end{verbatim}`.
- There can be no `verbatim` environment within a `verbatim` environment.

If you forget the first rule, there is a warning:

`LaTeX Warning: Characters dropped after '\end{verbatim}'.`

The violation of the second rule will result in environment delimiters that do not match. You will get an error message of the type:

`! \begin{document} ended by \end{verbatim}.`

`verbatim` also has an "inline" version, the command `\verb`. Here is an example:

```
Some European email addresses also contain \%;
recall that  you have to type \verb+\%+ to get \%.
```

which prints:

Some European email addresses also contain %; recall that you have to type `\%` to get %.

The character following the command `\verb` is the delimiter; in the example we used +. The argument starts with the character following the delimiter, and it is terminated by the next occurrence of the delimiter. So in the example, the argument is `\%`.

Choose the delimiter character carefully. For instance, if you want to show $\sin(\pi/2 + \alpha)$ (which prints $\sin(\pi/2 + \alpha)$) and you type

```
\verb+\( \sin(\pi/2 + \alpha) \)+
```

then you get the error message:

```
! Missing $ inserted.
<inserted text>
                 $
...
1.4606 ...\( \sin(\pi/2 + \alpha
                          ) \)+.
```

Indeed, the argument of `\verb` is `\( \sin(\pi/2 `, and then $\mathcal{A}_{\mathcal{M}}\mathcal{S}$-LaTeX tries to print `\alpha) \)+` but cannot because it is not in math mode. Use, for instance, % in place of +:

```
\verb%\( \sin(\pi/2 + \alpha) \)%
```

The whole `\verb` command must be in a single line. If it is not, as in

```
\verb%\( \sin(\pi/2 +
\alpha) \)%
```

you get the error message:

```
! \verb command ended by end of line..
```

# PART III

# CUSTOMIZING

# CHAPTER 10

# Customizing
# $\mathcal{AMS}$-LaTeX

There is a lot you can do to speed up typing and typesetting in $\mathcal{AMS}$-LaTeX. In this chapter, we cover some of the basic techniques.

## 10-1. User-defined commands

$\mathcal{AMS}$-LaTeX comes with a large number of commands. However, $\mathcal{AMS}$-LaTeX is much easier to use, if you judiciously add to this list of commands to satisfy your particular needs. Commands you define are called *user-defined commands*.

For instance, if you use the \rightarrow command a lot, you may want to define:

\newcommand{\ra}{\rightarrow}

and then you only have to type \ra (or whatever code you choose) to obtain a right arrow. Instead of

\widetilde{a}

you can simply type \wa if you define:

\newcommand{\wa}{\widetilde{a}}

Or to use **Trunc** as an operator with limits (see Section 4-11.2), you have to type:

\operatornamewithlimits{\bold{Trunc}}

Would it not be nice to type \Trunc instead? You can do that with the following user-defined command:

\newcommand{\Trunc}{\operatornamewithlimits{\bold{Trunc}}}

You can use new commands also as a shorthand. For instance, if you use the phrase "subdirectly irreducible" many times in your article, you may choose to define

\newcommand{\si}{subdirectly irreducible}

and then "\si" becomes the shorthand for "subdirectly irreducible".

**Rule 1.** To set up a user-defined command:

    (1) Issue the command \newcommand.

(2) In braces, give the name of the new command, including the \.

(3) Again, in braces, give what the new command stands for.

**Tip.** Be very careful to follow Rule **1** to the letter. Dropping a single brace will cause an error that the error message is unlikely to clear up. Introduce user-defined commands one at a time, so if trouble develops you know which one to correct.

Here are some other typical examples:

```
\newcommand{\bv}{ \bold{v} }
```

defines \bv for a bold "v" in math mode.

```
\newcommand{\Ds}{ D^{\langle 2 \rangle} }
```

defines \Ds for $D^{\langle 2 \rangle}$ in math mode. What if you would like to use $D^{\langle 2 \rangle}$ also in text? Of course, you can type \( \Ds \), which is awkward. Or you could define

```
\newcommand{\Ds}{\( D^{\langle 2 \rangle} \)}
```

in which case, in text, \Ds produces $D^{\langle 2 \rangle}$; but this command now cannot be used in math mode.

However, if you define:

```
\newcommand{\Ds}{\text{\( D^{\langle 2 \rangle} \)} }
```

it can be used both in text and math mode.

This example also shows the editorial advantages of user-defined commands. Suppose the referee suggests that the notation be changed to $D^{[2]}$. To carry out the change we only have to change one line:

```
\newcommand{\Ds}{ \text{\( D^{[2]} \)} }
```

**Tip.** Place the user-defined commands in the Command section of the Preamble. Then you know where to look for the definition of a command.

**Tip.** Suppose you want to define a command for the warning: *Do not redefine this variable!* It is very easy to make the following error:

```
\newcommand{\VarWarn}{\em Do not redefine this variable!}
```

Then variable warning: \VarWarn will present the warning, but everything thereafter will also be emphasized. The correct definition is:

```
\newcommand{\VarWarn}{ {\em Do not redefine this variable!} }
```

**Tip.** Make sure the name of the new command is not already in use. If it is, you get an error message. To redefine a command, see Section 10-1.2.

More examples of user-defined commands can be found in Section 11-2.

**10-1.1. Arguments.** Although, defining

`\newcommand{\Ahh}{ \Hat{ \Hat{A} } }`

is very convenient, we may also need a command for double hats in general. Here is how we do it:

`\newcommand{\hh}[1]{ \Hat{ \Hat{#1} } }`

and then to print $\hat{\hat{A}}$, type `\( \hh{A} \)`. The form of this `\newcommand` is the same as before, except that after the name of the command: `{\hh}` we put in brackets **the number of arguments**; in this example: `[1]`. This allows us to use #1 in the definition of the command. When the command is invoked, the user provides an argument, which replaces #1 in the definition. So type `\hh{B}` to get $\hat{\hat{B}}$.

In several articles, we need formulas of the type $\mathrm{Con}_c L$ to designate the lattice of complete congruences of a complete lattice $L$. Define the command

`\newcommand{\Com}[1]{\operatorname{Con_c}#1}`

and then $\mathrm{Con}_c L$ is typed as `\( \Com L \)`.

In the Preamble of the manuscript of this book, we define

`\newcommand{\en}[1]{ {\tt #1} }`

The command `\en` is used to typeset environment names. So the environment `center` is typed

`\en{center}`

Again the editorial advantage is obvious; if the editor wants the environment names emphasized, just one line in the book has to be changed:

`\newcommand{\en}[1]{ {\em #1} }`

If you want to use the command `\index` (see Section 6-4.2) to assist you in compiling an index, you may wish to introduce the user-defined command

`\newcommand{\ie}[1]{#1\index{#1}}`

The argument of this command ("`ie`" stands for index entry) is a word (or phrase) in the source file to be included in the Index. For instance, if the word "PostScript" is in the source file, and we want it in the Index, then we write `\ie{PostScript}`. This command has the same effect as typing

`PostScript\index{PostScript}`

Let us define a command with three arguments for congruences:

`\newcommand{\con}[3]{#1 \equiv #2 \pmod{#3}}`

Then to print the congruence $a \equiv b \pmod{\theta}$, type `\( \con{a}{b}{\theta} \)`. In Section 11-1.4, we present another command (macro) for congruences.

We mentioned in Section 6-3 that in this book all sections have labels starting with "S:"; see also Section 11-2. To refer to a section with label xxx we have to type: `Section \ref{S:xxx}`. So we define

`\newcommand{\refS}[1]{Section~\ref{S:#1}}`

and then the reference is \refS{xxx}.

We give a final example from the sample article. In that article, there are a lot of vectors with one nonzero entry: $\langle \ldots, 0, \ldots, \overset{i}{d}, \ldots, 0, \ldots \rangle$; the $i$ on top of $d$ indicates from which component $D_i$ the element $d$ comes from. A command producing this symbol can be defined by

```
\newcommand{\vct}[2]{\langle \dotsc, 0, \dotsc,
    \overset{#1}{#2}, \dotsc, 0, \dotsc \rangle}
```

So to print $\langle \ldots, 0, \ldots, \overset{i}{d}, \ldots, 0, \ldots \rangle$, we type \vct{i}{d}.

**10-1.2. Redefining commands.** $\mathcal{AMS}$-LaTeX makes sure that you do not define inadvertently a new command with the name of an existing command. To test this, define

```
\newcommand{\vct}{vct}
```

You get the error message

```
! Command name 'vct' already used.
\@latexerr ....}\errmessage {#1}
```

```
1.40 \newcommand{\vct}{vct}
```

To redefine \vct, use the command \renewcommand:

```
\renewcommand{\vct}{vct}
```

You can use \renewcommand to redefine the way $\mathcal{AMS}$-LaTeX was programmed to do things. For instance, the end of proof symbol is \qedsymbol. To change that to the symbol many people prefer, \blacksquare, issue the command:

```
\renewcommand{\qedsymbol}{\( \blacksquare \)}
```

$\mathcal{AMS}$-LaTeX checks only the syntax of a command when the command is read. Other mistakes will not be found until the command is used. For instance, the symbol \blacksquare can only be used in math mode. If you define

```
\renewcommand{\qedsymbol}{\blacksquare}%Mistake!
```

$\mathcal{AMS}$-LaTeX will accept the definition. But when you try to use a pf environment, you will get the message:

```
! Missing $ inserted.
<inserted text>
                $
...
```

```
1.27 \end{pf}
```

**Tip.** Use the command \renewcommand very sparingly. Make sure that you know the consequences of redefining the command. Redefining $\mathcal{AMS}$-LaTeX commands may cause $\mathcal{AMS}$-LaTeX to behave in unexpected ways, or in fact to crash altogether.

**10-1.3. Showing the origin of commands.** If you are defining a new command with \newcommand, and an error message advises that the command name is already in use, then it is useful to find out who defined the command and what is its meaning. For instance, in article2.tex (see the DISK and Section 11-3) we define the new command:

```
\newcommand{\vct}[2]{\v<\dotsc, 0, \dotsc,\overset{#1}{#2},
    \dotsc, 0, \dotsc>}% special vector
```

It would have been more logical to call this new command \vec. If you do, you get the error message

```
! Command name 'vec' already used.
\@latexerr ....}\errmessage {#1}


1.40     \dotsc, 0, \dotsc>}
                        % special vector
```

So who defined \vec?

Get into interactive mode with the ∗ prompt (see Sections 1-3.6 and 1-4.4), type \show \vec:

```
*\show \vec


> \vec=macro:
->\mathaccent "017E .
<*> \show \vec
```

informing you that \vec is a macro, and it is a math accent; see Sections 4-8 and A-11. Now try \hangafter (see Section 3-7.2):

```
*\show \hangafter


> \hangafter=\hangafter.
<*> \show \hangafter
```

The response indicates that \hangafter is a primitive command, defined in TEX itself. Redefining a primitive command does not seem like such a good idea.

We try one more command, \medskip (see Section 3-8.2) to find out how big it is:

```
*\show \medskip


> \medskip=macro:
->\vspace \medskipamount .
```

This indicates that the amount is in \medskipamount. So let us use \show to ask what \medskipamount is:

```
*\show \medskipamount


> \medskipamount=\skip14.
```

which does not give much information. In fact, \medskipamount is different from
the commands we have seen so far; it is a *parameter*, containing the amount of skip
\medskip will do. We ask for the meaning of such a parameter with the command
\showthe:

```
*\showthe \medskipamount
```

```
> 6.0pt plus 2.0pt minus 2.0pt.
```

So \medskip is a vertical space of 6pt.

$\mathcal{AMS}$-LaTeX has hundreds of registers containing numbers, and parameters containing integers (such as 3), dimensions (such as 0.1pt), or distances written in the form
6.0pt plus 2.0pt minus 2.0pt (so called *glues*; see Section C-2.2). Use \showthe for
all these.

## 10-2. User-defined environments

User-defined commands are brand new commands. *User-defined environments*, as
a rule, **modify** existing environments.

The simplest application of user-defined environments is to rename environments.
If you are not comfortable with pf but would prefer proof, define

```
\newenvironment{proof}{ \begin{pf} }{ \end{pf} }
```

and then

```
\begin{proof}
\end{proof}
```

will bracket your proofs.

The general form of \newenvironment is

```
\newenvironment{name}{begin text}{end text}
```

where begin text should contain a \begin{oldname} and end text should contain \end{oldname}, where oldname is the name of the modified environment.

For instance, the command,

```
\newenvironment{proof}{ \begin{pf} \em }{ \end{pf} }
```

defines the proof environment which typesets the proof in emphasized style. Note
that the scope of \em is the special braces provided by the environment.

If an error shows up in such a user-defined environment, the message refers to the
environment that was modified. For instance, if you misspell pf as prf when you
define

```
\newenvironment{proof}{ \begin{prf} \em }{ \end{pf} }
```

then at the first use of proof you get the message:

```
! Environment prf undefined.
\@latexerr ....}\errmessage {#1}
```

```
...
```

```
l.26 \begin{proof}
```

Or if you define:

`\newenvironment{proof}{\begin{pf} \em}{\end{prf}}`

at the first use of proof you get the message:

```
! \begin{pf} ended by \end{prf}.
\@latexerr ....}\errmessage {#1}
```

```
...
```

`1.27 \end{proof}`

`\newenvironment` can have arguments; they can only be used in the begin text. Here is a typical example:

`\newenvironment{ThmRef}[1]{ \begin{Thm}\label{T:#1} }{ \end{Thm} }`

which is invoked with

```
\begin{ThmRef}{label}
\end{ThmRef}
```

`ThmRef` is a modification of the `Thm` environment, defined in the Preamble; see Section 5-2. It is a `Thm` that can be Referenced (of course, with the command `\ref`). `ThmRef` invokes the `Thm` environment and defines `T:label` to be the label for the theorem for cross-referencing. See Section 11-2 for an enhanced version.

Some environments (for instance, `equation`) cannot be modified.

**Tip**. Do not give a new environment the name of a command/macro. For instance, if you define

```
\newenvironment{small}
   {\tiny}
   {\relax}
```

then you get the error message:

```
LaTeX error.  See LaTeX manual for explanation.
            Type  H <return>  for immediate help.
! Command name 'small' already used.
\@latexerr ....}\errmessage {#1}
```

```
...
```

`1.21    {\tiny}`

Next we present two examples of user-defined environments that are not modifications of $\mathcal{AMS}$-LaTeX environments. Recall the command `\samepage` from Section 3-7.3. Now define:

```
\newenvironment{together}
   {\par \samepage}
   {\par}
```

The `together` environment allows you to designate paragraphs that have to be on the same page.

Recall that a newly defined command remains effective only within its scope (see Section 3-3.1). Now suppose that you want to define some commands to be used only in a few paragraphs. Of course, you can place braces around these paragraphs or define

```
\newenvironment{exception}
    {\relax}
    {\relax}
```

and then

```
\begin{exception}
    new commands
    text
\end{exception}
```

stands out better than a pair of braces.

The `\relax` means "do nothing"; we placed it in the definition to make it more readable.

### 10-3.  Custom format files

At some point, you will have a great deal of experience writing your own articles, and will probably be annoyed at how long it takes $\mathcal{A}\mathcal{M}\mathcal{S}$-L#TEX to process the line

```
\documentstyle[amscd,amssymb,verbatim]{amsart}
```

Type the file:

```
\input lplain
\documentstyle[amscd,amssymb,verbatim]{amsart}
```

and call it cform.tex (you can find this file on the DISK). Now make an $\mathcal{A}\mathcal{M}\mathcal{S}$-L#TEX format file (see Section 1-3.3 and Section 1-4.2) starting not with the file lplain.tex but with the file cform.tex. Name this format file amsart. (For the **PC**, amsart.fmt.)

In your article, comment out the line

```
\documentstyle[amscd,amssymb,verbatim]{amsart}
```

to read

```
%\documentstyle[amscd,amssymb,verbatim]{amsart}
```

and add the comment:

```
%Typeset with amsart format file.
```

as a reminder.

Now if you work with a **PC** implementation of TEX, you typeset the article, say test.tex, with

```
tex &amsart test
```

or you modify the batch file, t.bat (see Section 1-3.4) to read

```
tex &amsart %1
```

and then you can typeset test.tex with

```
t test
```

If you work on a **Mac** with TEXTURES, simply select the amsart format, and typeset test.tex. You will be surprised at the speed of the typesetting. In fact, the second typesetting will be even faster, because TEXTURES keeps the format file amsart in memory.

Before you submit the article for publication, undo these changes. The editor of the journal does not have the amsart format file.

Of course, you can make lots of other format files. For instance, if you use macros02.tex in every article (see Section 11-2), add a last line

```
\input{macros02.tex}
```

to cform.tex. (Note that macros02.tex is in braces.) Then your standard macros are in the format file, and they do not have to be \input-ed with the article.

You may make a separate format file for transparencies by changing the line

```
\documentstyle[amscd,amssymb,verbatim]{amsart}
```

in cform.tex to

```
\documentstyle[amscd,amssymb,verbatim,12pt]{amsart}
```

You find this file on the DISK under the name cform12.tex. The format file this creates typesets in 12pt size, suitable for transparencies.

# CHAPTER 11

# T*E*X Macros

There are some tasks that cannot be accomplished in *AMS*-L*A*T*E*X but can easily be done with T*E*X macros. Since *AMS*-L*A*T*E*X allows us to mix *AMS*-L*A*T*E*X commands and T*E*X macros, we learn some applications of T*E*X macros in this chapter.

*AMS*-L*A*T*E*X is all about automatic numbering. In the last section, we take up this topic in a bit more detail.

This is not an introduction to T*E*X; we only cover a very few topics of immediate use to us. For more about T*E*X, consult the references discussed in Appendix G.

### 11-1. Macros in T*E*X

*AMS*-L*A*T*E*X makes the definition of a new command safe, but it loses some of the flexibility T*E*X provides.

**11-1.1. Macro definition.** T*E*X defines a new command, which we call a *macro*, with one of several commands. We start with \def (and give a few examples of \let and one example of \chardef later). The first command we defined in Section 10-1:

```
\newcommand{\ra}{\rightarrow}
```

is done in T*E*X as follows

```
\def\ra{\rightarrow}
```

Instead of \newcommand we write \def, and the new macro defined **is not in braces**.

T*E*X does not check whether the new macro name is already in use, so \def serves as \renewcommand (see Section 11-1.2) as well.

**Tip**. The responsibility is **yours** when you rename a macro with \def.

**11-1.2. Renaming macros.** \newcommand can be used to provide shorthand for long command names, or simply renaming commands.

To rename \operatornamewithlimits simply as \ol:

```
\newcommand{\ol}{\operatornamewithlimits}
```

However, this does not work out if you want to rename a command, and use the old name for some new task. For instance, some like to have one letter commands available for often used symbols. Unfortunately, many of the one letter commands are reserved for quaint accents; for instance, \u is used for the accent in ŏ; see Sections 3-4.6 and B-2. To rename this accent \au so that \u becomes available for other command names, use the form:

`\let\au=\u`

Now \au is the accent, and \u is available for redefinition; see Section 11-2.

**11-1.3. A special macro.** There are many macros that can only be defined in TEX. For instance, if you want to typeset the symbol \, you need a special macro because of the role played by \ in TEX. The following macro defines \ as the macro \bslash in the typewriter style:

`\chardef\bslash='\\ % p. 424, TeXbook backslash`

Now {\tt \bslash} prints \. (Without \tt, \bslash prints ".)

**11-1.4. Delimited macros.** In Section 10-1.1, we defined a command with three arguments for typing congruences:

`\newcommand{\con}[3]{#1 \equiv #2 \pod{#3}}`

And then \( \con{a}{b}{\theta} \) prints: $a \equiv b \ (\theta)$. This saves a lot of typing, but it does not make it easier to read the source file. We can use *delimited macros* to make the manuscript easier to read.

Let us start with a simple example; we define a macro for vectors:

`\def\v<#1>{\langle #1 \rangle}`

\v is the name of the macro; it has one argument: #1. When invoked it will print the delimiter ⟨, then the argument, then the delimiter ⟩.

Note that in the definition of \v, the argument is delimited by < and >. When the macro is invoked, **the argument must be delimited the same way**.

So for the vector $\langle a, b \rangle$ you invoke \v with

`\v<a, b>`

which looks like a vector.

You have to be careful with delimited macros, because the space rules (see Section 3-2 and Section 4-4.1) do not hold; both in the definition and in the invocation space is a regular character. So if in the definition

`\def\v< #1>{\langle #1 \rangle}`

there is a space before #1, then \( \v<a, b> \) gives the error message:

`! Use of \v doesn't match its definition.`
`l.11 A vector \( \v<a`
`                    , b> \)`

which is clear enough. Now if the space is on the other side:

`\def\v<#1 >{\langle #1 \rangle}`

the error message is:

```
Runaway argument?
a, b> \) \end {document}
! File ended while scanning use of \v.
<inserted text>
                \par
```

or

```
! Something's wrong--perhaps a missing \item.
\@latexerr ....}\errmessage {#1}
```

or something else ...

Anyhow, the moral is that if you use delimited macros, be very careful that the invocation completely matches the definition.

Now the congruence example:

```
\def\con#1=#2(#3){#1 \equiv #2 \pod{#3}}%
```

So \( \con a=b(\theta) \) prints: $a \equiv b\ (\theta)$. For me, \con a=b(\theta) looks like a congruence, and it is easy to read.

There is only one catch. Suppose that you want to type the formula

$$x = a \equiv b \quad (\theta)$$

If you type \( \con x=a=b(\theta) \), then it will print $x \equiv a = b\ (\theta)$. Indeed, the first argument is delimited on the right by =; hence the first argument is x. The second argument is delimited by = and (; hence the second argument is a=b. In such cases, to help TEX find the correct first argument, type

```
\( \con  {x=a}=b(\theta) \)
```

In Section 3-3, we discussed the problem of typing a command such as \TeX in the form: \TeX\␣ (where ␣ is the space character obtained by pressing the spacebar) so that TEX will be typeset as a separate word. The problem is that if we just type \TeX, then TEX is merged with the next word, and there is no error message. A solution is to define such commands with a delimited macro:

```
\def\tex/{\TeX}
```

Now to get TEX, type \tex/; if a space is needed after it, then type \tex/␣. And if you forget the closing /, you get an error message.

**11-1.5. A label printing macro.** In the Command section of the Preamble of the sample article, article2.tex (see the DISK and Section 11-3), there is the line

```
%\ShowLabelsfalse% comment this out if labels should be printed
```

If this line is not touched, the labels marking the sections, theorems, equations, and so on, are printed on the margin. The macro doing this (contained in macros02.tex) is listed now:

```
\newif\ifShowLabels
\ShowLabelstrue
\newdimen\theight
\def\TeXref#1{%by M. Doob
    \leavevmode\vadjust{\setbox0=\hbox{{\tt
        \quad\quad  {\small \rm #1}}}%
    \theight=\ht0
    \advance\theight by \dp0
    \advance\theight by \lineskip
    \kern -\theight \vbox to
    \theight{\rightline{\rlap{\box0}}%
     \vss}%
     }}%
```

The first line defines \ShowLabels as an entity that can be set True or False. The next line sets it True. The next eight lines define the macro \TeXref, which prints its argument on the margin.

These macros are used in \SecRef, \SSecRef, \ThmRef, and so on. For instance, \SecRef (section with reference) is defined in macros02.tex as follows:

```
\newcommand{\SecRef}[2]{\section{#1}\label{S:#2}%
    \ifShowLabels \TeXref{{S:#2}} \fi}
```

which defines the section title and the label, then a simple conditional

```
\ifShowLabels
```

decides whether \TeXRef prints the label.

We shall not discuss the macro \TeXref; this would require a discussion of programming in TₑX which is beyond the scope of this book; see Section G-2.

### 11-2. A sample macro file

We give here a commented version of the macro file, macros02.tex (which you can find on the DISK). Macros, of course, are a matter of individual need and taste. This file is not presented for your use; we hope, however, that this model will help you to develop one of your own.

Commands/macros should be *mnemonic*; if you cannot easily remember one, rename it. They should be easily recalled even after weeks and months. This implies that you cannot have too large a command/macro file unless you have an unusual ability to recall abbreviations.

To avoid confusion, command/macro files should seldom be changed. Make sure that the name of the macro file reflects the version number, and that your article contains the information which macro file is to be used.

The macro file macros02.tex:

```
% Macros for AMS-LaTeX
% Version 02
```

```
% February 1991
```

The first section makes all the one-letter commands available for our use. Note that all the new accent commands start with \a.

```
% Accents
    \let\au=\u% breve accent
    \let\av=\v% check accent
    \let\aH=\H% long umlaut accent
    \let\aB=\B% bar accent
    \let\ab=\b% bar under accent
    \let\aD=\D% dot accent
    \let\ad=\d% dot under accent
    \let\ac=\c% cedilla accent
    \let\ai=\i% dotless i
    \let\aj=\j% dotless j
    \let\at=\t% tie accent
    \let\al=\l% Polish l
    \let\aL=\L% Polish L
    \let\ao=\o% Scandinavian slashed o
    \let\aO=\O% Scandinavian slashed O
```

While before the accents worked as in Section B-2, after these redefinitions, for instance, the Polish l becomes \al, the Hungarian umlaut is \aH, so Erd\H os becomes Erd\aH os, and prints Erdős.

Since the author of this book works in lattice theory, some of these one letter commands are utilized for lattice operations. For every "small" operation there is a corresponding "big" one using a capitalized name.

```
% Lattice operations
    \renewcommand{\j}{\vee}% join
    \newcommand{\m}{\wedge}% meet
    \newcommand{\J}{\bigvee}% big join
    \newcommand{\M}{\bigwedge}% big meet

% Set operations
    \renewcommand{\u}{\cup}% union; original breve accent
    \renewcommand{\i}{\cap}% intersection; original dotless i
    \newcommand{\U}{\bigcup}% big union
    \newcommand{\I}{\bigcap}% big intersection

% Sets
    \newcommand{\ci}{\subseteq}% contained in with equality
    \newcommand{\nc}{\nsubseteq}% not \ci
    \newcommand{\nci}{\nc}% not \ci
    \newcommand{\ce}{\supseteq}% containing with equality
```

```
\newcommand{\nce}{\nsupseteq}% not \ce
\newcommand{\nin}{\notin}% not of membership \in
\newcommand{\es}{\varnothing}% the empty set
\newcommand{\set}[1]{ \{ #1 \} }% set, invoke with \set{...}
\def\v<#1>{\langle #1 \rangle}% vector e.g.: \v<A;F>
```

```
% Partial ordering
    \newcommand{\nle}{\nleq}% not \le
```

```
% Text
    \renewcommand{\t}{\text}
    \newcommand{\tif}{\t{if }}
    \newcommand{\tin}{\t{in }}
    \newcommand{\tiff}{\t{iff }}
    \newcommand{\tand}{\t{and }}
    \newcommand{\tbut}{\t{but }}
    \newcommand{\tor}{\t{or }}
    \newcommand{\tfor}{\t{for }}
    \newcommand{\toth}{\t{otherwise}}
    \newcommand{\tthen}{\t{then }}
    \newcommand{\twith}{\t{with }}
```

So a \j b prints $a \vee b$, A \ci B prints $A \subseteq B$, and so on. Note that the original commands are not redefined; if your co-author prefers a \vee b for $a \vee b$, it is still available.

Note that we can use \v for a vector because we freed it up as an accent.

With the command \set we type the set $\{a, b\}$ as \set{a, b} which is easy to read. Similarly, we type the vector $\langle a, b \rangle$ as \v<a, b>, so it looks like a vector.

The text commands give abbreviations to text that have to be inserted often in math formulas.

Next we map the Greek letters to the keyboard. Note that \g starts a lowercase and \G starts an uppercase letter. For some Greek letters, I prefer to use the variants, a matter of individual taste.

```
% Greek letters
    \newcommand{\ga}{\alpha}
    \newcommand{\gb}{\beta}
    \newcommand{\gc}{\chi}
    \newcommand{\gd}{\delta}
    \renewcommand{\ge}{\varepsilon}% use \geq for >=
    \newcommand{\gf}{\varphi}
    \renewcommand{\gg}{\gamma}% old use >>
    \newcommand{\gh}{\eta}
    \newcommand{\gi}{\iota}
    \newcommand{\gj}{\theta}
```

```
\newcommand{\gk}{\kappa}
\newcommand{\gl}{\lambda}
\newcommand{\gm}{\mu}
\newcommand{\gn}{\nu}
\newcommand{\go}{\omega}
\newcommand{\gp}{\pi}
\newcommand{\gq}{\theta}
\newcommand{\gr}{\varrho}
\newcommand{\gs}{\sigma}
\newcommand{\gt}{\tau}
\newcommand{\gu}{\upsilon}
\newcommand{\gv}{\vartheta}
\newcommand{\gw}{\omega}
\newcommand{\gx}{\xi}
\newcommand{\gy}{\psi}
\newcommand{\gz}{\zeta}

\newcommand{\gC}{\Xi}
\newcommand{\gG}{\Gamma}
\newcommand{\gD}{\Delta}
\newcommand{\gF}{\Phi}
\newcommand{\gL}{\Lambda}
\newcommand{\gO}{\Omega}
\newcommand{\gP}{\Pi}
\newcommand{\gQ}{\Theta}
\newcommand{\gS}{\Sigma}
\newcommand{\gU}{\Upsilon}
\newcommand{\gW}{\Omega}
\newcommand{\gX}{\Xi}
\newcommand{\gY}{\Psi}
```

All the other math fonts are commands with arguments; the command is a single uppercase letter: \B for bold, \C for Calligraphic, \D for blackboard bold (double), \E for Euler script, \F for Fraktur (German Gothic); see Section 4-13.1.

```
% Math fonts
\newcommand{\B}[1]{{\bold#1}}% Bold math
\newmathalphabet*{\Bi}{cmm}{b}{it}% Bold math italic
\newcommand{\C}[1]{{\cal#1}}% Calligraphic - only caps
\newcommand{\D}[1]{{\Bbb#1}}%
    % Doubled - blackboard bold - only caps
\newmathalphabet*{\E}{eus}{m}{n}
    % Euler script - only caps
\newcommand{\F}[1]{{\frak#1}}% Fraktur
```

And some others:

```
% Misc.
    \newcommand{\nl}{\newline}
    \newcommand{\ol}{\overline}
    \newcommand{\ul}{\underline}
    \newcommand{\SS}{\S \S}% Sections
    \def\con#1=#2(#3){#1\equiv#2\pod{#3}}
        % congruence: \con a=b(\gQ)
    \newcommand{\q}{\quad}
    \newcommand{\qq}{\qquad}
    \renewcommand{\rm}{\normalshape}%
        % redefining \rm to mean: change to roman style
```

Finally, the $\mathcal{AMS}$-LATEX specific macros:

```
% Labeling macros
\newif\ifShowLabels
\ShowLabelstrue
\newdimen\theight
\def\TeXref#1{%
    \leavevmode\vadjust{\setbox0=\hbox{{\tt
        \quad\quad  {\small \rm #1}}}%
    \theight=\ht0
    \advance\theight by \dp0
    \advance\theight by \lineskip
    \kern -\theight \vbox to
    \theight{\rightline{\rlap{\box0}}%
    \vss}%
    }}%


% Section titles that can be referenced
\newcommand{\SecRef}[2]{\section{#1}\label{S:#2}%
    \ifShowLabels \TeXref{{S:#2}} \fi}
\newcommand{\SSecRef}[2]{\subsection{#1}\label{SS:#2}%
    \ifShowLabels \TeXref{{SS:#2}} \fi}


% Referencing sections and declarations
    \newcommand{\refS}[1]{Section ~\ref{S:#1}}
    \newcommand{\refSS}[1]{Section ~\ref{SS:#1}}
    \newcommand{\refT}[1]{Theorem ~\ref{T:#1}}
    \newcommand{\refL}[1]{Lemma ~\ref{L:#1}}
    \newcommand{\refD}[1]{Definition ~\ref{D:#1}}
    \newcommand{\refC}[1]{Corollary ~\ref{C:#1}}


% New environments for declarations that can be referenced
```

```
\newenvironment{ThmRef}[1]%
    { \begin{Thm} \label{T:#1} \ifShowLabels \TeXref{T:#1} \fi }%
    { \end{Thm} }

\newenvironment{DefRef}[1]%
    { \begin{Def} \label{D:#1} \ifShowLabels \TeXref{D:#1} \fi }%
    { \end{Def} }

\newenvironment{LemRef}[1]%
    { \begin{Lem} \label{L:#1} \ifShowLabels \TeXref{L:#1} \fi }%
    { \end{Lem} }

\newenvironment{CorRef}[1]%
    { \begin{Cor} \label{L:#1} \ifShowLabels \TeXref{C:#1} \fi }%
    { \end{Cor} }

\newcommand{\EqRef}[1]%
    { \ifShowLabels \TeXref{E:#1} \fi
      \begin{equation} \label{E:#1} }

% Misc. environments
  \newenvironment{together}% To keep lines on same page
  {\par \samepage}%
  {\par}
```

The section titles are commands with two arguments:

`\SecRef{title}{label}`

The Theorem environment `\ThmRef` is invoked with

`\begin{ThmRef}{label}`

and concluded with

`\end{ThmRef}`

Equations are handled slightly differently. They are introduced with the command:

`\EqRef{label}`

and ended with

`\end{equation}`

Sections and declarations are referenced with `\refX{label}`, where X is S for sections, SS for subsections, T for Theorem, L for Lemma, D for definition, and C for Corollary.

To keep paragraphs on the same page, enclose them within `\begin{together}` and `\end{together}`.

## 11-3. Sample article with macros

The use of these commands and macros is illustrated in article2.tex (see the DISK) which is a rewriting of article1.tex with these macros:

```
% Sample file: article2.tex
% The sample article with macros
% Typeset with AMSLaTeX format file

% Preamble
% Style section
   \documentstyle[amscd,amssymb,verbatim]{amsart}

% Declaration section
   \theoremstyle{plain}
   \newtheorem{Thm}{Theorem}
   \newtheorem{Cor}{Corollary}
   \newtheorem{Main}{Main Theorem}
   \renewcommand{\theMain}{}
   \newtheorem{Lem}{Lemma}
   \newtheorem{Prop}{Proposition}

   \theoremstyle{definition}
   \newtheorem{Def}{Definition}

   \theoremstyle{remark}
   \newtheorem{notation}{Notation}
   \renewcommand{\thenotation}{}

% Command section
   \errorcontextlines=0
   \input{macros02}
   %\ShowLabelsfalse% comment this out if labels should be printed

% Commands for this article
   \newcommand{\Jm}[2]{\J( #1 \mid #2  )}%
      % big join with middle used as: \Jm{a}{a < 2}
   \newcommand{\setm}[2]{ \{  #1 \mid #2  \}}
      % set with a middle used as: \setm{a}{a < 2}
   \newcommand{\Prodm}[2]{\gP(  #1 \mid #2  )}
      % product with a middle
   \newcommand{\Prodsm}[2]{\gP^{*}(  #1 \mid #2  )}
   \newcommand{\vct}[2]{\v<\dotsc, 0, \dotsc,\overset{#1}{#2},
   \dotsc, 0, \dotsc>}% special vector
```

```
    \newcommand{\fp}{\t{\( \F p \)}}% fraktur p
    \newcommand{\Ds}{ \t{\( D^{\langle 2 \rangle} \)} }

\begin{document}

% Topmatter
\title[Complete-simple distributive lattices]%
    {A construction of complete-simple\\
    distributive lattices}
\author{G.~ A.~ Menuhin}
\address{Computer Science Department\\
    University of Winebago \\
    Winebago, Minnesota 23714}
\email{menuhin@@ccw.uwinebago.edu}
\thanks{Research supported by the NSF under grant number ~23466.}
\keywords{Complete lattice, distributive lattice, complete
    congruence, congruence lattice}
\subjclass{Primary: 06B10; Secondary: 06D05}
\date{March 15, 1991}

\begin{abstract}
    In this note we prove that there exist {\em complete-simple
    distributive lattices}, that is, complete distributive
    lattices in which there are only two complete congruences.
\end{abstract}
% End topmatter
\maketitle

\SecRef{Introduction}{intro}
In this note we prove the following result:

\begin{Main}
    There exists an infinite complete distributive lattice
    \( K \) with only the two trivial complete  congruence
    relations.
\end{Main}

\SecRef{The \Ds\ construction}{Ds}
For the basic notation in lattice theory and universal algebra,
see F.~ R.~ Richard\-son \cite{fR82} and G.~ A.~ Menuhin
\cite{gM68}.  We start with a definition:
```

```
\begin{DefRef}{prime}
    Let \( V \) be a complete lattice, and let \( \fp = [u, v] \)
    be an interval of \( V \).  Then \fp\ is called {\em
    complete-prime\/} if the following three conditions are
    satisfied:

    (M)  \( u \) is meet-irreducible but \( u \) is\/ {\em not}
         completely meet-irreducible;

    (J) \( v \) is join-irreducible but \( v \) is\/ {\em not}
        completely join-irreducible;

    (C) \( [u, v] \) is a complete-simple lattice.
\end{DefRef}


Now we prove

\begin{LemRef}{ds}
    Let \( D \) be a complete distributive lattice satisfying
    Conditions {\rm (M)} and  {\rm (J)}.   Then \( \Ds \) is a
    sublattice of \( D^{2} \), hence \( \Ds \) is a lattice, and
    \Ds\ is  a complete distributive lattice satisfying
    Conditions  {\rm (M)} and {\rm (J)}.
\end{LemRef}

\begin{pf}
    By  Conditions  (M) and (J), \Ds\ is a sublattice of
    \( D^{2} \).  Hence, \Ds is a lattice.

    Since \Ds\ is a sublattice of a distributive lattice, \Ds\ is
    a distributive lattice.  Using the characterization of
    standard ideals in E.~T.~Moynahan \cite{eM57}, obviously,
    \Ds\ has a zero and a unit element, namely,
    \( \v<0, 0> \) and \( \v<1, 1> \).  To show that \Ds\ is
    complete, let \( \es \ne A \ci \Ds \), and let \( a = \J A \)
    in \( D^{2} \).  If \( a \in \Ds \), then
    \( a = \J A \) in \Ds.  Otherwise, \( a \) is of the form
    \( \v<b, 1> \) for some  \( b \in D \), \( b < 1 \).  Then
    \( \J A = \v<1, 1> \) in \( D^{2} \).
    The dual argument shows that \( \M A \) also exists in
    \( D^{2} \).  Hence \( D \) is complete. Conditions (M) and (J)
    are obvious for \Ds.
\end{pf}
```

```
\begin{CorRef}{prime}
   If \( D \) is complete-prime, then so is \Ds.
\end{CorRef}
```

```
The motivation for the following result comes from S.-K. Foo
\cite{sF90}.
```

```
\begin{LemRef}{ccr}
   Let \( \gQ \) be a complete congruence relation of \Ds\ such
   that
   \EqRef{rigid}
      \con{\v<1, d>}={\v<1, 1>}(\gQ),
   \end{equation}
   for some \( d \in D \), \( d < 1 \). Then \( \gQ = \gi \).
\end{LemRef}
```

```
\begin{pf}
   Let \( \gQ \) be a complete congruence relation  of \Ds\
   satisfying \eqref{E:rigid}. Then \( \gQ = \gi \).
\end{pf}
```

```
\SecRef{The \( \gP^{*} \) construction}{P*}
The following construction is crucial in our proof of the Main
Theorem:
```

```
\begin{DefRef}{P*}
   Let \( D_{i} \), \( i \in I \), be complete distributive
   lattices satisfying Condition (J).  Their \( \gP^{*} \)
   product is defined as follows:
   \[
      \Prodsm{ D_{i} }{i \in I} = \Prodm{ D_{i}^{-} }{i \in I} +1;
   \]
   that is, \( \Prodsm{ D_{i} }{i \in I} \) is
   \( \Prodm{ D_{i}^{-} }{i \in I} \) with a new unit element.
\end{DefRef}
```

```
\begin{notation}
   If \( i \in I \) and \( d \in D_{i}^{-} \), then
   \[
      \vct{i}{d}
   \]
   is the element of \( \Prodsm{ D_{i} }{i \in I} \) whose
```

```
   \( i \)-th component is \( d \) and all the other
   components are \( 0 \).
\end{notation}


See also  E.~T.~Moynahan \cite{eM57a}.


Now we can prove:


\begin{ThmRef}{P*}
   Let \( D_{i} \), \( i \in I \), be complete distributive
   lattices satisfying Condition {\rm (J)}.  Let \( \gQ \) be a
   complete congruence relation on
   \( \Prodsm{ D_{i} }{i \in I} \).  If there exists an
   \( i \in I \) and a \( d \in D_{i} \) with \( d < 1_{i} \) such
   that for all  \( d \le c < 1_{i} \),
   \EqRef{}
      \con\vct{i}{d}=\vct{i}{c}(\gQ),
   \end{equation}
   then \( \gQ = \gi \).
\end{ThmRef}


\begin{pf}
   Since
   \EqRef{cong2}
      \con\vct{i}{d}=\vct{i}{c}(\gQ),
   \end{equation}
   and \( \gQ \) is a complete congruence relation, it follows
   from Condition (C) that
   \begin{align}\label{E:cong}
      &\con{\vct{i}{d}}=\notag\\
      &\qq\qq\q{\Jm{\vct{i}{c}}{d \le c < 1}=1}(\gQ).
   \end{align}
   Let \( j \in I \), \( j \neq i \), and let
   \( a \in D_{j}^{-}\).  Meeting both sides of the congruence
   \eqref{E:cong} with \( \vct{j}{a} \), we obtain
   \begin{align}\label{E:comp}
       0 = &\vct{i}{d} \m \vct{j}{a} \equiv \\
           &\vct{j}{a}\pod{\gQ}, \notag
   \end{align}
   Using the completeness of \( \gQ \) and \eqref{E:comp}, we
   get:
   \EqRef{cong3}
      \con 0=\Jm{ \vct{j}{a} }{ a \in D_{j}^{-} }=1(\gQ),
```

```
   \end{equation}
   hence \( \gQ = \gi \).
\end{pf}

\begin{ThmRef}{P*a}
   Let \( D_{i} \), \( i \in I \), be complete distributive
   lattices satisfying
   Conditions  {\rm (J)} and {\rm (C)}.  Then
   \( \Prodsm{ D_{i} }{i \in I} \) also satisfies Conditions
   {\rm (J)} and {\rm (C)}.
\end{ThmRef}

\begin{pf}
   Let \( \gQ \) be a complete congruence on
   \( \Prodsm{ D_{i} }{i \in I} \). Let \( i \in I \).  Define
   \EqRef{dihat}
      \widehat{D}_{i} = \setm{ \vct{i}{d} }{ d \in D_{i}^{-} }
         \u \set{1}.
   \end{equation}
   Then \( \widehat{D}_{i} \)  is a complete sublattice of
   \( \Prodsm{ D_{i} }{i \in I} \), and  \( \widehat{D}_{i} \)
   is isomorphic to \( D_{i} \).  Let \( \gQ_{i} \) be the
   restriction of \( \gQ \) to \( \widehat{D}_{i} \).  Since
   \( D_{i} \) is complete-simple, so is
   \( \widehat{D}_{i} \),
   hence \( \gQ_{i} \) is \( \go \) or \( \gi \).  If
   \( \gQ_{i} = \go \) for all \( i \in I \), then
   \( \gQ = \go \).
   If there is an \( i \in I \), such that  \( \gQ_{i} = \gi \),
   then \( \con 0=1(\gQ) \), hence \( \gQ = \gi \).
\end{pf}

The Main Theorem easily follows from Theorems \ref{T:P*} and
\ref{T:P*a}.

\bibliographystyle{amsplain}
\bibliography{article2}

\end{document}
```

**11-4. Numbering**

**11-4.1. Counters.** $\mathcal{A}_{\mathcal{M}}\mathcal{S}$-LATEX generates numbers for equations, sections, theorems, and so on, automatically. Each such number is associated with a *counter*:

```
equation  footnote  figure      page            table
part      section   subsection  subsubsection
enumi     enumii    enumiii     enumiv
```

All are self-explanatory; the third line shows that you can use four levels of enumerated environments. In addition, for every declaration name, there is a counter called name.

These counters are handled by $\mathcal{A}_{\mathcal{M}}\mathcal{S}$-LATEX: initialized and incremented. But sometimes you may want to manipulate them yourself. Here is an example. We work on a book with a number of chapters (using the amsbook style which also provides chapters; see Section G-1.1). The main document book.tex contains the lines:

```
\include{intro}
\include{ch1}
\include{ch2}

. . .
```

When working on Chapter 3, add the line

```
\includonly{ch3}
```

as explained in Section 3-11.2. This will process Chapter 3 only; however, any time the book is typeset, all the aux files will be read, and at the end, written out. An alternate strategy is to have a file book3.tex containing the lines

```
\setcounter{chapter}{2}
\include{ch3}
```

and then the chapter will be properly numbered. We can also set

```
\setcounter{page}{31}
```

if the first page of Chapter 3 is supposed to be 31.

The command for setting a counter is \setcounter. A number is generated by $\mathcal{A}_{\mathcal{M}}\mathcal{S}$-LATEX by incrementing the appropriate counter; so if you want Chapter 3, you set the chapter counter to 2. The only exception is the page number, which is first used to number the current page, and then incremented.

```
\newcounter{numb}
```

makes numb a new counter. You can use an optional argument:

```
\newcounter{numb}[sec]
```

which will reset numb to 0 whenever sec changes value.

```
\stepcounter{numb}
```

increments the counter; use the form

```
\refstepcounter{sec}
```

to increment the counter and set to 0 all the counters that were defined with the optional argument sec.

You can do more complicated arithmetic with

```
\setcounter{counter}{number}
\addtocounter{counter}{number}
```

The value of the counter numb can be used with

```
\thenumb
```

Setting one counter numb equal to the value of another one oldnumb:

```
\setcounter{numb}{\value{oldnumb}}
```

Here is a typical example. As is customary, you may want your Theorems (the Thm environment) followed by Corollaries (the Cor environment) always starting with Corollary 1. So you have Theorem 1 followed by Corollary 1, Corollary 2, Corollary 3. Next comes Theorem 2. The Corollary would be numbered Corollary 4. To avoid this, precede the Corollary with the command:

```
\setcounter{theCor}{0}
```

Would you want the equations to be numbered from 1 in Part II? At the beginning of Part II issue the command

```
\setcounter{equation}{0}
```

Two counters control which sectional units are numbered (secnumdepth) and which are listed in the Table of Contents (tocdepth). For instance,

```
\setcounter{secnumdepth}{2}
```

sets secnumdepth to 2. As a result, sections and subsections are numbered, but subsubsections are not. This command must be placed in the Preamble of the article; preferably, in the Command section.

**11-4.2. Counter styles.** The counter numb can be displayed with the command

```
\thenumb
```

in five different styles:

        **arabic:** \arabic{numb} (1, 2, ... )
        **lowercase roman:** \roman{numb} (i, ii, ... )
        **uppercase roman:** \Roman{numb} (I, II, ... )
        **lowercase letters:** \alph{numb} (a, b, ... , z)
        **uppercase letters:** \Alph{numb} (A, B, ... , Z)

The default is arabic. For instance, to set the page numbering lowercase roman in the introduction, arabic in the rest of the book, book.tex should contain the lines:

```
\pagenumbering{roman}
\maketitle
\tableofcontents
\listoftables
\include{intro}
```

```
\pagenumbering{arabic}
\include{ch1}
\include{ch2}
```

...

where

```
\pagenumbering{roman}
```

is defined in $\mathcal{A}_{\mathcal{M}}S$-LaTeX as

```
\renewcommand{\thepage}{\roman{page}}
```

The style of the sectioning numbers in this book are defined by the following commands:

```
\renewcommand{\thechapter}{\arabic{chapter}}
\renewcommand{\thesection}{\thechapter-\arabic{section}}
\renewcommand{\thesubsection}{\thechapter-\arabic{section}%
.\arabic{subsection}}
```

**11-4.3. Numbering in TₑX.** Of course, if you use TₑX macros, you get much greater flexibility in numbering. The following example shows how to set up a counter, initialize it, increment and display it.

Define the counter \numb:

```
\newcount\numb
```

To initialize or reset it:

```
\numb=0
```

Define the macro to increment and display \numb:

```
\def\enum{\global \advance \numb by 1 \relax \the \numb}
```

A TₑX macro can only be used within the scope of the definition. Moreover, the effect of the invocation is limited to its scope. To make the effect global, the arithmetic operation has to be preceded by the \global command, as in the example.

So \enum will display and increment \numb. So to get #1, #2, ... , type:

```
\# \enum
```

TₑX can also multiply with \multiply and (integer) divide with \divide as in

```
\multiply \numb by 2
```

or

```
\divide \numb by 2
```

## 11-5. Pitfalls

As a rule, you should have little difficulty incorporating TₑX code into an $\mathcal{A}_{\mathcal{M}}S$-LaTeX article. After all, $\mathcal{A}_{\mathcal{M}}S$-LaTeX *is* TₑX with a large layer of macros on top of TₑX. However, what can go wrong, will, so we give you some guidelines.

There are a number of reasons why a (Plain) TₑX command may not work as expected in $\mathcal{A}_{\mathcal{M}}S$-LaTeX.

- $\mathcal{A}_{\mathcal{M}}S$-LATEX rewrote the "output" routines of TEX, that is, the way paragraphs and pages are formatted. Avoid all TEX commands that directly affect output (see Chapter 15 of [14]).
- $\mathcal{A}_{\mathcal{M}}S$-LATEX provides a number of environments that make some TEX commands obsolete: `tabbing` and `center` are two examples.
- A number of TEX font size change commands are not defined in $\mathcal{A}_{\mathcal{M}}S$-LATEX.
- Some TEX commands change parameters that are also used in $\mathcal{A}_{\mathcal{M}}S$-LATEX. For instance, \hangindent in an $\mathcal{A}_{\mathcal{M}}S$-LATEX list environment will change the shape of the list.

Here is a short list of TEX commands to avoid:

| | | | |
|---|---|---|---|
| \+ | \fivei | \midinsert | \sevensy |
| \advancepageno | \fiverm | \nopagenumbers | \tabalign |
| \beginsection | \fivesy | \normalbottom | \tabsdone |
| \bye | \folio | \oldstyle | \tabset |
| \centering | \footline | \pagebody | \tabs |
| \cleartabs | \footstrut | \pagecontents | \teni |
| \dosupereject | \headline | \pageinsert | \topinsert |
| \endinsert | \leqalignno | \pageno | \topins |
| \end | \line | \plainoutput | \vfootnote |
| \eqalignno | \magnification | \settabs | |
| \eqalign | \makefootline | \sevenbf | |
| \fivebf | \makeheadline | \seveni | |

Also, remember that in Plain TEX displayed math is delimited by $$ and $$; if these occur in a macro, replace them with \[ and \].

# APPENDIX A

# Math Symbol Tables

## A-1. Greek characters

| Type: | Print: | Type: | Print: | Type: | Print: |
|-------|--------|-------|--------|-------|--------|
| \alpha | $\alpha$ | \beta | $\beta$ | \gamma | $\gamma$ |
| \digamma | $\digamma$ | \delta | $\delta$ | \epsilon | $\epsilon$ |
| \varepsilon | $\varepsilon$ | \zeta | $\zeta$ | \eta | $\eta$ |
| \theta | $\theta$ | \vartheta | $\vartheta$ | \iota | $\iota$ |
| \kappa | $\kappa$ | \varkappa | $\varkappa$ | \lambda | $\lambda$ |
| \mu | $\mu$ | \nu | $\nu$ | \xi | $\xi$ |
| \pi | $\pi$ | \varpi | $\varpi$ | \rho | $\rho$ |
| \varrho | $\varrho$ | \sigma | $\sigma$ | \varsigma | $\varsigma$ |
| \tau | $\tau$ | \upsilon | $\upsilon$ | \phi | $\phi$ |
| \varphi | $\varphi$ | \chi | $\chi$ | \psi | $\psi$ |
| \omega | $\omega$ | | | | |

| Type: | Print: | Type: | Print: |
|-------|--------|-------|--------|
| \Gamma | $\Gamma$ | \varGamma | $\varGamma$ |
| \Delta | $\Delta$ | \varDelta | $\varDelta$ |
| \Theta | $\Theta$ | \varTheta | $\varTheta$ |
| \Lambda | $\Lambda$ | \varLambda | $\varLambda$ |
| \Xi | $\Xi$ | \varXi | $\varXi$ |
| \Pi | $\Pi$ | \varPi | $\varPi$ |
| \Sigma | $\Sigma$ | \varSigma | $\varSigma$ |
| \Upsilon | $\Upsilon$ | \varUpsilon | $\varUpsilon$ |
| \Phi | $\Phi$ | \varPhi | $\varPhi$ |
| \Psi | $\Psi$ | \varPsi | $\varPsi$ |
| \Omega | $\Omega$ | \varOmega | $\varOmega$ |

## A-2. Hebrew letters

| Type: | Print: | Type: | Print: |
|-------|--------|-------|--------|
| \aleph | ℵ | \beth | ℶ |
| \daleth | ℸ | \gimel | ℷ |

## A-3. Binary operations

| Type: | Print: | Type: | Print: |
|-------|--------|-------|--------|
| \pm | ± | \mp | ∓ |
| \dotplus | ∔ | \cdot | · |
| \times | × | \centerdot | ▪ |
| \ltimes | ⋉ | \rtimes | ⋊ |
| \leftthreetimes | ⋋ | \rightthreetimes | ⋌ |
| \ast | * | \star | ⋆ |
| \diamond | ⋄ | \circ | ∘ |
| \bullet | • | \div | ÷ |
| \setminus | \ | \smallsetminus | ∖ |
| \cap | ∩ | \cup | ∪ |
| \Cap | ⋒ | \Cap | ⋒ |
| \sqcap | ⊓ | \sqcup | ⊔ |
| \wedge | ∧ | \vee | ∨ |
| \barwedge | ⊼ | \doublebarwedge | ⩞ |
| \curlywedge | ⋏ | \curlyvee | ⋎ |
| \veebar | ⊻ | \intercal | ⊺ |
| \oplus | ⊕ | \ominus | ⊖ |
| \otimes | ⊗ | \oslash | ⊘ |
| \odot | ⊙ | \circleddash | ⊝ |
| \circledast | ⊛ | \circledcirc | ⊚ |
| \boxminus | ⊟ | \boxtimes | ⊠ |
| \boxdot | ⊡ | \boxplus | ⊞ |
| \triangleleft | ◁ | \triangleright | ▷ |
| \bigtriangleup | △ | \bigtriangledown | ▽ |
| \dagger | † | \ddagger | ‡ |
| \wr | ≀ | \bigcirc | ◯ |
| \amalg | ⨿ | \divideontimes | ⋇ |
| \And | & | | |

## A-4. Binary relations

| Type: | Print: | Type: | Print: |
|-------|--------|-------|--------|
| \leq | ≤ | \geq | ≥ |
| \leqslant | ⩽ | \geqslant | ⩾ |
| \eqslantless | ⪕ | \eqslantgtr | ⪖ |
| \lesssim | ≲ | \gtrsim | ≳ |
| \lessapprox | ⪅ | \gtrapprox | ⪆ |
| \approxeq | ≊ | | |
| \lessdot | ⋖ | \gtrdot | ⋗ |
| \ll | ≪ | \gg | ≫ |
| \lll | ⋘ | \ggg | ⋙ |
| \lessgtr | ≶ | \gtrless | ≷ |
| \lesseqgtr | ⋚ | \gtreqless | ⋛ |
| \lesseqqgtr | ⪋ | \gtreqqless | ⪌ |
| \prec | ≺ | \succ | ≻ |
| \preceq | ≼ | \succeq | ≽ |
| \doteqdot | ≑ | \eqcirc | ≖ |
| \circeq | ≗ | \fallingdotseq | ≒ |
| \risingdotseq | ≓ | \triangleq | ≜ |
| \equiv | ≡ | \sim | ∼ |
| \simeq | ≃ | \backsim | ∽ |
| \thicksim | ∼ | \backsimeq | ⋍ |
| \approx | ≈ | \thickapprox | ≈ |
| \preccurlyeq | ≼ | \succcurlyeq | ≽ |
| \curlyeqprec | ⋞ | \curlyeqsucc | ⋟ |
| \precsim | ≾ | \succsim | ≿ |
| \precapprox | ⪷ | \succapprox | ⪸ |
| \subset | ⊂ | \supset | ⊃ |
| \subseteq | ⊆ | \supseteq | ⊇ |
| \subseteqq | ⫅ | \supseteqq | ⫆ |
| \Subset | ⋐ | \Supset | ⋑ |
| \sqsubseteq | ⊑ | \sqsupseteq | ⊒ |
| \sqsubset | ⊏ | \sqsupset | ⊐ |
| \vartriangleleft | ◁ | \vartriangleright | ▷ |
| \trianglelefteq | ⊴ | \trianglerighteq | ⊵ |
| \vdash | ⊢ | \dashv | ⊣ |
| \vDash | ⊨ | \Vdash | ⊩ |
| \Vvdash | ⊪ | \models | ⊨ |
| \smile | ⌣ | \smallsmile | ⌣ |
| \frown | ⌢ | \smallfrown | ⌢ |
| \mid | ∣ | \shortmid | ∣ |
| \parallel | ∥ | \shortparallel | ∥ |
| \asymp | ≍ | \cong | ≅ |

Binary relations, continued

| Type: | Print: | Type: | Print: |
|-------|--------|-------|--------|
| \bumpeq | ≏ | \Bumpeq | ≎ |
| \between | ≬ | \pitchfork | ⋔ |
| \propto | ∝ | \varpropto | ∝ |
| \in | ∈ | \ni | ∋ |
| \backepsilon | ϶ | \doteq | ≐ |
| \blacktriangleleft | ◀ | \blacktriangleright | ▶ |
| \therefore | ∴ | \because | ∵ |
| \perp | ⊥ | | |

## A-5. Negated binary relations

| Type: | Print: | Type: | Print: |
|-------|--------|-------|--------|
| \ne | ≠ | \notin | ∉ |
| \nless | ≮ | \ngtr | ≯ |
| \nleq | ≰ | \ngeq | ≱ |
| \nleqslant | ⪇ | \ngeqslant | ⪈ |
| \nleqq | ≨ | \ngeqq | ≩ |
| \lneq | ⪇ | \gneq | ⪈ |
| \lneqq | ≨ | \gneqq | ≩ |
| \lvertneqq | ≨ | \gvertneqq | ≩ |
| \lnsim | ⋦ | \gnsim | ⋧ |
| \lnapprox | ⪉ | \gnapprox | ⪊ |
| \nprec | ⊀ | \nsucc | ⊁ |
| \npreceq | ⋠ | \nsucceq | ⋡ |
| \precneqq | ⪵ | \succneqq | ⪶ |
| \precnsim | ⋨ | \succnsim | ⋩ |
| \precnapprox | ⪹ | \succnapprox | ⪺ |
| \nsim | ≁ | \ncong | ≇ |
| \nshortmid | ∤ | \nshortparallel | ∦ |
| \nmid | ∤ | \nparallel | ∦ |
| \nvdash | ⊬ | \nvDash | ⊭ |
| \nVdash | ⊮ | \nVDash | ⊯ |
| \ntriangleleft | ⋪ | \ntriangleright | ⋫ |
| \ntrianglelefteq | ⋬ | \ntrianglerighteq | ⋭ |
| \nsubseteq | ⊈ | \nsupseteq | ⊉ |
| \nsubseteqq | ⊈ | \nsupseteqq | ⊉ |
| \subsetneq | ⊊ | \supsetneq | ⊋ |
| \varsubsetneq | ⊊ | \varsupsetneq | ⊋ |
| \subsetneqq | ⫋ | \supsetneqq | ⫌ |
| \varsubsetneqq | ⫋ | \varsupsetneqq | ⫌ |

## A-6. Arrows

| Type: | Print: | Type: | Print: |
|---|---|---|---|
| \leftarrow | ← | \rightarrow or \to | → |
| \longleftarrow | ⟵ | \longrightarrow | ⟶ |
| \Leftarrow | ⇐ | \Rightarrow | ⇒ |
| \Longleftarrow | ⟸ | \Longrightarrow | ⟹ |
| \leftrightarrow | ↔ | \longleftrightarrow | ⟷ |
| \Leftrightarrow | ⇔ | \Longleftrightarrow | ⟺ |
| \leftleftarrows | ⇇ | \rightrightarrows | ⇉ |
| \leftrightarrows | ⇆ | \rightleftarrows | ⇄ |
| \Lleftarrow | ⇚ | \Rrightarrow | ⇛ |
| \twoheadleftarrow | ↞ | \twoheadrightarrow | ↠ |
| \leftarrowtail | ↢ | \rightarrowtail | ↣ |
| \looparrowleft | ↫ | \looparrowright | ↬ |
| \uparrow | ↑ | \downarrow | ↓ |
| \Uparrow | ⇑ | \Downarrow | ⇓ |
| \upuparrows | ⇈ | \downdownarrows | ⇊ |
| \updownarrow | ↕ | \Updownarrow | ⇕ |
| \nearrow | ↗ | \searrow | ↘ |
| \swarrow | ↙ | \nwarrow | ↖ |
| \mapsto | ↦ | \longmapsto | ⟼ |
| \hookleftarrow | ↩ | \hookrightarrow | ↪ |
| \leftharpoonup | ↼ | \rightharpoonup | ⇀ |
| \leftharpoondown | ↽ | \rightharpoondown | ⇁ |
| \upharpoonleft | ↿ | \upharpoonright | ↾ |
| \downharpoonleft | ⇃ | \downharpoonright | ⇂ |
| \multimap | ⊸ | \rightsquigarrow | ⇝ |
| \leftrightsquigarrow | ↭ | | |

| Type | Print | Type | Print |
|---|---|---|---|
| \nleftarrow | ↚ | \nrightarrow | ↛ |
| \nLeftarrow | ⇍ | \nRightarrow | ⇏ |
| \nleftrightarrow | ↮ | \nLeftrightarrow | ⇎ |

## A-7. Miscellaneous symbols

| Type: | Print: | Type: | Print: |
|-------|--------|-------|--------|
| \hbar | ℏ | \hslash | ℏ |
| \imath | ı | \jmath | ȷ |
| \ell | ℓ | \complement | ∁ |
| \wp | ℘ | \Re | ℜ |
| \Im | ℑ | \partial | ∂ |
| \infty | ∞ | \smallint | ∫ |
| \P | ¶ | \S | § |
| \prime | ′ | \backprime | ‵ |
| \emptyset | ∅ | \varnothing | ∅ |
| \Bbbk | k | \backslash | \ |
| \diagup | ╱ | \diagdown | ╲ |
| \triangle | △ | | |
| \vartriangle | △ | \blacktriangle | ▲ |
| \triangledown | ▽ | \blacktriangledown | ▼ |
| \square | □ | \blacksquare | ■ |
| \lozenge | ◊ | \blacklozenge | ◆ |
| \forall | ∀ | \exists | ∃ |
| \nexists | ∄ | \neg | ¬ |
| \angle | ∠ | \sphericalangle | ∢ |
| \measuredangle | ∡ | | |
| \surd | √ | \Vert | ‖ |
| \top | ⊤ | \bot | ⊥ |
| \dag | † | \ddag | ‡ |
| \flat | ♭ | \natural | ♮ |
| \sharp | ♯ | | |
| \clubsuit | ♣ | \diamondsuit | ◇ |
| \heartsuit | ♡ | \spadesuit | ♠ |
| \circledS | Ⓢ | \bigstar | ★ |
| \mho | ℧ | \eth | ð |
| \Finv | ⅃ | \Game | ⅁ |

### A-8. Spacing commands

| Short form: | Full form: | Short form: | Full form: |
|---|---|---|---|
| \, | \thinspace | \! | \negthinspace |
| \: | \medspace | | \negmedspace |
| \; | \thickspace | | \negthickspace |
| @, | | @! | |
| | \quad | | |
| | \qquad | | |

### A-9. Delimiters

| Name: | Type: | Print: | Name: | Type: | Print: |
|---|---|---|---|---|---|
| Left paren. | ( | ( | Right paren. | ) | ) |
| Left bracket | [ | [ | Right bracket | ] | ] |
| Left brace | \{ | { | Right brace | \} | } |
| Reverse slash | \backslash | \ | Forward slash | / | / |
| Left angle br. | \langle | ⟨ | Right angle br. | \rangle | ⟩ |
| Vertical line | | | | | Double vert. line | \| | ‖ |
| Left floor br. | \lfloor | ⌊ | Right floor br. | \rfloor | ⌋ |
| Left ceiling br. | \lceil | ⌈ | Right ceiling br. | \rceil | ⌉ |

| Name: | Type: | Print: |
|---|---|---|
| Upward arrow | \uparrow | ↑ |
| Double upward arrow | \Uparrow | ⇑ |
| Downward arrow | \downarrow | ↓ |
| Double downward arrow | \Downarrow | ⇓ |
| Up-and-down arrow | \updownarrow | ↕ |
| Double up-and-down arrow | \Updownarrow | ⇕ |

### A-10. Operators

| \arccos | \arcsin | \arctan | \arg |
|---|---|---|---|
| \cos | \cosh | \cot | \coth |
| \csc | \dim | \exp | \hom |
| \ker | \lg | \ln | \log |
| \sec | \sin | \sinh | \tan |
| \tanh | | | |
| \varliminf | \varlimsup | \varinjlim | \varprojlim |

| \det | \gcd | \inf | \injlim |
|---|---|---|---|
| \lim | \liminf | \limsup | \max |
| \min | \projlim | \Pr | \sup |

Large operators

| Type: | Print: | Type: | Print: |
|-------|--------|-------|--------|
| `\prod_{i=1}^{n}` | $\prod_{i=1}^{n}$ | `\coprod_{i=1}^{n}` | $\coprod_{i=1}^{n}$ |
| `\bigcap_{i=1}^{n}` | $\bigcap_{i=1}^{n}$ | `\bigcup_{i=1}^{n}` | $\bigcup_{i=1}^{n}$ |
| `\bigvee_{i=1}^{n}` | $\bigvee_{i=1}^{n}$ | `\bigwedge_{i=1}^{n}` | $\bigwedge_{i=1}^{n}$ |
| `\bigsqcup_{i=1}^{n}` | $\bigsqcup_{i=1}^{n}$ | `\biguplus_{i=1}^{n}` | $\biguplus_{i=1}^{n}$ |
| `\bigotimes_{i=1}^{n}` | $\bigotimes_{i=1}^{n}$ | `\bigoplus_{i=1}^{n}` | $\bigoplus_{i=1}^{n}$ |
| `\bigodot_{i=1}^{n}` | $\bigodot_{i=1}^{n}$ | `\sum_{i=1}^{n}` | $\sum_{i=1}^{n}$ |

$$\prod_{i=1}^{n} \quad \coprod_{i=1}^{n} \quad \bigcap_{i=1}^{n} \quad \bigcup_{i=1}^{n} \quad \bigvee_{i=1}^{n} \quad \bigwedge_{i=1}^{n} \quad \bigsqcup_{i=1}^{n} \quad \biguplus_{i=1}^{n} \quad \bigotimes_{i=1}^{n} \quad \bigoplus_{i=1}^{n} \quad \bigodot_{i=1}^{n} \quad \sum_{i=1}^{n}$$

## A-11.  Math accents

| | | | | | | | |
|---|---|---|---|---|---|---|---|
| `\hat{a}` | $\hat{a}$ | `\Hat{a}` | $\hat{a}$ | `\widehat{a}` | $\widehat{a}$ | `a\sphat` | $a^\frown$ |
| `\tilde{a}` | $\tilde{a}$ | `\Tilde{a}` | $\tilde{a}$ | `\widetilde{a}` | $\widetilde{a}$ | `a\sptilde` | $a^\sim$ |
| `\acute{a}` | $\acute{a}$ | `\Acute{a}` | $\acute{a}$ | | | | |
| `\bar{a}` | $\bar{a}$ | `\Bar{a}` | $\bar{a}$ | | | | |
| `\breve{a}` | $\breve{a}$ | `\Breve{a}` | $\breve{a}$ | | | `a\spbreve` | $a^\smallsmile$ |
| `\check{a}` | $\check{a}$ | `\Check{a}` | $\check{a}$ | | | `a\spcheck` | $a^\vee$ |
| `\dot{a}` | $\dot{a}$ | `\Dot{a}` | $\dot{a}$ | | | `a\spdot` | $a^\cdot$ |
| `\ddot{a}` | $\ddot{a}$ | `\Ddot{a}` | $\ddot{a}$ | | | `a\spddot` | $a^{\cdot\cdot}$ |
| `\dddot{a}` | $\dddot{a}$ | | | | | `a\spdddot` | $a^{\cdot\cdot\cdot}$ |
| `\grave{a}` | $\grave{a}$ | `\Grave{a}` | $\grave{a}$ | | | | |
| `\vec{a}` | $\vec{a}$ | `\Vec{a}` | $\vec{a}$ | | | | |

| `\imath` | $\imath$ | `\jmath` | $\jmath$ |
|---|---|---|---|

# APPENDIX B

# Text Symbol Tables

### B-1. Special characters

| Type: | Print: | Type: | Print: | Type: | Print: |
|-------|--------|-------|--------|-------|--------|
| \# | # | \$ | $ | \% | % |
| \& | & | \~{} | ~ | \_ | _ |
| \^{} | ^ | \{ | { | \} | } |
| @@ | @ | \( \backslash \) | \ | \( * \) | * |

| Type: | Print: |
|-------|--------|
| $\|$ | \| |

### B-2. Accents

| Type: | Print: | Type: | Print: | Type: | Print: | Type: | Print: |
|-------|--------|-------|--------|-------|--------|-------|--------|
| \`{o} | ò | \'{o} | ó | \"{o} | ö | \H{o} | ő |
| \^{o} | ô | \~{o} | õ | \v{o} | ǒ | \u{o} | ŏ |
| \={o} | ō | \b{o} | o̲ | \.{o} | ȯ | \d{o} | ọ |
| \c{o} | ǫ | \t{oo} | o͡o | | | | |

| \i | ı | \j | ȷ |
|----|---|----|---|

### B-3. Extra text symbols

| Type: | Print: | Type: | Print: | Type: | Print |
|-------|--------|-------|--------|-------|-------|
| \dag | † | \ddag | ‡ | \S | § |
| \P | ¶ | \copyright | © | \pounds | £ |

## B-4. Foreign characters

| Type: | Print: | Type: | Print: | Type: | Print: | Type: | Print: | Type: | Print: |
|-------|--------|-------|--------|-------|--------|-------|--------|-------|--------|
| \aa   | å      | \AA   | Å      | \ae   | æ      | \AE   | Æ      | \o    | ø      |
| \O    | Ø      | \oe   | œ      | \OE   | Œ      | \l    | ł      | \L    | Ł      |
| \ss   | ß      | ?`    | ¿      | !`    | ¡      |       |        |       |        |

## B-5. Fonts

Type:                                         Print:
{\rm This is roman.}                          This is roman.
{\bf This is bold.}                           **This is bold.**
{\sf This is sans serif.}                     This is sans serif.
{\sl This is slanted.}                        *This is slanted.*
{\em This is emphasized.}                     *This is emphasized.*
{\it This is italic.}                         *This is italic.*
{\sc This is Small Caps.}                     THIS IS SMALL CAPS.
{\tt This is the typewriter.}                 This is the typewriter.
(using the redefinition of \rm in Section 3-6.2)

## B-6. Spacing commands

| Short form: | Full form:    | Short form: | Full form:      |
|-------------|---------------|-------------|-----------------|
| \,          | \thinspace    | \!          | \negthinspace   |
| \:          | \medspace     |             | \negmedspace    |
| \;          | \thickspace   |             | \negthickspace  |
| @,          |               | @!          |                 |

| | | |
|---------|---|---|
| \␣      | \| \||
| \quad   | \|  \||
| \qquad  | \|   \||

# APPENDIX C

# $\mathcal{A}_{\mathcal{M}}\mathcal{S}$-L&TeX
# Background

## C-1. A short history

Donald E. Knuth's multi-volume epic: *The Art of Computer Programming* [13] caused a great deal of frustration to its author. It seemed very difficult to keep the various volumes typographically uniform. Out of this frustration, the TeX mathematical typesetting language was born; see [14]–[18].

A mathematical typesetting language takes care of the multitude of little details that are so important in mathematical typesetting: it properly spaces the formulas; breaks up the text into pleasing lines and paragraphs—hyphenates words as necessary; provides the hundreds of symbols without which you cannot do mathematics. TeX does all this and more on most any computer: **PC, Mac**, Atari, Amiga, workstations, minicomputers, and mainframes. You can typeset your work on a **PC**, and email it to your coworker who will do the corrections on a **Mac**; the final result is emailed to your publisher who probably uses a minicomputer to print the result on a Linotype printer.

Knuth realized that typesetting is only half the solution to producing a manuscript. You also need a style designer—a specialist, who will decide what fonts to use, how large an interline gap is needed after a theorem, and the million and one other parameters that go into a style. TeX was designed to work with a "document style", so you do not have to worry about style design problems.

Knuth also realized that it requires knowledgeable users to typeset in TeX an article of any complexity. So TeX was designed as a "platform" on which *convenient work environments*—so called "macro packages"—can be built.

It is somewhat unfortunate that **two** such macro packages, $\mathcal{A}_{\mathcal{M}}\mathcal{S}$-TeX and L&TeX, were made available to the mathematical community in the early eighties.

$\mathcal{A}_{\mathcal{M}}\mathcal{S}$-TeX was written by M. D. Spivak for the $\mathcal{A}_{\mathcal{M}}\mathcal{S}$, while L&TeX was developed by L. Lamport. Both systems became very popular, causing a split in the mathematical community. The strengths of the two systems are somewhat complementary. $\mathcal{A}_{\mathcal{M}}\mathcal{S}$-TeX (now in its version 2.1) provides many features, necessary for mathematical articles, including:

- Excellent formatting of multiline formulas, especially the use of aligned columns.
- Flexible bibliographic references.
- Articles written in $\mathcal{A}_{\mathcal{M}}S$-TEX can be submitted for publication to a number of journals.

LATEX also provides many features that are very convenient for authors, including:

- Automatic numbering and cross-referencing.
- Bibliographic databases.

$\mathcal{A}_{\mathcal{M}}S$-LATEX was developed for the $\mathcal{A}_{\mathcal{M}}S$ by R. Kumar, F. Mittelbach, R. Schöpf, with assistance from M. Downes. It successfully **unifies the two macro packages**. $\mathcal{A}_{\mathcal{M}}S$-LATEX is a LATEX *option*, called amstex.sty which contains the $\mathcal{A}_{\mathcal{M}}S$-TEX constructs and a *document style*, called amsart.sty.

## C-2. How does it work?

In this section, we present a somewhat simplified overview of the working of $\mathcal{A}_{\mathcal{M}}S$-LATEX. It is hoped that this will help you to better understand error messages and in isolating and resolving problems.

### C-2.1. The layers. $\mathcal{A}_{\mathcal{M}}S$-LATEX has many layers.

virtex. At the core is the TEX with only the most primitive commands; this is called virtex. It knows about 300 basic commands such as \input, \accent, and \hsize. It has the ability to read in *format files*, which are "precompiled" sets of macros. Basically, $\mathcal{A}_{\mathcal{M}}S$-LATEX is virtex reading in a large set of macros, built layer on layer.

plain.tex. The most basic layer on top of virtex was created alongside with TEX by D. E. Knuth; it is called plain.tex. It adds about 600 commands to virtex. When you give the tex command, it really executes virtex with the plain format file. This is made clear on the **Mac**: the plain format is the default format.

plain.tex is described in detail in Appendix B of D. E. Knuth [14]. You can read plain.tex; it is a text file in the TEX distribution. It is sufficiently powerful so that you could do all your work in plain.tex. This view is advocated by many; for instance, by M. Doob [10].

virtex cannot build format files. For that you need another version of TEX, called initex. This calls in the most basic information, such as the hyphenation tables and plain.tex, and creates a format file.

In the TEXTURES distribution, virtex has be used to make a format file.

PCTEX does not distribute a separate initex; rather, run TEX with the /I switch.

LATEX. LATEX is a set of macros written by L. Lamport, see the latex.tex file. It gives us automatic numbering and cross-referencing, Table of Contents, and lots of other features.

LATEX requires some changes in plain.tex; the modified version, lplain.tex, comes with the LATEX distribution.

amsart document style. The \documentstyle command of LATEX demands a document style; it may also have options (listed in square brackets).

In this book for all articles we use:

\documentstyle[amscd,amssymb,verbatim]{amsart}

amsart is the article document style by $\mathcal{AMS}$, amsart.sty. This document style determines which fonts are used, how a theorem is displayed; how the Topmatter is defined and where is it placed, and many other stylistic matters.

The $\mathcal{AMS}$-TEX option. There is one option we do not have to specify if we use the amsart document style. It is the amstex option (amstex.sty) which is automatically read in by the amsart document style. This option emulates the $\mathcal{AMS}$-TEX macro package of the $\mathcal{AMS}$ giving us the multiline math formulas and the other $\mathcal{AMS}$-TEX features.

**C-2.2. Typesetting.** When $\mathcal{AMS}$-LATEX does the typesetting, it uses two basic files: the source file(s) and the font metric file(s).

There is a font metric file for each font used (one for each size); it contains the size of each character; the measurements for "kerning" (the space between two characters), the length of the "italic correction", the size of the "interword space", and so on.

For the **PC**, all the font metric files are in the directories textfms and amstfms. A typical file is msam9.tfm which is the font metric file for the font msam at size 9 points.

On the **Mac**, the font metric files are combined into two files: TeX metrics and AMSFonts 2.1 Metrics

$\mathcal{AMS}$-LATEX reads the source file one character at a time, until the end of the paragraph. It then converts the character sequence into a token sequence; a "token" is either a character (and what role the character plays) or a macro. The argument of a macro is the token following the macro, unless a group enclosed in braces follows the macro (in which case the contents of the group becomes the argument). This explains why \( 2^3 \) and \( 2^\alpha \) work out well, but \( 2^\frak m \) does not (3 and \alpha turn into a single token each; \frak m turns into two tokens). Of course, if you always use groups

\( \( 2^{3} \), \( 2^{\alpha} \), \( 2^{\frak m} \)

then you do not have to remember what tokens are.

In the next step, TEX reads from the font metric files the measurements for the characters, kerning, spacing; hyphenates the text and then attempts to split the paragraph into lines of the required length. The measurements of the characters are absolute, so are the distances between characters (kerning); however, the spaces (interword space, intersentence space, and so on) are "glues". A glue has three dimensions: the length of the space, the stretchability (the amount with which it can be made longer), and shrinkability (the amount with which it can be made shorter); see Section 10-1.3 for an example. TEX will stretch and shrink the glues to make lines of equal length.

TᴇX uses a formula to measure how much stretching and shrinking was necessary in a line. The result is called "badness". Badness 0 is perfect; badness 10,000 is very bad.

Lines that are too wide are reported with

```
Overfull \hbox (5.61168pt too wide) in paragraph at lines 49
--57
```

and the badness is not shown. Lines that are too much stretched out show the badness:

```
Underfull \hbox (badness 1189) in paragraph at lines 993--99
3
```

Once enough paragraphs are put together, TᴇX composes a page from the typeset paragraph following the same principles using "vertical glue". A page too short is marked with an Underfull \vbox message, for instance:

```
Underfull \vbox (badness 10000) has
occurred while \output is active
```

The typeset file is stored as a dvi file. On the **PC**, it has the same name as the source file but with the extension dvi. On the **Mac**, the dvi file becomes a "resource" of the source file.

**C-2.3. Viewing and printing.** Viewing and printing is not really part of TᴇX; but it is obviously a part of your $\mathcal{AMS}$-LᴬTᴇX work environment. Separate programs print the dvi files and let you view them on the screen. These programs use, for the **PC**, the pk files and, for the **Mac**, the font files.

For the **PC**, there is a pk file for each font used, one for each size, one for each resolution. They are in the subdirectory pixel of the directory pctex. The directory pixel has a subdirectory for each resolution, for instance, dpi300 for the 300 dots per inch resolution. A typical file in dpi300 is msam9.pk which is the pk file for the font msam at size 9 points at 300 dots per inch resolution.

On the **Mac**, the font files are in "suitcases"; the exact arrangement (how many suitcases there are and which suitcase contains which fonts) depends on the installation.

**C-2.4. The files of** $\mathcal{AMS}$**-LᴬTᴇX.** $\mathcal{AMS}$-LᴬTᴇX is a "one-pass compiler", that is, it reads the source file only once for typesetting. Therefore, it is necessary for $\mathcal{AMS}$-LᴬTᴇX to use auxiliary files in which to store information. For the **current** typesetting, $\mathcal{AMS}$-LᴬTᴇX uses the auxiliary files compiled during the **last** typesetting. This explains why we have to typeset **twice** to make sure that changes we have made are reflected in the typeset article.

These auxiliary files have the same name as the source file; the extension indicates the type of the auxiliary file.

The most important auxiliary file is the aux file. It contains a lot of information, most importantly, all the data relevant to symbolic referencing. Here are two typical entries:

```
\newlabel{struct}{{1-1}{4}}
\bibcite{dk86c}{8}
```

The first entry indicates that we introduced a new symbol with

`\label{struct}`

It is in Section 1-1, on page 4. The command

`\ref{struct}`

will produce 1-1, while

`\pageref{struct}`

will yield 4.

There is an aux file for the source file being processed, and there is one for each file included in the main file with an `\include` command.

No aux is written if the `\nofiles` command is given; the message

`No auxiliary output files.`

in the log file reminds you that `\nofiles` is in effect.

The aux file also contains information about the Table of Contents.

The `log` file contains all the information shown on the screen during the typesetting.

The `dvi` file contains the typeset version of the source file; for the TEXTURES setup on the **Mac**, the `dvi` file becomes a "resource" of the source file.

There are five auxiliary files which store information for special tasks. They are written only if that special task is invoked by a command. They are all suppressed if there is a `\nofiles` command. They are

> `glo`: Contains the glossary entries produced by the `\glossary` commands. A new file is written only if there is a `\makeglossary` command in the source file.
>
> `idx`: Contains the index entries produced by the `\index` commands. A new file is written only if there is a `\makeindex` command in the source file.
>
> `lof`: Contains the list-of-figures entries produced by the `\caption` commands in the `figure` environment. A new file is written only if there is a `\listoffigures` command in the source file.
>
> `lot`: Contains the list-of-tables entries produced by the `\caption` commands in the `table` environment. A new file is written provided that there is a `\listoftables` command in the source file.
>
> `toc`: Contains the Table-of-Contents entries produced by the sectioning commands. A new file is written only if there is a `\tableofcontents` command in the source file.

BIBTEX uses four auxiliary files; see Section C-2.4.

# Keeping In Touch

If your PC (personal computer) can communicate with a mini or mainframe computer (we shall call this the "local" computer) that uses the UNIX operating system and is connected to the Internet computer network, then you can access the $\mathcal{AMS}$ computer and obtain the most up-to-date version of the $\mathcal{AMS}$-LaTeX and AMSFonts files. This appendix explains how to do this.

We make the assumption that you know how to "sign on" to the local computer, and that you know how to "download" from the local computer to your PC (typically this would be done with the program Kermit).

In this appendix, we reproduce some typical parts of a session that gets us all the necessary files.

You should also keep in touch with TUG: the TeX user group. The last section tells you how.

### D-1. Some UNIX commands

After you sign on, first you have to create on the local computer the directory structure into which you will copy the files from the $\mathcal{AMS}$ computer. Here is the part of the directory structure of the $\mathcal{AMS}$ computer that contains the information needed for $\mathcal{AMS}$-LaTeX:

```
ams
    amsfonts
        doc
        pk-files
            300-dpi
    amslatex
        doc
        fontsel
        inputs
        latex
    author-info
```

```
macintosh
   guidelines
   sty-files
tfm-files
```

A **PC** user needs the contents of all these directories except, of course, the macintosh directory; the contents of the author-info directory is optional. We assume that you have a 300 dpi (dot per inch) laser printer; if you have a dot matrix printer, replace the 300-dpi directory with 180-dpi. There are also directories for higher and lower resolution printers.

A **Mac** user only needs the contents of the macintosh directory; and optionally, the contents of the author-info directory.

To create a directory structure on the local computer, you need the following UNIX commands:

| | |
|---|---|
| cd | change directory |
| cd .. | move up one in the directory structure |
| ls | list files and subdirectories |
| mkdir | make directory |
| rm | remove file |
| pwd | current path |
| rmdir | remove directory |

Once connected with the $\mathcal{AMS}$ computer, use the following commands:

| | |
|---|---|
| get | get a file |
| lcd | change directory in the local computer |
| mget | get multiple files |
| prompt | do not prompt which files to get |
| ascii | file to get is ascii file |
| binary | file to get is binary file |
| bye | disconnect ftp |

### D-2. PC users

In this section, we show how to get the files needed for a **PC** user.

The local computer. The first part of the session creates the directory structure. What the computer displays on the screen is shown in this style; what you type is shown *in this style*.

```
ccu% pwd
/home/u1/gratzer
ccu% mkdir ams
ccu% cd ams
ccu% pwd
/home/u1/gratzer/ams
```

```
ccu% mkdir amsfonts
ccu% mkdir amslatex
ccu% mkdir author-info
ccu% mkdir tfm-files
ccu% cd amsfonts
ccu% pwd
/home/u1/gratzer/ams/amsfonts
ccu% mkdir doc
ccu% mkdir pk-files
ccu% cd pk-files
ccu% pwd
/home/u1/gratzer/ams/amsfonts/pk-files
ccu% mkdir 300-dpi
ccu% cd ..
ccu% cd ..
ccu% pwd
/home/u1/gratzer/ams
ccu% cd amslatex
ccu% pwd
/home/u1/gratzer/ams/amslatex
ccu% mkdir doc
ccu% mkdir fontsel
ccu% mkdir inputs
ccu% mkdir latex
ccu% cd ..
ccu% cd author-info
ccu% pwd
/home/u1/gratzer/ams/author-info
ccu% mkdir guidelines
ccu% mkdir sty-files
ccu% cd ..
ccu% pwd
/home/u1/gratzer/ams
```

The $\mathcal{A}\mathcal{M}\mathcal{S}$ computer. We use the method called *ftp anonymous* to log on to the $\mathcal{A}\mathcal{M}\mathcal{S}$ computer:

```
ccu% ftp e-math.ams.com
Connected to e-math.ams.com.
220 e-math FTP server (Ultrix Version 4.36
Thu Dec 29 22:53:11 EST 1988) ready.
Name (e-math.ams.com:gratzer): anonymous
331 Guest login ok, send ident as password.
Password:
```

```
230 Guest login ok, access restrictions apply.
```
ftp> *cd ams*
```
250 CWD command successful.
```
ftp> *cd tfm-files*
```
250 CWD command successful.
```

Some font files. Now we get the font metric files:

ftp> *lcd tfm-files*
```
Local directory now /home/u1/gratzer/ams/tfm-files
```
ftp> *prompt*
```
Interactive mode off.
```
ftp> *binary*
```
200 Type set to I.
```
ftp> *mget *.**
```
200 PORT command successful.
150 Opening data connection for cmbsy5.tfm
(130.179.16.8,4536) (1120 bytes).
226 Transfer complete.
  ...
  ...
```

Now all the tfm files are transferred from the $\mathcal{A}_{\mathcal{M}}\mathcal{S}$ computer to the local computer. Note the prompt command; without it you would be prompted for every file being transferred. Note also the binary command which informs ftp that the file is not a text file. The argument of the mget command: *.* means "all files in the subdirectory".

Some text files. Next we transfer the author-info guidelines; these are useful both for **PC** and **Mac** users:

ftp> *lcd ..*
```
Local directory now /home/u1/gratzer/ams
```
ftp> *lcd author-info*
```
Local directory now /home/u1/gratzer/ams/author-info
```
ftp> *lcd guidelines*
```
Local directory now /home/u1/gratzer/ams/author-info/guidelines
```
ftp> *pwd*
```
257 "/ams/tfm-files" is current directory.
```
ftp> *cd ..*
```
250 CWD command successful.
```
ftp> *cd author-info*
```
250 CWD command successful.
```
ftp> *cd guidelines*
```
250 CWD command successful.
```
ftp> *ascii*
```
200 Type set to A.
```

```
ftp> mget *.*
200 PORT command successful.
150 Opening data connection for READ.ME
(130.179.16.8,4679) (2993 bytes).
226 Transfer complete.
local:  READ.ME remote:  READ.ME
3071 bytes received in 4.1 seconds (0.73 Kbytes/s)
...

...
```

Now all the guideline files are being transferred from the $\mathcal{AMS}$ computer to the local computer. Note the `ascii` command which informs ftp that the files to be transferred are text files.

Of the files you want to transfer, all are ascii except the files in the directories: /ams/amsfonts/pk-files/300-dpi and /ams/tfm-files.

Kermit. The final step is transferring the files from the local computer to your PC. This step depends on what software is available on the local computer and on your PC.

The following would be typical: on the local computer, you locate in the subdirectory containing the files you wish to transfer.

```
ccu% kermit
C-Kermit, 4E(072) 24 Jan 89, SUNOS 4.x
Type ?  for help
C-Kermit> send *.*
Escape back to your local system and give a RECEIVE command...
```

At this point follow the instructions of the communication software on your PC on how to receive files sent by Kermit.

pk files. The pk files pose a special problem: we have to sort them out. As described in Section 1-3, in a typical **PC** setup, they are grouped into subdirectories; for instance, for a 300 dpi laserprinter, the subdirectories are: dpi300, dpi311, dpi329, dpi360, dpi373, dpi432, dpi518, dpi622, dpi746.

The pk files come to the local computer named:
cmbsy5.300pk, cmbsy5.329pk, cmbsy5.360pk, ... , cmbsy5.746pk, ...

Use Kermit to transfer the files to your **PC**. The transfer will rename the files: cmbsy5.300pk becomes cmbsy5.300. In the subdirectory into which all these files are transferred, place the batch file distr.bat (see the DISK):

```
copy *.300 c:\pctex\pixel\pk300\*.pk
copy *.311 c:\pctex\pixel\pk311\*.pk
copy *.329 c:\pctex\pixel\pk329\*.pk
copy *.360 c:\pctex\pixel\pk360\*.pk
copy *.373 c:\pctex\pixel\pk373\*.pk
copy *.432 c:\pctex\pixel\pk432\*.pk
copy *.518 c:\pctex\pixel\pk518\*.pk
```

```
copy *.622 c:\pctex\pixel\pk622\*.pk
copy *.746 c:\pctex\pixel\pk746\*.pk
```

Run this batch file with the command:

```
distr
```

and it will copy every file to the proper subdirectory and will rename them. The batch file assumes that all the necessary subdirectories exist; if not, first create them.

Compressed files. Most of the subdirectories we are interested in are available combined into a single tar file. You can recognize these files easily: they are marked by the extension tar. Text directories are, in addition, compressed, as signified by the extension Z. Ask an expert of the local computer how to use the UNIX tar and uncompress utilities to work with them. UNIX will provide assistance, if you ask, with the commands: `man tar` and `man compress` (man means "manual").

### D-3. Mac users

**Mac** users have to use compressed files: they come with extension hqx. On the local computer you need only two subdirectories for ams: macintosh and (optionally) author-info. So after logging on, we start creating them:

```
ccu% pwd
/home/u1/gratzer
ccu% mkdir ams
ccu% cd ams
ccu% pwd
/home/u1/gratzer/ams
ccu% mkdir macintosh
ccu% mkdir author-info
ccu% cd author-info
ccu% pwd
/home/u1/gratzer/ams/author-info
ccu% mkdir guidelines
ccu% mkdir sty-files
ccu% cd ..
ccu% cd ..
ccu% pwd
/home/u1/gratzer/ams
ccu% cd macintosh
```

Next, we log on to the $\mathcal{AMS}$ computer:

```
ccu% ftp e-math.ams.com
Connected to e-math.ams.com.
220 e-math FTP server (Ultrix Version 4.36
Thu Dec 29 22:53:11 EST 1988) ready.
```

```
Name (e-math.ams.com:gratzer): anonymous
331 Guest login ok, send ident as password.
Password:
230 Guest login ok, access restrictions apply.
ftp> cd ams
250 CWD command successful.
ftp> cd macintosh
250 CWD command successful.
ftp> ls
200 PORT command successful.
150 Opening data connection for /bin/ls
(130.179.16.8,2642) (0 bytes).
READ.ME
amsfonts_standard.hqx
amslatex1-1.hqx
amstex2-1.hqx
226 Transfer complete.
64 bytes received in 0.1 seconds (0.63 Kbytes/s)
ftp> ascii
200 Type set to A.
ftp> get amslatex1-1.hqx
200 PORT command successful.
150 Opening data connection for amslatex1-1.hqx
(130.179.16.8,2651) (992391 byt.
226 Transfer complete.
local:  amslatex1-1.hqx remote:  amslatex1-1.hqx
1007659 bytes received in 2.4e+02 seconds (4.1 Kbytes/s)
ftp> get amsfonts_standard.hqx
200 PORT command successful.
150 Opening data connection for amsfonts_standard.hqx
(130.179.16.8,2667) (2484.
226 Transfer complete.
local:  amsfonts_standard.hqx remote:  amsfonts_standard.hqx
2523014 bytes received in 6e+02 seconds (4.1 Kbytes/s)
ftp> bye
221 Goodbye.
```

Then you transfer the two files: amsfonts_standard.hqx and amslatex1-1.hqx to your **Mac** (as in Section D-2); remember to tell Kermit that you are transferring ascii files.

Move the file amsfonts_standard.hqx into the folder TeX fonts. The next step is to convert this ascii file to a binary file. For this you need the BinHex program which is available through ftp on many computers. Many of you have the StuffIt program, which includes BinHex. We assume that you have StuffIt.

Start StuffIt, and choose `Decode BinHex file ...` from the `Other` menu. In the file dialogue box locate amsfonts_standard.hqx, choose it, and click on Save. A new file AMSFonts_Standard.sit appears. Now you can delete amsfonts_standard.hqx. Double click on AMSFonts_Standard.sit, click on "Install" and you get five new items:

- AMSFonts 2.1 and AMSFonts 2.1 Metrics; you keep these in this folder; make sure you remove any earlier versions of AMSFonts.
- A READ ME file and TeachText. Read the READ ME file and remove both files from the folder.
- A folder named Textures files. Remove it from this folder, and transfer the contents of the folder into the folder TeX inputs.

Now you can delete the files:
amsfonts_standard.hqx and AMSFonts_Standard.sit.

Finally, you Kermit the file amslatex1-1.hqx from the local computer to your **Mac**, BinHex it, and then double click on AMS-LaTeX1.1.sit. You obtain a folder: AMS-LaTeX 1.1 distribution. This folder contains the following items:

- The file AMSFonts 2.1 Metrics; delete this, you already have it.
- The READ ME file; read it.
- The file AMSLATEX.BUG, of interest to those who used earlier versions, and want to know which bugs have been corrected.
- The folders INPUTS, FONTSEL, and LATEX; copy the contents of all three folders into the folder TeX inputs.
- The folder DOC. Place this folder into the Textures folder and rename it AMS-LaTeX 1.1 docs.

Finally, delete the files AMSLATEX1-1.HQX and AMS-LaTeX1.1.sit.

### D-4. The TeXfiles file

Once you have all the $\mathcal{A}_{\mathcal{M}}\mathcal{S}$-LaTeX files, it is your job to keep them up-to-date. After you sign on to the $\mathcal{A}_{\mathcal{M}}\mathcal{S}$ computer, transfer a single file from the /ams directory: TeXfiles. It lists all the files maintained in the $\mathcal{A}_{\mathcal{M}}\mathcal{S}$ directory with the time of the latest update.

Remember that when the files are updated, you may have to rebuild the format files.

### D-5. $\mathcal{A}_{\mathcal{M}}\mathcal{S}$ and user groups

The $\mathcal{A}_{\mathcal{M}}\mathcal{S}$ provides excellent technical advice. You can reach the $\mathcal{A}_{\mathcal{M}}\mathcal{S}$ Technical Support by email: tech-support@math.ams.com or by telephone: (800) 321-4267 or (401) 455-4080.

The TeX User's Group (TUG) does a tremendous job of maintaining TeX, developing LaTeX, and publishing a quarterly journal (*TUGboat*). Join TUG if you have an interest in TeX, LaTeX, or $\mathcal{A}_{\mathcal{M}}\mathcal{S}$-LaTeX. The address of TUG is P.O. Box 869, Santa Barbara, CA 93101; telephone: (805) 899-4673, email: tug@math.ams.org.

There are a large number of TEX user associations, geographic or linguistic in nature. The three largest are Dante (French), GUTenberg (German), and UK TUG (U.K.); they are represented on the TUG Board of Directors. As of this writing, there are seven more TEX user associations. They are all listed in the Resource Directory, a supplement to the *TUGboat*. For inquiries about TEX user associations, consult the Resource Directory, or write (email) TUG.

# APPENDIX E

# PostScript Fonts

Your computer and printer probably make a number of PostScript fonts available. In this appendix, we show how to use the PostScript font *Times* as the default font for text in articles.

We make the following assumptions:

- You have a PostScript printer and the Times font is available on this printer.
- You have the TeX font metrics files for the Times font under the names: Times (Times roman), TimesI (Times italic), TimesB (Times bold), TimesBI (Times bold italic).
- Your printer driver has a "substitution table" translating the names Times, TimesI, TimesB, TimesBI to the names used for these fonts by the printer (normally, Times-Roman, Times-Italic, Times-Bold, Times-BoldItalic). This table should also indicate that these fonts are resident in the printer. The printer should be instructed (*via* the metric file or if necessary, with an "encoding vector") to treat the Times characters so that accents and ligatures work correctly, text symbols print as requested.
- There is a substitution table in your system, translating the names Times, TimesI, TimesB, TimesBI to the names used for these fonts by the screen driver.

This is the setup in TEXTURES for the **Mac**. If you use a **PC**, ask an expert to get the TeX metric files and set up the substitution tables.

Now create in the Editor a style file named times.sty. Type the following lines:

```
% times.sty
% document style option for making the Times Post Script font
% the default text font

\new@fontshape{Times}{m}{n}{%
    <5>Times at 5pt%
    <6>Times at 6pt%
    <7>Times at 7pt%
```

```
   <8>Times at 8pt%
   <9>Times at 9pt%
   <10>Times at 10pt%
   <11>Times at 11pt%
   <12>Times at 12pt%
   <14>Times at 14pt%
   <17>Times at 17pt%
   <20>Times at 20pt%
   <25>Times at 25pt%
   }{}

\extra@def{Times}{}{}

\new@fontshape{Times}{m}{it}{%
   <5>TimesI at 5pt%
   <6>TimesI at 6pt%
   <7>TimesI at 7pt%
   <8>TimesI at 8pt%
   <9>TimesI at 9pt%
   <10>TimesI at 10pt%
   <11>TimesI at 11pt%
   <12>TimesI at 12pt%
   <14>TimesI at 14pt%
   <17>TimesI at 17pt%
   <20>TimesI at 20pt%
   <25>TimesI at 25pt
   }{}

\new@fontshape{Times}{b}{n}{%
   <5>TimesB at 5pt%
   <6>TimesB at 6pt%
   <7>TimesB at 7pt%
   <8>TimesB at 8pt%
   <9>TimesB at 9pt%
   <10>TimesB at 10pt%
   <11>TimesB at 11pt%
   <12>TimesB at 12pt%
   <14>TimesB at 14pt%
   <17>TimesB at 17pt%
   <20>TimesB at 20pt%
   <25>TimesB at 25pt%
   }{}
```

```
\new@fontshape{Times}{b}{it}{%
   <5>TimesBI at 5pt%
   <6>TimesBI at 6pt%
   <7>TimesBI at 7pt%
   <8>TimesBI at 8pt%
   <9>TimesBI at 9pt%
   <10>TimesBI at 10pt%
   <11>TimesBI at 11pt%
   <12>TimesBI at 12pt%
   <14>TimesBI at 14pt%
   <17>TimesBI at 17pt%
   <20>TimesBI at 20pt%
   <25>TimesBI at 25pt%
   }{}


\def\default@family{Times}
\def\Times{\def\bfdefault{b}\def\rmdefault{Times}%
   \family{Times}\selectfont}
\def\defaultfont{\Times}
\Times
```

Save this file in the texinputs directory/TeX inputs folder.

You can copy this file, times.sty, from the DISK.

To use the Times PostSript font as the default text font, include times.sty as a document-style option, so the Style section will read:

```
\documentstyle[times,amscd,amssymb,verbatim]{amsart}
```

You will find that the Times font works as expected, except that there is no dotless j (ȷ); there are only two ligatures (see Section 3-4.5) fi and fl. The \pounds command prints $; redefine it by

```
\renewcommand{\pounds}{\char163}
```

and then \pounds prints £. The Times font has no small capitals.

On the DISK, you will also find the stylesheet option: timesC.sty (Times Command style). It provides the \Times command but it does not change the default text font.

With both options, you may want to use the command

```
\newcommand{\CMR}{\family{cmr}\selectfont}
```

that invokes the Computer Modern Roman font (which is the default text font normally).

The next page shows page 1 of the sample article article.tex typeset with the times.sty option; compare it with page xviii.

# A CONSTRUCTION OF COMPLETE-SIMPLE
# DISTRIBUTIVE LATTICES

G. A. MENUHIN

March 15, 1991

ABSTRACT. In this note we prove that there exist *complete-simple distributive lattices*, that is, complete distributive lattices in which there are only two complete congruences.

## 1. INTRODUCTION

In this note we prove the following result:

**Main Theorem.** *There exists an infinite complete distributive lattice $K$ with only the two trivial complete congruence relations.*

## 2. THE $D^{(2)}$ CONSTRUCTION

For the basic notation in lattice theory and universal algebra, see F. R. Richardson [5] and G. A. Menuhin [2].

We start with some definitions:

**Definition 1.** Let $V$ be a complete lattice, and let $\mathfrak{p} = [u, v]$ be an interval of $V$. Then $\mathfrak{p}$ is called *complete-prime* if the following three conditions are satisfied:

(M) $u$ is meet-irreducible but $u$ is *not* completely meet-irreducible;

(J) $v$ is join-irreducible but $v$ is *not* completely join-irreducible;

(C) $[u, v]$ is a complete-simple lattice.

Now we prove

**Lemma 1.** *Let $D$ be a complete distributive lattice satisfying Conditions* (M) *and* (J). *Then $D^{(2)}$ is a sublattice of $D^2$, hence $D^{(2)}$ is a lattice, and $D^{(2)}$ is a complete distributive lattice satisfying Conditions* (M) *and* (J).

1991 *Mathematics Subject Classification.* Primary: 06B10; Secondary: 06D05.

*Key words and phrases.* Complete lattice, distributive lattice, complete congruence, congruence lattice.

Research supported by the NSF under grant number 23466.

1

# Conversions

There are three groups of experienced users who may want to convert to $\mathcal{A}_{\mathcal{M}}S$-LaTeX: users of Plain TeX, LaTeX, and $\mathcal{A}_{\mathcal{M}}S$-TeX.

By conversion we mean the reworking of an existing article in $\mathcal{A}_{\mathcal{M}}S$-LaTeX. Of course, the items we mention are very similar to the list of necessary changes to your working habits when converting to $\mathcal{A}_{\mathcal{M}}S$-LaTeX.

## F-1. From TeX

We discussed in Section 11-5 a number of Plain TeX commands that do not work in $\mathcal{A}_{\mathcal{M}}S$-LaTeX.

To convert an article from TeX to $\mathcal{A}_{\mathcal{M}}S$-LaTeX:

- Make sure that you do not use any of the commands listed in Section 11-5.
- Take your personalized article template (see Section 2-7), save it under a new name, and type in the article information. Then cut the TeX article and paste it in between \begin{document} and \end{document}.
- Replace the TeX displayed math delimiters $$ by \[ and \]. Optionally, also replace the math delimiters $ by \( and \).
- Redo all the section (and subsection) titles as in Section 2-8.1. Put in the cross-references.
- Redo the Bibliography as in Section 2-8.3. Put in the cross-references to the bibliographic items.
- Invoke all declarations in the form described in Section 2-8.2.
- Redesign, as necessary, the multiline formulas using the multiline math environments of $\mathcal{A}_{\mathcal{M}}S$-LaTeX.

## F-2. From LaTeX

There are just a few adjustments to make when switching from LaTeX to $\mathcal{A}_{\mathcal{M}}S$-LaTeX; after all, $\mathcal{A}_{\mathcal{M}}S$-LaTeX is a LaTeX option and a document style.

- Take your personalized article template (see Section 2-7), save it under a new name, and type in the article information. Then cut the LaTeX article from \begin{document} to \end{document} and paste it in between \begin{document} and \end{document} of the $\mathcal{AMS}$-LaTeX article.

- Check all the section titles to make sure that only those are used that are listed in Section 2-8.1 (LaTeX has section titles that are not in $\mathcal{AMS}$-LaTeX).

- Invoke all declarations in the form described in Section 2-8.2.

- Redesign, as necessary, the multiline formulas using the multiline math environments of $\mathcal{AMS}$-LaTeX. In particular, you should change the math environment eqnarray to an $\mathcal{AMS}$-LaTeX multiline math environment.

- Do not use the text style change commands (see Section 3-6.2) in math mode; use instead the math style change commands; see Section 4-13.2. For instance, instead of \bf, use \bold, \boldsymbol, or \boldmath. The command \bf is ignored in math mode.

- The @ character plays a special role in $\mathcal{AMS}$-LaTeX: it is used in forming unbreakable hyphens: @- (Section 3-4.8), long arrows @>>> and @<<< to accommodate labels (Section 4-10.1), and very tiny horizontal spaces: @, and @! (Section 4-4.2). You have to type @@ to get @ (Section 3-4.4).

- Do not use a LaTeX document style or bibliographic style. Use the $\mathcal{AMS}$-LaTeX version.

### F-3. From $\mathcal{AMS}$-TeX

Although $\mathcal{AMS}$-LaTeX is the amstex option for LaTeX, there are a number of differences the $\mathcal{AMS}$-TeX user has to get used to. They very seldom cause any difficulty since mistakes are caught by $\mathcal{AMS}$-LaTeX, as a rule, as undefined commands.

The major differences are:

- $\mathcal{AMS}$-TeX uses pairs of commands:

  \command and \endcommand

  to delimit environments; for instance,

  \document and \enddocument,
  \proclaim and \endproclaim.

- Some $\mathcal{AMS}$-TeX commands were dropped because there were LaTeX commands accomplishing the same task.

- Some $\mathcal{AMS}$-TeX commands became optional parameters.

- Some $\mathcal{AMS}$-TeX commands were renamed because there were LaTeX commands of the same name.

So here is what you should do when converting from $\mathcal{AMS}$-TeX to $\mathcal{AMS}$-LaTeX:

- Take your personalized article template (see Section 2-7), save it under a new name, and type in the article information. Then cut the $\mathcal{AMS}$-TeX article from \document to \enddocument and paste it in between \begin{document} and \end{document} of the $\mathcal{AMS}$-LaTeX article.

- Replace the $\mathcal{A}\mathcal{M}\mathcal{S}$-TeX displayed math delimiters $$ by \[ and \]. Optionally, also replace the math delimiters $ by \( and \).
- Look for $\mathcal{A}\mathcal{M}\mathcal{S}$-TeX commands that start with \end. Change all those to environments. In particular, redo each declaration as an environment.
- Completely redo the Bibliography. Change the \cite commands to references by labels.
- Redo every user-defined command. A \define becomes \newcommand, a \redefine becomes \renewcommand. Notice that the syntax changes substantially.

A number of $\mathcal{A}\mathcal{M}\mathcal{S}$-TeX commands that affect the style of the whole document became document style options:

| $\mathcal{A}\mathcal{M}\mathcal{S}$-TeX command | $\mathcal{A}\mathcal{M}\mathcal{S}$-LaTeX |
|---|---|
| \CenteredTagsOnSplits | ctagsplt document-style option |
| \LimitsOnInts | intlim document-style option |
| \LimitsOnNames | Dropped: the default |
| \LimitsOnSums | Dropped: the default |
| \NoLimitsOnInts | Dropped: the default |
| \NoLimitsOnNames | nonamelm document-style option |
| \NoLimitsOnSums | nosumlim document-style option |
| \TagsAsMath | Dropped |
| \TagsAsText | Dropped |
| \TagsOnLeft | Dropped: the default |
| \TagsOnRight | righttag document-style option |
| \TopOrBottomTagsOnSplits | Dropped: the default |

The following $\mathcal{A}\mathcal{M}\mathcal{S}$-TeX commands may create some difficulties:

| $\mathcal{A}_{\mathcal{M}}$S-TEX | $\mathcal{A}_{\mathcal{M}}$S-LATEX |
|---|---|
| \: | Conflict. Renamed: \colon |
| \adjustfootnotemark | Dropped: reset the counter footnote |
| \and | Renamed: \And |
| \boldkey (math style change) | Dropped: use \boldsymbol |
| \botsmash | Dropped: use the optional parameter of \smash |
| \caption | Changed: use the figure environment and the \caption command |
| \captionwidth | Dropped: use the figure environment and the \caption command |
| \cite | Different syntax |
| \displaybreak | Trap: place it before \\ |
| \dsize (math size change) | Dropped: use \displaystyle |
| \foldedtext | Dropped: use \parbox |
| \hdotsfor | Different syntax |
| \innerhdotsfor | Dropped |
| \italic (math style change) | Dropped: use \text{\it ... } |
| \midspace | Dropped: use the figure environment |
| \nopagebreak in multiline math environments | Dropped |
| \pretend ... \haswidth | Dropped: pad the label with blanks |
| \roman (math style change) | Conflict: use \mathrm |
| \slanted (math style change) | Dropped: use \text{\sl \dots} |
| \ssize (math size change) | Dropped: use \scriptstyle |
| \sssize (math size change) | Dropped: use \scriptscriptstyle |
| \spacehdotsfor | Dropped: use the optional parameter of \hdotsfor |
| \spaceinnerhdotsfor | Dropped: use the optional parameter of \hdotsfor |
| \spreadlines | Dropped |
| \thickfrac | Dropped: use the optional parameter of \frac |
| \thickfracwithdelims | Dropped: use the optional parameter of \fracwithdelims |
| \topsmash | Dropped: use the optional parameter of \smash |
| \topspace | Dropped: use the figure environment |
| \tsize (math size change) | Dropped: use \textstyle |
| \vspace in multiline math environments | Dropped: use the optional argument of \\ |

# Final Word

As we explained in the Introduction,

"This book is for you: the mathematician, engineer, or scientist who wants to write and typeset articles containing mathematical formulas without spending much time learning how to do it."

In this final appendix, we will outline what was left out of the presentation; and what should you read to learn more about $\mathcal{A}_{\mathcal{M}}\mathcal{S}$-LaTeX.

### G-1. What did we leave out from $\mathcal{A}_{\mathcal{M}}\mathcal{S}$-LaTeX

**G-1.1. Omitted from $\mathcal{A}_{\mathcal{M}}\mathcal{S}$-LaTeX.** LaTeX is in transition from Lamport's Version 2 to LaTeX3. This new Version 3 will contain amstex.sty in some form as the document-style option for mathematical formulas.

Frank Mittelbach and Rainer Schöpf have already coded many new and improved features of LaTeX3, and some of them have been included in $\mathcal{A}_{\mathcal{M}}\mathcal{S}$-LaTeX. For a more detailed exposition on declarations, see Frank Mittelbach [22], and on the comment and verbatim environments, see Rainer Schöpf [24].

A new feature of LaTeX3, already included in $\mathcal{A}_{\mathcal{M}}\mathcal{S}$-LaTeX, is the New Font Selection Scheme. It is discussed in Part II of $\mathcal{A}_{\mathcal{M}}\mathcal{S}$-LaTeX—User's Guide [5], and in more detail in Frank Mittelbach and Rainer Schöpf [23]. This represents a crucial departure from, and a great improvement over, Version 2 of LaTeX. We do not discuss the New Font Selection Scheme in this book for two reasons:

(1) Many professionals and secretaries who use $\mathcal{A}_{\mathcal{M}}\mathcal{S}$-LaTeX, may not have the background for understanding font families and attributes.

(2) $\mathcal{A}_{\mathcal{M}}\mathcal{S}$-LaTeX gives the commands to do all the necessary changes in font size and shape, without any reference to the commands of the New Font Selection Scheme. So for the target audience of this book, a study of the New Font Selection Scheme can be put off without a major penalty.

Nevertheless, those who want to use fonts other than the standard Computer Modern fonts, would do well to read [5] and [23].

In this book, we use the New Font Selection Scheme in two places. In the macro file, macros02.tex (see Section 11-2 and the DISK), the introduction of the math font, Euler script:

`\newmathalphabet*{\E}{eus}{m}{n}`

uses a command of the New Font Selection Scheme. And, of course, all the code in Appendix E is in the New Font Selection Scheme.

To my knowledge, we omitted only the following features of $\mathcal{AMS}$-L#T#X:

    (1) The document-style options:
        (a) nosumlim, no limits on sums.
        (b) intlim, limits on integrals.
        (c) nonamelm, no limit on operatorname.
        (d) ctagsplit, vertically centered tags on the `split` environment.
        (e) righttag, equation tags on the right.
    (2) The amsbook document style.
    (3) The amsalpha bibliographic style.

We omitted the document-style options, so that throughout the book the user works under exactly the same conditions; this avoids the necessity of discussing whether a particular feature is available because it is a part of T#X, L#T#X, $\mathcal{AMS}$-L#T#X, the document style, or the document-style options. We violate this principle only a few times; for instance, in Section 6-4.2, where we have to include the multicol.sty option to do an Index, and in Appendix E, where we use the times.sty option to utilize the Times PostScript font.

The amsbook document style is not a document style in the same sense as amsart is. The document style amsart does relieve you of worrying about the visual appearance of the article. The document style amsbook does not pretend to do the same for books; the demands of a book are too complicated to be handled by a single document style. amsbook does little more than provide an additional sectioning command, `\chapter`. The design of the book is left to the publisher.

**G-1.2. Omitted from L#T#X.** L#T#X has a number of features omitted from this book:

    (1) The `picture` environment is a major feature. It allows you to draw simple pictures with lines and circles.
    (2) The `list` environment makes all the parameters that go into making a list available to the user, so that a customized list format can be created.
    (3) The `tabbing` environment is quite sophisticated; only the simplest commands are discussed in this book.
    (4) L#T#X makes most of the style parameters available to the user; it provides the command, `\setlength` (and some others), to change them.

Drawing with the `picture` environment has the advantage of portability. However, we believe that the right approach today is to use a CAD (computer assisted drawing) program with PostScript picture saving capability, and include the drawing with the

\special command. Unfortunately, there is no uniformity as to how this is done in the various TEX implementations, so you will have to consult the TEX manual about the use of the \special command.

The style parameters for $\mathcal{A}_{\mathcal{M}}S$-LATEX are set in the document style. When the journal in which you publish changes the name of the document style, they change the style parameters to their specifications. If the style parameters are changed in the article, the journal has no easy way to mark up the source file to conform with their publishing style.

**G-1.3. Omitted from TEX.** Most everything. TEX is a powerful programming language; you can design any page layout and any formula in TEX. Remember, however, that to change the design features, you should be knowledgeable not only in TEX but also in document design. Also keep in mind our goal that the journal you publish in ought to be able to change the design to its own specifications.

### G-2. Further reading

To learn more about LATEX, of course, read Leslie Lamport [20].

It is a bit more complicated to learn TEX. You may want to start out with Wynter Snow [26]. It introduces many of the basic concepts of TEX in a very relaxed style with lots of examples. The LATEX notes make the book especially useful to users of $\mathcal{A}_{\mathcal{M}}S$-LATEX. The author gives many examples of macros. TEX as a programming language is not discussed.

Raymond Seroul and Silvio Levy [25] is another good introduction. It has a chapter on TEX programming.

Donald E. Knuth [14] also provides an easy introduction to TEX, as long as you avoid the difficult parts marked by dangerous bend signs.

Paul W. Abrahams, Karl Berry, and Kathryn A. Hargreaves [1] explain many TEX commands grouped by topics. It has a very useful, nonsequential, approach.

Victor Eijkhout [9] is an excellent reference book on TEX for experts.

For lots of tutorial examples, see the articles and columns in *TUGboat*.

On PostScript and TEX, read the article [11].

For advice to authors of mathematical articles, see Ellen Swanson [28]; it is interesting to note how many rules she states have been incorporated into $\mathcal{A}_{\mathcal{M}}S$-LATEX. The point of view on copy editing of the Cambridge and Oxford University Presses are presented in Judith Butcher [8] and Horace Hart [12], respectively.

Ruari McLean [21] gives a useful introduction to typography, the art of printing with type. See also Alison Black [7] for more about typefaces.

Paul W. Abrahams and Bruce L. Larson [2] provide a good introduction to UNIX.

Ed Krol [19] is my favourite introduction to ftp and Internet. There are many important ftp sites for $\mathcal{A}_{\mathcal{M}}S$-LATEX users; among the most important sites are

- The $\mathcal{A}_{\mathcal{M}}S$ computer at e-math.ams.com.
- The Stanford computer at sumex-aim.stanford.edu.
- The UK Source Archive at src.doc.ic.ac.uk.

- The official TEX archive at `labrea.stanford.edu`.
- The Houston archive at `niord.shsu.edu`.
- The Stuttgart archive at `rusvm1.rus.uni-stuttgart.de`, sponsored by DANTE e.V., the German TEX user group.

The Houston archive will email the $\mathcal{A}_{\mathcal{M}}S$-LATEX package; send an email message including the request:

`SENDME AMSLaTeX`

to

`FILESERV@SHSU.BITNET`

or to

`FILESERV@SHSU.edu`

# BIBLIOGRAPHY

[1] Paul W. Abrahams, Karl Berry, and Kathryn A. Hargreaves, TeX *for the Impatient*, Addison-Wesley, Reading, Massachusetts, 1990.

[2] Paul W. Abrahams and Bruce L. Larson, *UNIX for the Impatient*, Addison-Wesley, Reading, Massachusetts, 1992.

[3] American Mathematical Society, *AMSFonts Version 2.1—Installation Guide*, Providence, R.I., 1991.

[4] ――――, *AMSFonts Version 2.1—User's Guide*, Providence, R.I., 1991.

[5] ――――, *AMS-LATEX Version 1.1—User's Guide*, Providence, R.I., 1991.

[6] ――――, *Installation Guide for AMS-LATEX Version 1.1*, Providence, R.I., 1991.

[7] Alison Black, *Typefaces for desktop publishing; a user guide*, Architecture Design and Technology Press, London, 1990.

[8] Judith Butcher, *Copy editing: the Cambridge handbook*, 2nd ed., Cambridge University Press, London, 1981.

[9] Victor Eijkhout, TeX *by topic, A* TeX*nician's reference*, Addison-Wesley, Reading, Massachusetts, 1991.

[10] Michael Doob, *A Gentle Introduction to* TeX, Publications on TeX and its Environment, vol. 15, TeX Users Group, Providence, R.I., 1990.

[11] George Grätzer, *Advances in* TeX *implementations. I. PostScript fonts*. Notices Amer. Math. Soc. **40** (1993), July issue.

[12] Horace Hart, *Hart's Rules; For Compositors and Readers at the University Press, Oxford*, Oxford University Press, Oxford, 1991.

[13] Donald E. Knuth, *The Art of Computer Programming*, Volumes 1–4, Addison-Wesley, Reading, Massachusetts, 1968–.

[14] ――――, *The* TeX *book*, Computers and Typesetting, vol. A, Addison-Wesley, Reading, Massachusetts, 1984, 1990.

[15] ――――, TeX: *The Program*, Computers and Typesetting, vol. B, Addison-Wesley, Reading, Massachusetts, 1986.

[16] ――――, *The Metafont Book*, Computers and Typesetting, vol. C, Addison-Wesley, Reading, Massachusetts, 1986.

[17] ――――, *METAFONT: The Program*, Computers and Typesetting, vol. D, Addison-Wesley, Reading, Massachusetts, 1986.

[18] ――――, *Computer Modern Typefaces*, Computers and Typesetting, vol. E, Addison-Wesley, Reading, Massachusetts, 1987.

[19] Ed Krol, *The Whole Internet, User Guide & Catalog*, O'Reilly & Associates, Sebastopol CA, 1992.

[20] Leslie Lamport, LaTeX: *A Document Preparation System*, Addison-Wesley, Reading, Massachusetts, 1985.

[21] Ruari McLean, *The Thames and Hudson Manual of Typography*. Thames and Hudson, London, 1980.

[22] Frank Mittelbach, *An extension of the LaTeX theorem environment, TUGboat* **10** (1989), 416-426.

[23] Frank Mittelbach and Rainer Schöpf, *The new font family selection—user interface to standard LaTeX, TUGboat* **11** (1990), 297–305.

[24] Rainer Schöpf, *A new implementation of the LaTeX* `verbatim` *and* `verbatim*` *environments, TUGboat* **11** (1990), 284-296.

[25] Raymond Seroul and Silvio Levy, *A beginner's book of TeX*, Springer-Verlag, New York, 1991.

[26] Wynter Snow, TeX *for the beginner*, Addison-Wesley, Reading, Massachusetts, 1992.

[27] Michael Spivak, *The Joy of TeX*, 2nd ed., American Mathematical Society, Providence, R.I., 1990.

[28] Ellen Swanson, *Mathematics into Type; Copy Editing and Proofreading of Mathematics for Editorial Assistants and Authors*, American Mathematical Society, Providence, R.I., 1986.

# INDEX

If there are several page numbers for an item, consult the boldfaced numbers first.

## Trademarks and Copyrights

# Instructions for Macintosh users

There is only one DISK included with this book---the IBM compatible DISK. The following steps are for Macintosh users.

1. Start up the **Apple File Exchange.**
2. Insert the DISK.
3. In the menu: **MS-DOS to MAC**, select **Text translation.** A dialogue box appears; click on **OK.** Now in the **MS-DOS to MAC** menu, **Text translation** is highlighted.
4. In the panel showing the directory of the DISK, while holding down the shift key, click on **PARTI, PARTII,** and **PARTIII.**
5. Click on **Translate.**
6. **Apple File Exchange** informs you that the translation is text translation and performs the translation.
7. There will be three folders created on your hard disk, called **PARTI, PARTII,** and **PARTIII.** In the last step of the Mac installation procedure (Section 1-4.1), drag these three folders into the **DISK** folder.